ACADEMIC BELONGING IN HIGHER EDUCATION

The concept of belonging has been increasingly understood as the missing piece in diversity, equity, and inclusion efforts in higher education. This book explores the need to recognize and account for institutional-level factors that shape academic belonging, thereby improving student experience and outcomes.

Though recent scholarship has identified several factors that are associated with student belonging in academics, there is little research that addresses what faculty can do in concrete terms to promote belonging, particularly in the domains where they have the most influence. The 12 chapters in this volume introduce readers to an array of collaborative, cutting-edge efforts to develop pedagogies, programs, strategies, and environments that help students develop academic belonging; that is, a sense of connection, competence, and confidence in academic domains.

This book is written for higher education faculty, administrators, and researchers who wish to enhance their students' sense of academic belonging by taking informed, practical measures to make them feel valued and supported.

Eréndira Rueda is associate professor of sociology and the director of the Latin American and Latinx Studies multidisciplinary program at Vassar College.

Candice Lowe Swift is associate professor of anthropology and serves on the steering committees of Africana Studies and International Studies at Vassar College.

ACADEMIC BELONGING IN HIGHER EDUCATION

Fostering Student Connection, Competence, and Confidence

*Edited by Eréndira Rueda and
Candice Lowe Swift*

Routledge
Taylor & Francis Group

NEW YORK AND LONDON

Designed cover image: Getty Images/Qvasimodo

First published 2024
by Routledge
605 Third Avenue, New York, NY 10158

and by Routledge
4 Park Square, Milton Park, Abingdon, Oxon OX14 4RN

Routledge is an imprint of the Taylor & Francis Group, an informa business

© 2024 Taylor & Francis

The right of Eréndira Rueda and Candice Lowe Swift to be identified as
the authors of the editorial material, and of the authors for their individual
chapters, has been asserted in accordance with sections 77 and 78 of the
Copyright, Designs and Patents Act 1988.

ISBN: 978-1-642-67528-3 (hbk)
ISBN: 978-1-642-67529-0 (pbk)
ISBN: 978-1-003-44373-5 (ebk)

DOI: 10.4324/9781003443735

Typeset in Galliard
by Taylor & Francis Books

CONTENTS

ILLUSTRATIONS

Figures

Tables

PREFACE

The calls for increased attention to matters of diversity, equity, inclusion, and belonging (DEIB) throughout higher education convey an important shift in our understanding of our roles as faculty members. The requirement that all job candidates for teaching positions of various sorts submit materials that include diversity statements demonstrating an awareness of and sustained commitment to DEIB efforts makes clear that our faculty roles now go well beyond demonstrating expertise on a given subject or in a particular discipline. When we hire new colleagues, we more often expect statements of teaching philosophy that reflect the use of cutting-edge and inclusive pedagogical approaches, the ability to cultivate a sense of community in the classroom, and an awareness of wide-ranging student needs and experiences. The expectations for faculty are high – as they should be, given that students' experiences in college and their ability to persist to graduation are at stake – yet faculty rarely receive extensive pedagogical training as graduate students, and professional development that focuses on inclusive pedagogies is not often a requirement once faculty are hired. In recent years, we have seen a growing emphasis throughout higher education on the importance of fostering a sense of belonging among our students, especially those from historically under-represented backgrounds, which may feel profoundly intuitive and necessary to some faculty but daunting to others. This book responds to both. Faculty who feel that their pedagogy has always been aligned with the spirit of DEIB efforts may take away new ideas from what authors share in their chapters. Faculty who feel that they are newcomers to this work will hopefully feel inclined to learn about this work in a way that feels safe and inviting.

Our own efforts to raise awareness regarding the importance of belonging and find increasingly effective ways of cultivating a sense of belonging in our classrooms, in our relationships with students, and in our roles as campus leaders are precisely what led to this book. One of the most commonly expressed sentiments in conversations with colleagues from across academic disciplines over the years has been the concern over not knowing what to do or what to change, in concrete terms, despite a desire to see all of their students succeed. As leaders on our campus in DEIB efforts (e.g., Eréndira co-chaired the Committee on Inclusion and Equity for 6 years, and Candice was an advisor to two college presidents on race, equity, and inclusion and director of the Mellon-funded Engaged Pluralism Initiative for 4 years), we had a bird's-eye view of the array of approaches, initiatives, and programs that were underway at various levels of the college to address matters of student belonging. Additionally, when we dug into the scholarship on belonging, we discovered that research on the topic has explored a range of factors that are associated with belonging at various levels (e.g., academic, social, and campus community belonging), but there is less research that addresses what faculty can do in concrete terms to promote a sense of belonging, particularly where they have the most influence – academic belonging.

Our research into the concept of belonging, our experience in campus leadership roles related to the work of DEIB, and our conversations with colleagues about the challenges we often faced in our efforts to foster a sense of belonging among our students made us curious about the kinds of efforts that exist at other institutions. The idea for this book originates in this desire to foster dialogue across institutions and learn from what our colleagues at other colleges and universities have been doing. *Academic Belonging in Higher Education* introduces readers to a variety of collaborative, cutting-edge efforts pursued by faculty, students, administrators, and researchers to develop pedagogies, programs, strategies, and environments that help students develop academic belonging; that is, a sense of connection, competence, and confidence in academic domains.

The volume is divided into five parts that introduce readers to the collaborative work happening across colleges and universities to prioritize and facilitate academic belonging among undergraduate students, particularly those from historically underrepresented backgrounds. Part I focuses on pedagogies of belonging and provides readers with examples of the kinds of modifications they can make to how they teach, what they teach, and the culture of their classrooms. The chapters in Part II introduce readers to efforts that promote academic belonging more broadly in curricula, by way of a campus-wide first-year seminar model and department-wide interventions. Part III demonstrates how educators are supporting students' sense of belonging by engaging with them in supportive learning communities that provide academic, civic, leadership, and research opportunities. The chapters in Part IV introduce case studies of institutional strategies and campus-wide efforts to address students' belonging needs at minority-serving institutions. The two chapters in Part V invite readers to think about the opportunities and limits of belonging by proposing a creative method for gathering information about students' experiences of belonging and interrogating the relationship between belonging and mattering.

ABOUT THE EDITORS

Eréndira Rueda is associate professor of sociology and the director of the Latin American and Latinx Studies multidisciplinary program at Vassar College. Her primary areas of research and teaching are the sociology of education, immigration, and childhoods. She has been a key leader in diversity, equity, inclusion, and belonging work at Vassar for the past decade. She has been a member of the President's Diversity Council, co-chair of the Committee on Admissions and Financial Aid, a founding member of the Engaged Pluralism Initiative's working group focused on inclusive pedagogies and curriculum development, and a Core Team member of the Howard Hughes Medical Institute Grand Challenges Program. She served as the co-chair of the Committee on Inclusion and Equity for 6 years, a presidential advisory committee tasked with identifying college practices and campus issues that require a clearer articulation of the institution's stance on diversity, equity, and inclusion. She has also been an active mentor and dedicated member of the Advisory Board for the Vassar Transitions Program, which serves first-generation, low-income, and/or undocumented and DACA students. She has directed the Transitions Research Team since 2017, which trains first-generation and low-income (FGLI) Vassar students in participatory action research and provides college administrators, offices, and programs with recommendations that help foster a sense of belonging among FGLI students on campus.

Candice Lowe Swift is associate professor of anthropology and serves on the steering committees of Africana Studies and International Studies at Vassar College. Her research focuses on multiculturalism and heritage in Mauritius and on the relationships between diasporans from Africa, India, China, Europe, and the Middle East within the context of the Indian Ocean.

She has served in the roles of liaison to president for race and inclusion and advisor to the College on Inclusion and Engaged Pluralism for the past 6 years, during which time she became a co-principal investigator on a Mellon Foundation grant to address Vassar's interest in becoming a more welcoming and generative learning community for all, with a concentration on students from historically underrepresented groups on campus. The successful funding of the Mellon proposal allowed Vassar College to launch the Engaged Pluralism Initiative, which Candice directed until December 2020. She also initiated, co-founded, and directed Summer Immersion in the Liberal Arts, which was designed primarily to serve first-generation and lower income students.

ACKNOWLEDGEMENTS

We would like to extend our heartfelt gratitude to volume contributors for sharing their knowledge about how the concept of belonging functions in academic settings and making explicit the links between their efforts to promote belonging and their influences on the academic lives of students. In reflecting on their efforts, they have brought to light the challenges, limitations, and successes of the sense of belonging framework in ways that we hope will help us build on each other's knowledge and successes, learn from those efforts, and promote more conversation and action around the limits and potential of sense of belonging and how it can better serve students.

A special thanks goes to the students in our lives as educators who push our thinking and pedagogy in much-needed ways.

Finally, we would be remiss if we did not thank our spouses and families for their unconditional support and patience and for being incredible sources of inspiration. A special thanks to Dr. Jesse Moya for providing us with a fresh set of eyes on the introduction to this volume.

1

INTRODUCTION

Eréndira Rueda and Candice Lowe Swift

The concept of belonging has been increasingly touted as the missing piece in diversity, equity, and inclusion efforts throughout the field of higher education. An increasing number of colleges and universities have created offices of diversity, equity, inclusion, and belonging (e.g., Harvard University, The Julliard School, University of California Berkeley) or offices whose titles include the term *belonging* (e.g., Montclair State University, Mount Holyoke College). Many more institutions incorporate the language of belonging in descriptions of campus programs and initiatives (e.g., University of Illinois Chicago, Vassar College), in their strategic plans (e.g., Cornell University, Kansas State University, University of Texas at Austin), and in faculty development websites (e. g., Iowa State University, Massachusetts Institute of Technology, University of Colorado Boulder). Some institutions have developed institution-wide research initiatives that explore, measure, and track belonging (e.g., Georgetown University, Imperial College London, Stanford University). The findings from these research initiatives have produced recommendations that are helping to reshape curricula, faculty development, programming decisions, and campus policies (e.g., Cohen & Viola, 2022; Joy, 2019; Morrison et al., 2019, 2020).

The expanding focus on belonging signals an awareness that diversity efforts – that is, recruiting a more heterogeneous campus population and working to "value difference" – are not enough to ensure equitable outcomes across groups. The new set of acronyms is also intended to convey that there is additional work to be done beyond providing varied forms of support and resources (i.e., equity efforts) and ensuring that everyone has a seat at the table (i.e., inclusion efforts). The growing attention to student sense of belonging on college campuses encourages institutions to pay attention to students' subjective experiences of campus climates and

DOI: 10.4324/9781003443735-1

classroom cultures, which are often shaped by diversity, equity, and inclusion (DEI) efforts. The concept of belonging expands the focus of DEI efforts and encourages educators and administrators to consider the extent to which students feel connected, valued, supported, and respected. For these reasons, the concept of belonging has been framed as the next step in ongoing commitments throughout the field of higher education to ensure successful outcomes for all students, particularly students from historically excluded, marginalized, and minoritized groups (e.g., Conway, 2021; Kurfist, 2022; West, 2022).

Contributions of the volume

Academic Belonging in Higher Education engages with the important shift that the growing attention to belonging signals, one that seeks to reframe the problem in need of addressing in a way that also reframes solutions. Historically, issues of student retention and success have been framed, understood, and addressed from a deficit perspective, one that locates the "problem" as inherent in students; for example, a lack of preparation, grit, or help-seeking behaviors (Beattie, 2018). Scholarship on student sense of belonging has highlighted the need to understand the contextual factors that help students benefit from intended institutional supports and feel valued, safe, and connected in college settings (Hurtado & Carter, 1997; Nunn, 2021; Strayhorn, 2012; Vaccaro & Newman, 2016, 2022; Walton & Cohen, 2011). Of particular importance is the need to recognize institutional-level factors that shape student sense of belonging, rather than focusing primarily or exclusively on individual-level factors that shape student experience and outcomes. The contributors to this volume do just that. The chapters encourage readers to move away from questions and approaches that focus on what *students* should do differently to those that focus on what *institutions* can do differently to create systemic change that ensures student success.

The present volume also contributes to an understanding of belonging as a multifaceted experience, one that requires that a wide array of campus community members share the responsibility for helping students develop connections and communicate to students that they are valued and supported. Recent scholarship has highlighted the need to recognize that belonging varies across time (e.g., from one point in an academic career to another) and place (e.g., some spaces on campus help students feel safer, valued, and more connected than others) and that while students might feel like they belong in some campus spaces, they still may not feel like they belong at the institution as a whole or in academic spaces (Nunn, 2021). Attention to the conceptual distinctions between belonging to the campus community as a whole, social belonging, and academic belonging marks an important development in this line of research and offers a promising way to frame future institutional efforts.

Faculty have a particular responsibility to ensure that students are able to develop a sense of belonging in academic settings given the influence that faculty have on students' academic experiences. While the ability to develop a sense of belonging in academic domains does not guarantee belonging in other domains, the experience of belonging in one context may promote belonging in others (Miller et al., 2019; Nunn, 2021). The chapters in this volume introduce readers to an array of collaborative, cutting-edge efforts pursued by faculty, administrators, researchers, and students to develop pedagogies, programs, strategies, and environments that help students develop academic belonging; that is, a sense of connection, competence, and confidence in academic domains.

Evolving understandings of student success: From integration to belonging

Research from across disciplinary fields confirms that a sense of belonging is an important factor in supporting student success in higher education, particularly for students from historically underrepresented backgrounds (see Baumeister & Leary, 1995; Jack, 2019; Strayhorn, 2012; Vaccaro & Newman, 2016). One of the earliest conceptualizations of belonging that had a strong influence on discourses of belonging for several decades was developed by Vincent Tinto (1987, 1993). The original model that he proposed for understanding why students succeed – or leave college before obtaining a degree – pivoted on the concepts of *integration* and *fit* and was grounded in a linear process, one in which students intentionally distanced themselves from their home communities to successfully embed themselves in their college communities. The initial focus on integration and individual student behaviors and abilities was a generative starting point for considering students' academic trajectories. Subsequent scholars found that other factors, such as campus climate, student interactions and perceptions, and the affirmation (or not) of student backgrounds, also played important roles in retention and the ability of students to succeed academically.

In reviewing the research on studies of campus culture and its influence on students from marginalized backgrounds, Solorzano et al. (2000) found that when a racial climate is positive,

> it includes at least four elements: (a) the inclusion of students, faculty, and administrators of color; (b) a curriculum that reflects the historical and contemporary experiences of people of color; (c) programs to support recruitment, retention, and graduation of students of color; and (d) a college/university mission that reinforces the institution's commitment to pluralism.

> *(p. 62)*

In their own study of 34 African American students' experiences of racial climate at three predominantly White institutions, Solorzano et al. (2000) found that subtle forms of racism, such as microaggressions and having to educate peers about one's social group, can lead to experiences of isolation and energy drain, which diverted students' attention away from academics. In contrast, being in an environment where students feel a sense of belonging is associated with retention and academic achievement (Feagin & Sikes, 1995; Fischer, 2007; Fries-Britt & Turner, 2002; Harper, 2013; Hausmann et al., 2007; Museus & Maramba, 2011; Solorzano et al., 2000; Strayhorn, 2012).

In addition to campus culture, interactions with peers, faculty, and administrators shape students' perceptions of themselves and their abilities. For example, questions and statements from peers that imply that minoritized students are less academically qualified or interactions with faculty that are perceived by students to be unsupportive can contribute to feelings of self-doubt and lead students to feel less motivated to persist or to expend their energy on trying to prove their worth (Davis et al., 2004; Lewis & Hodges, 2015; Vaccaro & Newman, 2016). By contrast, students who feel seen by their professors and who feel that their work is acknowledged – regardless of the outcome in terms of grades – feel a greater sense of confidence and self-efficacy as they pursue their academic goals (Freeman et al., 2007; Kahu et al., 2022; Nunn, 2021). Student perceptions, campus culture, and student achievement are interrelated, and they contribute collectively to a student's ability to experience academic success and belonging.

Empirical research confirms that when students from historically underrepresented groups are even subtly reminded of the minoritized groups to which they belong, they can experience stress and stereotype threat (Steele, 2010; Steele & Aronson, 1995). When their behavior or performance is at risk of being attributed to stigmas that are associated with the social groups with which they identify, students can underperform on intellectual tasks, such as scoring poorly on standardized tests (Steele, 2010; Steele & Aronson 1995). Perceived threats to students' identities are directly linked to the situations and academic environments in which they find themselves, and such threats can undermine confidence, academic success, and belonging for students from marginalized backgrounds.

By contrast, research suggests that affirming the identities of marginalized groups can be important to supporting student success. For example, maintaining ties to home communities can support students' ability to succeed and persist (Hurtado & Carter, 1997; Museus & Maramba, 2011). Far from necessitating that students separate themselves from their family and community cultures, cultural integrity can be a critical factor in supporting student success. Tierney and Jun (2001) defined *cultural integrity* as "those programs and teaching strategies that call upon students' racial and ethnic backgrounds in a positive manner in the development of their pedagogies and learning activities" and assert that "cultural background is a critical ingredient for acquiring cultural capital and achieving success" (p. 211). These scholars articulate a compelling critique of the assumption that success in college requires the acceptance of dominant norms.

Campus culture, student interactions and perceptions, and the affirmation of communities of origin are all important factors in promoting persistence and success in college – especially for students attending institutions that were not designed with their cultural, social, and economic backgrounds in mind. Sense of belonging has become a salient construct that contemporary researchers use to integrate these factors and to highlight the relationships between student experience and institutional environments.

The role of belonging in promoting student success

Sense of belonging is a multidimensional phenomenon, one that is relational and directly tied to student motivation and success (Baumeister & Leary, 1995; Freeman et al., 2007; Strayhorn, 2019). Core elements of this construct are "perceived social support on campus, a feeling or sensation of connectedness, the experience of mattering or feeling cared about, accepted, respected, valued by, and important to the group (e.g., campus community) or others on campus" (Strayhorn, 2012, p. 3). In addition, "[u]nder optimal conditions, members feel that the group is important to them *and that they are important to the group* [emphasis added]" (Strayhorn, 2019, p. 4). The multiple, interrelated components within the framework of belonging suggest that institutional actors have different, yet complementary, roles to play in working with students to create the most ideal conditions for their success and wellness (Nunn, 2021; Strayhorn, 2019).

Though the research on belonging is expansive, we know much less about how faculty, in collaboration with administrators, researchers, and students, are applying the knowledge that we are acquiring regarding the invaluable role that sense of belonging has for academic success and holistic well-being. This is not to say that the literature is silent on the role of faculty in promoting student sense of belonging and academic success. The literature suggests that faculty are critical to this area of student outcomes and experience, but less is known about what faculty are doing to facilitate academic belonging among students.

Researchers and students describe academic belonging as feeling comfortable in class, being in a learning community where their questions and contributions are welcomed, where mastery of course material is not assumed, and where students feel seen, heard, acknowledged, and able to succeed (Kahu et al., 2022; Lewis & Hodges, 2015; Means & Pyne, 2017; Nunn, 2021; Versteeg et al., 2022). Faculty are particularly important when it comes to helping students feel connected to, and competent in, the subject matter being studied and confident in their ability to complete academic tasks successfully (Engle & Tinto, 2008; Freeman et al., 2007; Lewis & Hodges, 2015; McCallen & Johnson, 2020; Miller et al., 2019; Nunn, 2021; Schademan & Thompson, 2016). Among the factors that shape academic belonging are positive relationships and interactions with faculty, inclusive and affirming teaching practices that communicate an ethic of care, efforts to foster communities of connectedness in classrooms and among students, and opportunities to participate in research with faculty (Kirby & Thomas, 2022; Miller et al., 2019; Morrison et al., 2020; Rueda et al., 2017).

The promise of academic belonging: Fostering connection, competence, and confidence

This volume articulates an evolving understanding of *academic* belonging as one that operates along social and intellectual dimensions. The feeling that one matters to others in a given academic setting and that one is an accepted member of that setting speaks to the importance of *connection*. The quality of interactions and the strength of relationships that students experience with peers and faculty in academic settings are of great importance for the ability to experience a sense of connection. Mattering and feeling accepted can also be shaped by the ability to connect with what is being taught, how it is being taught, and who is doing the teaching. Course content and pedagogical approaches that allow students to see connections between course material and their own lives, that allow students to feel that their knowledge and experience add value to classroom interactions and intellectual spaces, and that make students feel like they are accepted for who they are (rather than their ability to assimilate) are key to facilitating a sense of connection. In short, connections to faculty, peers, and content are key elements of the social dimension of academic belonging.

Of equal importance to the social dimension of academic belonging are the two elements that we see as constituting its intellectual dimension: *competence* and *confidence*. Having the knowledge and skill set necessary to handle coursework and meet the standards in a disciplinary field is at the core of what it means to be competent. Students often look to grades and GPAs as a measure of their competence. However, attention to the notion of confidence offers a more holistic understanding of the intellectual dimension of academic belonging, one that also takes into account how students feel about their intellectual skills and capacity to meet standards. Taking into account students' feelings of self-efficacy also helps us take into account the important role of interactions with others – the feedback, support, and encouragement from others – that shapes students' subjective sense of whether or not they have what it takes to make it in a particular field. In describing and reflecting on existing efforts to understand and cultivate academic belonging, the contributors to this volume provide concrete examples of how they have been working with students to develop a sense of connection, competence, and confidence in academic settings.

Based on studies of the impact of belonging on retention and academic success and on student perceptions and perspectives on the role that faculty can play in their sense of self-efficacy and desire to engage and persist, it is clear that academic belonging is important to students and directly tied to the educational missions of institutions of higher education. The influence of faculty on students' academic experience is well established in the literature. The chapters that follow provide examples of what faculty are actually doing, in collaboration with administrators, researchers, and students, to promote academic belonging.

Chapter overview

The volume is divided into five sections that provide concrete examples of the kind of proactive and collaborative work that faculty, students, administrators, and researchers are doing to ensure that students are increasingly able to develop a sense of belonging in an array of academic contexts.

Part I focuses on pedagogies of belonging and provides readers with a sense of what faculty have done to modify how they teach, what they teach, and the culture of their classrooms.

Chapter 2 introduces readers to the Infusing Inclusion workshop, which is grounded in the fearless teaching framework created by the authors (Donlan et al., 2019). The chapter features a series of reflection questions and evidence-based strategies that faculty can make use of to be intentionally inclusive in their design of classroom climate, course content, teaching practice, and assessment strategies.

In Chapter 3, the authors address the importance of interactive learning opportunities in introductory undergraduate calculus courses, especially for the purpose of improving undergraduate women's sense of belonging and contributing to their retention in STEM majors. Drawing on surveys of students in two types of calculus courses at the University of Delaware (lecture-based instruction vs. interactive learning approach), the authors reflect on findings that indicate a greater sense of belonging among women enrolled in the courses that took an interactive approach to learning.

In Chapter 4, the authors share insights from their work at Dougherty Family College, which is housed within the University of St. Thomas in Minnesota and serves primarily BIPOC and first-generation college students. Faculty reflect on how they make use of culturally sustaining pedagogies to honor the perspective and knowledge that students bring to learning contexts to foster academic belonging in their classes.

The chapters in Part II introduce readers to broader curricular efforts to foster academic belonging – in this case, among first-year students and through department-wide interventions.

In Chapter 5, the authors share insights from the work they did to develop and implement a first-year seminar program at California State University, Dominguez Hills, a Hispanic-serving institution that enrolls high percentages of BIPOC, low-income, and first-generation college students. The chapter emphasizes the importance of the type of ongoing professional development necessary to provide students with opportunities to work closely with faculty, explore the curriculum, participate in co-curricular activities, receive academic and whole-person support, and develop a sense of belonging as they transition to college.

Chapter 6 introduces readers to the Strengthening Learning Communities (SLC) project, which is helping faculty understand student achievement and belonging in a large UK-based, research-intensive physics department. The five subprojects described in this chapter highlight the ways in which faculty can involve students as researchers or active research participants to learn more about student academic experiences within a department, develop interventions that address students' needs, and help students develop a sense of belonging in the field of physics education.

In Chapter 7, faculty from the Early Childhood Studies Department at California State Polytechnic University, Pomona, reflect on their experiences with a department-wide curriculum overhaul. The chapter provides readers with details regarding the changes that faculty made to address student input regarding their academic needs and professional goals – from restructuring concentrations within the major, revising program and course learning outcomes, embedding anti-racist and linguistically and culturally responsive pedagogies throughout all courses, and developing a recruitment plan to attract underrepresented Native and Black students to the major.

The chapters in Part III demonstrate how educators are supporting students' sense of belonging by engaging with them in supportive learning communities that provide academic, civic, leadership, and research opportunities.

In Chapter 8, educators from the Brotherhood Initiative introduce a theory of action that addresses the challenges faced by undergraduate men of color at the University of Washington. Articulating a cross-organizational collaborative approach, the authors illustrate how curricular and co-curricular activities can operate synergistically to assist students in achieving their academic goals and facilitate a sense of belonging.

In Chapter 9, readers learn how intentionally incorporating undergraduate students into communities of research can play a significant role in supporting students' sense of academic belonging. The student and faculty authors of this chapter assert that by engaging students in collaborative research, faculty and graduate students can act as mentors, empowering students to learn valuable research skills, and provide them with an experience that positions undergraduates as agents in an academic community of practice.

Part IV provides examples of institutional strategies and campus-wide efforts to address students' belonging needs at minority-serving institutions.

In Chapter 10, authors illustrate how they employ an asset-based approach to promote a sense of belonging at The University of Texas at El Paso, a Hispanic-serving institution that enrolls a high percentage of Latinx, low-income, and first-generation college students. The authors describe a collaboratively developed framework for belonging that engages students primarily through applied learning and pedagogical practices that build on students' strengths and that favor the cultural and linguistic practices of participants' home communities.

In Chapter 11, the author presents a case study of a historically Black college/university that launched a multifaceted, college-wide effort to promote academic success by engendering a sense of belonging during the global pandemic of 2020, while members of the campus community remained physically distant. The chapter reflects on the methods used to meet students' basic physiological and learning needs and shares insights into which strategies were most effective in sustaining a sense of belonging and promoting academic success.

The work featured in Part V invites readers to engage in creative methods for gathering information about students' experiences of belonging and to interrogate the relationship between belonging and mattering.

Chapter 12 introduces the "walking interview" as a novel mixed methods approach that can serve as a generative method for learning about what sites on campus students associate with a sense of belonging. The authors reflect on their participation in an institution-wide effort at Imperial College London to cultivate the practice of research as a method for learning about how to better support student belonging and success.

Chapter 13 draws on the experiences of faculty and undergraduate student partners at a community college and two liberal arts colleges to explore the relationship between the constructs of belonging and mattering. The student and faculty authors of this chapter suggest that mattering may be a more generative framework for supporting student success and empowerment, especially among students from historically underrepresented groups.

Conclusion

Taken as a whole, the volume combines insights from faculty, administrators, students, and researchers across disciplines and from an array of institutional settings (e.g., small colleges and universities, 2-year and 4-year institutions, predominantly White institutions and minority-serving institutions). In doing so, *Academic Belonging in Higher Education* provides readers with a sense of how collaborative efforts are evolving on the ground as faculty take a critical look at the power they have to shape student sense of belonging in academic domains. Readers will benefit from what the authors share about the process of collaborating, how efforts evolve across academic contexts and institutional levels, the challenges and successes these efforts encounter, how students experience these efforts, and how programs and initiatives can be assessed and improved to ensure that students are feeling connected, competent, and confident across academic settings.

References

Baumeister, R. F., & Leary, M. R. (1995). The need to belong: Desire for inter-personal attachment as a fundamental human motivation. *Psychological Bulletin*, 117, 497–529. doi:10.1037/0033-2909.117.3.497

Beattie, I. R. (2018). Sociological perspectives on first-generation college students. In B. Schneider & G. K. Shaw (Eds.), *Handbook of the sociology of education in the 21st century* (pp. 171–191). Springer. doi:10.1007/978-3-319-76694-2_8

Cohen, E., & Viola, J. (2022). The role of pedagogy and the curriculum in university students' sense of belonging. *Journal of University Teaching & Learning Practice*, 19(4), 06. doi:19/iss4/06

Conway, A. J. (2021, November 10). *Prioritizing diversity, equity, inclusion, and belonging in higher education.* Today's Learner Cengage. https://todayslearner.cengage.com/prioritizing-diversity-equity-inclusion-and-belonging-in-higher-education/

Davis, M., Dias-Bowie, Y., Greenberg, K., Klukken, G., Pollio, H. R., Thomas, S. P., & Thompson, C. L. (2004). "A fly in the buttermilk": Descriptions of university life by successful Black undergraduate students at a predominately White south-eastern university. *The Journal of Higher Education*, 75(4), 420–445. doi:10.1353/jhe.2004.0018

Donlan, A. E., Loughlin, S., & Byrne, V. L. (2019). The fearless teaching framework: A model to synthesize foundational education research for university instructors. *To Improve the Academy: A Journal of Educational Development*, 38(1), 33–49. doi:10.1002/tia2.20087

Engle, J., & Tinto, V. (2008). *Moving beyond access: College success for low-income, first-generation students.* Pell Institute for the Study of Opportunity in Higher Education.

Feagin, J., & Sikes, M. (1995). How Black students cope with racism on White campuses. *Journal of Blacks in Higher Education*, 8, 91–97.

Fischer, E. M. J. (2007). Settling into campus life: Differences by race/ethnicity in college involvement and outcomes. *The Journal of Higher Education*, 78(2), 125–161.

Freeman, T. M., Anderman, L. H., & Jensen, J. M. (2007). Sense of belonging in college freshmen at the classroom and campus levels. *The Journal of Experimental Education*, 75(3), 203–220.

Fries-Britt, S., & Turner, B. (2002). Uneven stories: Successful Black collegians at a Black and a White campus. *Review of Higher Education: Journal of the Association for the Study of Higher Education*, 25(3), 315–330. doi:10.1353/rhe.2002.0012

Harper, S. R. (2013). Am I my brother's teacher? Black undergraduates, racial socialization, and peer pedagogies in predominantly White postsecondary contexts. *Review of Research in Education*, 37(1), 183–211.

Hausmann, L. R., Schofield, J. W., & Woods, R. L. (2007). Sense of belonging as a predictor of intentions to persist among African American and White first-year college students. *Research in Higher Education*, 48, 803–839.

Hurtado, S., & Carter, D. F. (1997). Effects of college transition and perceptions of the campus racial climate on Latino college students' sense of belonging. *Sociology of Education*, 70(4), 324–345. doi:10.2307/2673270

Jack, A. A. (2019). *The privileged poor: How elite colleges are failing disadvantaged students (2019)*. Harvard University Press.

Joy, M. (2019, January 14). *Mastering the hidden curriculum (½)*. The Hub for Equity and Innovation in Higher Education. http://thehub.georgetown.doma ins/realhub/experience/mastering-the-hidden-curriculum-1-2/

Kahu, E. R., Ashley, N., & Picton, C. (2022). Exploring the complexity of first-year student belonging in higher education: Familiarity, interpersonal, and academic belonging. *Student Success*, 13(2), 10–20.

Kirby, L. A., & Thomas, C. L. (2022). High-impact teaching practices foster a greater sense of belonging in the college classroom. *Journal of Further and Higher Education*, 46(3), 368–381. doi:10.1080/0309877X.2021.1950659

Kurfist, A. (2022, April 29). *Student belonging: The next DEI frontier in higher education*. Hanover Research. https://www.hanoverresearch.com/insights-blog/stu dent-belonging-the-next-dei-frontier-in-higher-education/?org=higher-education

Lewis, K. L., & Hodges, S. D. (2015). Expanding the concept of belonging in academic domains: Development and validation of the Ability Uncertainty Scale. *Learning and Individual Differences*, 37, 197–202. doi:10.1016/j.lindif.2014.12.002

McCallen, L. S., & Johnson, H. L. (2020). The role of institutional agents in promoting higher education success among first-generation college students at a public urban university. *Journal of Diversity in Higher Education*, 13(4), 320. doi:10.1037/dhe0000143

Means, D. R., & Pyne, K. B. (2017). Finding my way: Perceptions of institutional support and belonging in low-income, first-generation, first-year college students. *Journal of College Student Development*, 58(6), 907–924. doi:10.1353/csd.2017.0071

Miller, A. L., Williams, L. M., & Silberstein, S. M. (2019). Found my place: The importance of faculty relationships for seniors' sense of belonging. *Higher Education Research & Development*, 38(3), 594–608. doi:10.1080/07294360.2018.1551333

Morrison, M., Young, T., Johnson, A., & Elmendorf, H. (2019). *TLISI 2019: The student sense of belonging at Georgetown: What we've learned from the data and where we go next*. Georgetown University. http://hdl.handle.net/10822/1055286

Morrison, M., Young, T., Johnson, A., & Elmendorf, H. (2020, January 20). *A student sense of belonging at Georgetown: First generation undergraduate student experiences*. The Hub for Equity and Innovation in Higher Education, Georgetown University. https://thehub.georgetown.domains/realhub/experience/student-sense-of-belong ing-at-georgetown-first-generation-undergraduate-student-experiences/

Museus, S. D., & Maramba, D. C. (2011). The impact of culture on Filipino American students' sense of belonging. *Review of Higher Education*, 34(2), 231–258. https://doi.org/10.1353/rhe.2010.0022

Nunn, L. (2021). *College belonging: How first-year and first-generation students navigate campus life*. Rutgers University Press.

Rueda, E., Ballard, T., Gonzalez, K., Gutierrez, A., Herrera, J., Magdaleno, L., Majarali, V., Martinez, J., Molina, J., & Walker, A. (2017). *In search of belonging:*

First generation, low-income students navigating financial, bureaucratic, and academic experiences at Vassar (Faculty Research Report No. 112). Vassar College. https://digitalwindow.vassar.edu/faculty_research_reports/112/

Schademan, A. R., & Thompson, M. R. (2016). Are college faculty and first-generation, low-income students ready for each other? *Journal of College Student Retention: Research, Theory & Practice*, 18(2), 194–216.

Solorzano, D., Ceja, M., & Yosso, T. (2000). Critical race theory, racial micro-aggressions, and campus racial climate: The experiences of African American college students. *Journal of Negro Education*, 69(1–2), 60–73.

Steele, C. M. (2010). *Whistling Vivaldi: How stereotypes affect us and what we can do.* W.W. Norton & Company.

Steele, C. M., & Aronson, J. (1995). Stereotype threat and the intellectual test performance of African Americans. *Journal of Personality and Social Psychology*, 69(5), 797.

Strayhorn, T. L. (2012). *College students' sense of belonging: A key to educational success for all students.* Routledge.

Strayhorn, T. L. (2019). *College students' sense of belonging: A key to educational success for all students* (2nd ed.). Routledge.

Tierney, W. G., & Jun, A. (2001). A university helps prepare low income youths for college: Tracking school success. *The Journal of Higher Education*, 72(2), 205–225.

Tinto, V. (1987). *Leaving college: Rethinking the causes and cures of student attrition.* University of Chicago Press.

Tinto, V. (1993). *Leaving college: Rethinking the causes and cures of student attrition* (2nd ed.). University of Chicago Press.

Vaccaro, A., & Newman, B. M. (2016). Development of a sense of belonging for privileged and minoritized students: An emergent model. *Journal of College Student Development*, 57(8), 925–942. https://muse.jhu.edu/article/638558

Vaccaro, A., & Newman, B. M. (2022). Theoretical foundations for sense of belonging in college. In E. M. Bentrim & G. W. Henning (Eds.), *The impact of a sense of belonging in college: Implications for student persistence, retention, and success* (pp. 3–20). Stylus.

Versteeg, M., Kappe, R. F., & Knuiman, C. (2022). Predicting student engagement: The role of academic belonging, social integration, and resilience during COVID-19 emergency remote teaching. *Frontiers in Public Health*, 10, 1–14. https://www.ncbi.nlm.nih.gov/pmc/articles/PMC8971557/

Walton, G. M., & Cohen, G. L. (2011). A brief social-belonging intervention improves academic and health outcomes of minority students. *Science*, 331(6023), 1447–1451. doi:10.1126/science.1198364

West, J. (2022, April 28). Belonging: Why it is the next step on the equity, diversity and inclusion ladder. *The Times Higher Education.* https://www.timeshighereducation.com/campus/belonging-why-it-next-step-equity-diversity-and-inclusion-ladder

PART I
Pedagogies of belonging

2

SENSE OF BELONGING IN THE COLLEGE CLASSROOM

Strategies for instructors

Alice E. Donlan, Carlton E. Green and Virginia L. Byrne

School belonging has been defined as the extent to which students feel that they are accepted, respected, and supported members of the campus system and community (Goodenow, 1993). The need for students to feel a strong sense of belonging in higher education has been well established (Davis et al., 2019; T. M. Freeman et al., 2010). We recommend that instructors develop an iterative approach to fostering a sense of belonging in their courses. We developed a workshop called Infusing Inclusion that guides instructors to think about why inclusion work must be done explicitly and intentionally across multiple dimensions of the course. Workshop participants reflect on a series of questions meant to stimulate attitudes and behaviors related to creating more inclusive courses in their own contexts, in ways that work for their courses, styles of teaching, and cohorts of students. Originally presented as one workshop in a series leading to a diversity and inclusion certificate, the workshop has been attended by hundreds of individuals with teaching responsibilities, including graduate teaching assistants, as well as tenure- and professional-track faculty. Designed as a highly interactive experience, the facilitators encourage questions throughout the workshop. Additionally, small-group work among participants affords them the opportunity to pose questions in a low-risk learning environment, share best practices from past experience, and generate additional strategies for navigating classroom challenges. Across multiple presentations of the workshop, feedback has been consistently favorable.

We aim to translate that workshop into this chapter, so that readers can go through the reflection questions on their own. In addition, we share findings from interviews with undergraduate students from underrepresented groups (i.e., Black, Latinx, LGBTQ+, low-income, and/or first-generation college

DOI: 10.4324/9781003443735-3

students) to provide real-life examples of students' experiences that can help educators rethink their approaches to teaching.

Fearless teaching framework

Instructors who are trying to foster belonging and infuse inclusion into their courses can benefit from using a conceptual model that prompts them to think about multiple dimensions of their teaching. We ground the Infusing Inclusion workshop in a model for effective teaching in higher education called the fearless teaching framework (Donlan et al., 2019). The framework was designed by reviewing the empirical teaching and learning literature and organizing findings into four interdependent pieces of effective teaching that encourage students' motivation and engagement: classroom climate, course content, teaching practice, and assessment strategies.

Climate refers to the extent to which students perceive the classroom to be a supportive, inclusive, accessible, and power-conscious space (whether online or face to face) and has been found to be supportive of students' sense of belonging and motivation (e.g., Baumeister & Leary, 1995; Zubrunn et al., 2014). *Content* encompasses the course objectives, topics, materials, and examples selected by the instructor. When students see these content decisions as being relevant to their lives, interests, and cultures, there is a positive impact on their motivation, engagement, and belonging (e.g., Frymier & Shulman, 1995; Howard, 2001). *Practices* include all teaching moves, learning activities, facilitated decisions, and lessons used during class time. Students are more likely to engage in class activities, enjoy the learning process, and feel a sense of belonging to the class community when the instructor uses organized, purposeful, accessible, and active teaching practices (e.g., Ambrose et al., 2010; Wentzel & Brophy, 2014). *Assessments* include all projects, tests, and assignments used as formative or summative evaluations of student learning. Students' motivation, engagement, and belonging are related to the degree to which they see themselves as meeting the expectations of the environment – a measure that is often determined by graded assessments, instructor feedback, and class standing (e.g., Hattie & Timperley, 2007; Pellegrino et al., 2016).

We have found this framework to be effective for working with higher education instructors in discussing and evaluating their teaching both in person and online (Byrne & Donlan, 2020; Donlan & Byrne, 2020). It has also been useful to think about the framework as an inclusion tool for promoting belonging in a multidimensional way. In the Infusing Inclusion workshop, we prompt instructors to think deeply about how they are engaging in inclusion work across the course climate, content, practice, and assessment.

Connecting instructor strategies to students' stories

In the Infusing Inclusion workshop, we ask instructor participants to share stories describing times their students taught them lessons about inclusion. Instructors share times they realized that they needed to change a common practice to make the class more relevant or accessible to their students. They also share reflections on their own identities as students and instructors, in terms of both dominant group identities and marginalized identities. These stories provide a richness and ground the workshop in the real world. Since we cannot elicit stories from the reader here, we offer student quotations from a research project on college student belonging to give examples of student experiences with inclusion and exclusion in class.

To understand the experiences of campus belonging among students from historically marginalized groups, the first author conducted interviews with 20 undergraduate students from October 2016 to October 2017 ($n = 20$; mean age = 20.45; 65% women, 20% men, 15% non-binary or other gender identity; 55% Black/African American, 20% Asian, 25% other racial identity). We recruited students who belonged to five identity groups: Black/African American ($n = 6$), Latinx ($n = 3$), LGBTQ+ ($n = 6$), low-income/Pell Grant–eligible ($n = 10$), and first-generation ($n = 6$) college students. In the sample, 12 students identified with more than one of these groups. Students received a $10 gift card as an incentive for participating. All of the interviews were conducted at the same large, public university.

In private, recorded one-on-one interviews and focus groups, students were asked about their general experiences with belonging in multiple campus contexts, including with peers and in classroom settings. Example questions included "Is there a place on campus where you feel a strong sense of belonging?" and "What are things that faculty and staff could do to show you that you belong in class and on campus?" Students reported a variety of experiences related to belonging and exclusion on campus.

Infusing Inclusion workshop

The Infusing Inclusion workshop was co-developed and co-facilitated by the first and second authors. Two primary factors contributed to the formulation of the workshop. First, the workshop developers heard from many instructors that they were interested in discussing ways in which they could foster a sense of academic belonging among students, and they were having difficulties coming up with concrete ideas supported by literature. Second, through campus climate study data and informal interactions with staff, students from marginalized backgrounds indicated that they were experiencing microaggressions and other forms of identity-related maltreatment in classrooms. Sometimes, the offenses were committed by faculty, and other times faculty passively observed as students made prejudiced remarks or exhibited discriminatory behaviors. The first two authors created a professional development experience to address both of these concerns.

Institutional context

The workshop begins with a discussion of the institutional context, including the recent current racial and gender demographics of the students and faculty. As a note, though we present some demographic data (e.g., race, gender), we also explicitly state that we cannot share data on other categories (e.g., percentage of people who are sexual and gender minorities), because those data are not collected at our institution. We highlight how this could be an institutional shortcoming that might compromise a sense of belonging for groups neglected in data collection, and instructors should be sensitive to replicating this dynamic in the classroom.

The workshop was developed at an institution that is a large, historically White land-grant university in the mid-Atlantic United States. The campus community consists of approximately 50,000 students, staff, and faculty from diverse racial, gender, and geographic backgrounds. Designated as a Carnegie Doctoral/Research University, the institution offers undergraduate and graduate degrees. Though most students reported being White men, the student population has become less White and male in recent years. Additionally, the teaching faculty continues to be predominantly White and male.

At inception, American higher education focused on the "rigorous education of the 'gentleman scholar'" (Thelin & Gasman, 2017, p. 6). Initially, all college presidents and faculty were White men, many of whom were men of the cloth. New College – now Harvard College – opened in 1636, followed by the College of William and Mary in 1693 (Geiger, 2014). Heavily influenced by the English education tradition that emerged out of the universities of Oxford and Cambridge, early colonial education became a living and learning experience that attended to the character development of its White male students. Using a curriculum that emphasized analytic thinking and writing (Thelin & Gasman, 2017), early higher education sought to create a pathway to church and state leadership.

Students who benefited from higher education were primarily White and male. Though most of these students hailed from wealthy families, there was some socioeconomic diversity. Schools borrowed from the Oxford tradition of marking students by social class. "Academic robes reflected socioeconomic position, delineating the 'commoners' (those who dined at college commons) from the 'servitors' (those who waited tables)" (Thelin & Gasman, 2017, p. 5). Students also represented the Protestant religious affiliations that were present among the colonists. Whereas the modern university purports to promote upward social mobility, the early collegiate experience marked a White man's social location.

The confluence of the early emphasis on restricting higher education to White men from wealthy and religious families, the introduction of the campus living environment, and the focus on training for public life excluded large swaths of the population. Specifically, the legacy of settler colonialism, beginning with Columbus's "discovery" of America, extended to higher education as the early educators erased the educational needs of White women, Indigenous people, and enslaved Africans (Museus et al., 2015). Thus, the early colonial colleges institutionalized both climate and curriculum that focused on the needs of its population: White, mostly Protestant men.

Understanding the history of purposeful exclusion in higher education of students who are not White, cisgender, Protestant, and able-bodied men provides a powerful lens to the work of inclusion. We use this history to argue that to promote academic belonging, instructors must intentionally and actively engage in inclusion work to combat the exclusive structures that were baked into the design of higher education.

The fearless teaching framework as a tool for inclusion

After describing the institutional context, we go through each piece of the fearless teaching framework and pose reflection questions to be discussed in small groups. Then, we choose one reflection question to discuss as a full group. We do not provide a checklist of strategies since each course, instructor, discipline, and institution is different. Instead, we offer the list of reflection questions and recommendations from students from historically excluded groups to illustrate the relationship between inclusion work and academic belonging and provide ideas to the reader.

Climate

Climate is the dimension of the fearless teaching framework that likely comes to mind first when discussing belonging and inclusion and encompasses what the instructors and students do to create an inclusive context that promotes belonging. We challenge instructors to consider:

1. What plans do you have to prioritize relationship building at the start of the semester?
2. What efforts are you making to use inclusive language?
3. What work are you prepared to do to create a context where difficult discussions can be productive?
4. How are you planning to address hurtful or harmful language?
5. How are you meeting students' needs for accessibility?

These questions are intended to prompt instructors to think about how they design their course to foster acceptance, respect, and support by learning their students' pronouns and interests and constructing helpful norms for engagement and repair. In the session, instructors often share how they start the semester with good intentions for doing this work, and they leave the workshop acknowledging that many times they do not reinforce class norms throughout the course, as needed. Often, we hear from educators who are grappling with learning up-to-date language themselves and balancing the time to create a positive learning environment with time dedicated to course content. In addition, sometimes instructors struggle with ways to hold students to high academic standards while maintaining a supportive environment.

The data collected from students highlighted the need for faculty to engage climate-related inclusion strategies that facilitate a sense of belonging. For instance, when building relationships early on, students suggest that faculty consider the role of racial bias:

> ... one thing I would let professors know is that it's part of your job ... to step out of your comfort zone as a professor. I think a lot of professors stay in their comfort zone. Like, first of all, there's a lot more White professors than Black professors and a lot more White students than Black students. ... With professors sometimes it's like they are really comfortable with being more around White students than Black students. ... They'll make more jokes with the White students, they'll have more conversations with White students than with Black students. It's kind of just like, "Okay, here's your homework."
>
> *(Black man, engineering student)*

Students also suggest that instructors stay up-to-date with inclusive language and establish community guidelines for respect and care in the class:

> So one of the things my professors do there is they'll ask for people's pronouns and how they identify it and we would write it down on little cards. ... That was helpful 'cause then they ended up remembering stuff about you and what things are important to you. ... It would be helpful also talking about inclusive language and when we're doing discussions and stuff like not even for large classes for discussion sessions. It would be nice to have people set ground rules for this is how we're going to meet, talk to you about or just not being rude in class. ... It makes me feel like the professor cares more. ... So definitely the classes where I liked my professors and I feel comfortable and I want to do better at.
>
> *(Latina, first-generation computer science student)*

Many students, particularly Pell Grant–eligible students, requested that instructors recognize that not all students have financial means to buy resources or print readings, an accessibility issue that can negate their meaningful participation in the class:

> A lot of teachers have an assumption that we can afford to go to certain things. And so when they are telling us that we've got to go and check this out, got to go to that show … the people that don't have money are like yeah. … Even the asking us to print stuff, even asking us to – that one is something that kind of really bugs me because if I don't have money on my [account] and if I'm already in the red for the month, I'm like, fuck, we have to print this thing? Great. [sarcasm]
> *(Mixed-race, non-binary, LGBTQ, first-generation, Pell Grant–eligible*
> *art student)*

Finally, students wanted instructors to acknowledge within-group differences and not act as if all marginalized students have the same experiences or needs:

> I have to think about it for a bit because me not coming from, I would say a traditional minority student or Black student's background, my experiences are a little bit different.
> *(Black man, LGBTQ questioning, Pell Grant–eligible engineering*
> *student)*

The interviewed students and the workshop participants agreed about the importance of creating an accepting, supportive classroom climate. Instructors were interested in how to go beyond simple care (e.g., learning students' names) and also include other aspects mentioned by students, such as learning their backgrounds and goals, establishing and revisiting community guidelines for class discussions, and understanding the heterogeneity within groups of students.

Content

We see inclusive content when the instructor chooses content that students can see themselves in or connect to. Using names from a wide array of cultures in word problems, choosing novels with main characters from many backgrounds, or highlighting the contributions of scholars from minoritized and marginalized identities in a field are all ways to increase inclusivity and belonging using content. Our reflection questions for this area include:

1. How do you select course material that relates to students' own lived experiences?

2. Whose identities are you centering?
3. Whose voices (e.g., theorists, researchers, authors) are you presenting as experts?
4. What resources are you providing to help students access required course materials?
5. How can you help your students see gaps in the field where there are not enough resources related to a particular identity group?

These questions prompt a discussion of examples and artifacts discussed in the course. Most disciplines include a cannon that disproportionately relies on scholars who are White men, and these questions lead to conversations about how to disrupt that overreliance. We often hear from instructors who have a hard time finding resources that center the experiences of historically marginalized groups, and we encourage them to share that difficulty with their students and explore the reasons and implications behind the gap in the literature and research. It is also important to note that selecting relevant course material requires instructors to get to know their students and understand their prior knowledge and future goals.

Students we spoke to were particularly excited when instructors included information from multiple perspectives:

> One of my teachers is a part of the LGBTQ community. So, like, every day, we'll talk about different things. And she'll make sure to try to include all different types of people. So that's always nice. Especially around the election time, when there was all this stuff happening. She was just very … inclusive with that.
>
> *(Black woman, Pell Grant–eligible family science student)*

When trying to make content relevant and connected to students' prior knowledge, the students we spoke to also asked that instructors consider that students may have different preexisting knowledge and preparation:

> The high school I went to, it was pretty diverse. … It's a magnet school, but if you compare that school to private school, I would say the academic resources you had back then affect where you are now. I was talking about this to one of the professors here on campus. About when you have minorities who come to [university], they're really smart students. They have the ability to do very well, but since their foundation is a little bit more rocky, it affects when they move up.
>
> *(Black man, LGBTQ questioning, Pell Grant–eligible engineering student)*

An impactful way to make sure students can see that they belong in class is when instructors include content that is relevant to the lives of the students:

> I'm way more motivated to inject myself into everything [in] my American Studies class. I don't know my professor a whole lot, but everything that she's teaching about is stuff that feels super-relevant to me. ... [S]he's talking about abuse in the labor system and it's a global economy and how it's affected by race and gender. ... [W]hat she's been teaching about is about me, as I see it, and I've been really noisy in my discussion group all the time.
>
> *(Mixed-race, non-binary, LGBTQ, first-generation, Pell Grant–eligible art student)*

Bringing in expertise from different identities and perspectives has been discussed as decolonizing the cannon of academia (Stein & Andreotti, 2016) and can require considerable effort on the part of instructors. Further, departments and colleges need to support instructors' choice of course content, which can facilitate the transition away from a this-is-the-way-it's-always-been-done mentality. However, even engaging in the question of *who* counts as an expert, and *why*, can help students recognize gaps in the field that they could potentially remedy and shows the need for multiple perspectives within fields.

Practice

The next piece of the fearless teaching framework is practice, which includes all of the techniques instructors engage to teach students the course content. In the most positive case, instructors utilize evidence-based teaching practices (e.g., active learning) and make an effort to refine their skills. Teaching practices can be infused with inclusion by choosing course activities and lecture styles that incorporate small-group discussions, reflection prompts, and poll questions that help students connect what they are learning to their own lives and identities and to structure activities to create opportunities for positive peer relationships. We encourage instructors to explore:

1. What would it look like to teach as though your goal is to expand your field to more students?
2. What are your lenses, identities, and approaches to the material, and can these be shared with your students?
3. How do you help students connect the material to their own lived experiences?
4. How can peers interact with each other during the course? How are you structuring those interactions?

Many disciplines weed students out of programs through cultures of competition (e.g., Hatfield et al., 2022), which are arguably exclusionary practices. The workshop questions are designed to help instructors reflect on ways to support all students in collaborative ways and show students the relevance of the discipline to their lives. Participants have shared strategies to incorporate the recognition of power and privilege in group work and discussions, as well as active learning strategies that bring students' thoughts and contributions into the forefront of the lesson.

In the workshop, we heard from many instructors who are wary to talk about their personal lives with students (e.g., self-disclosing as first-generation college students). However, students noted that when instructors share their identities with their students in discussions related to diversity and inclusion, it enriches the conversation and makes students feel a sense of belonging:

> I took [a course] first semester of my freshman year and we did all sorts of activities, sort of like that other class where it was interesting because, first of all, a really diverse class, and then also our teacher was really cool, so he kind of also just facilitated it a lot. ... He was gay, and I think he [had a] Latino background, so he was just all about diversity and everything, so that made it a cool class.
>
> *(Black woman, nursing student)*

Active learning strategies – strategies that engage students directly with learning instead of listening as passive receivers of knowledge – have been shown to predict increases in student grades by about half a letter grade (S. Freeman et al., 2014; Chapter 3). Some examples include debates, small-group discussions, jigsaw activities that ask students to teach each other one puzzle piece of a topic to learn the whole lesson, and many other strategies.

Students indicated that these active learning practices contribute to their sense of academic belonging:

> [The instructor] did a lot of, like, fishbowls where we had our assigned readings from the evening and she would ask if anybody had any major questions. And then she would have two or three seats in the middle and all of the other chairs would be around and people would all come in. And she would put a couple questions on the board and ask everybody to write their responses just to think about the stuff they read the night before. And then she told everybody that three people would have to get up and go sit in those middle tables and just as if it were just the three of them just talk about the first question. ... Her efforts to, like, make people have discussions in

class was, like, heroic, because that's really something that's missing in a lot of classes.

(Mixed-race, non-binary, LGBTQ, first-generation, Pell Grant–eligible art student)

When instructors take the lead in broaching identity-related topics, some students reported increased classroom engagement, as well as a sense of acknowledgment in the classroom:

I've been very active in that class because it feels so relevant to me, and the TA for that one is really nice. She started off the semester in a cute way where she like everybody had to do like … she put signs up around the room that was, like, Gender, Race, Religion, Political Beliefs. And it was like "Blank is the part of my identity that I think people misunderstand the most," and then you had to go and stand in that corner. … It was really cool, and so that helped set me up throughout the semester to want to be more chatty in class.

(Mixed-race, non-binary, LGBTQ, first-generation, Pell Grant–eligible art student)

Finally, students noted that instructors often assume that students will independently find others with whom they will form groups. Unfortunately, students from historically marginalized groups are often subtly or overtly ignored by their classmates during organic group formation. Students instead suggested that instructors assist in the formation of study groups, which is likely to foster greater connection among students while minimizing exclusion and discrimination:

Once you find a group of people to study with, you study with them. You have access to oral exams. You have people to bounce ideas off of. But if you have minorities or other people that feel like they don't belong, they don't really have that, so it's less likely for them to do well because they don't have the same type of community, the same type of resources that these groups share amongst each other. They might have exams from the past three semesters, whereas that one student alone, who could be a transfer student, who didn't start the program with these people, or a minority student who just can't really relate to some of the experiences, they're alone, so they only can rely on their textbook, the professor, and themselves. … Students do it on their own. The thing is, with engineering, you can't get through it alone. I feel like that might be why you see a small percentage of minorities actually making it through to graduation, because you can't do it alone.

(Black man, LGBTQ questioning, Pell Grant–eligible engineering student)

Teaching practices include a broad range of activities designed to help students learn the course content. Student data indicated that long, impersonal lectures that allowed them to remain anonymous did not positively impact academic belonging. Instead, they recommended that instructors share their own personal stories, include active practices, and direct interventions with students on group work. These practices facilitate connections to instructors, peers, and content.

Assessment

The final piece of the fearless teaching framework is assessment, which should be clear, valid, and appropriate for the level of learning. Students should know the expectations of any assessments in advance, and they should have ample opportunities to build the skills necessary to be successful on the assessments. The workshop reflection questions we pose are:

1. Does the timing of your assessments make assumptions about the students' schedules?
2. What cultures and prior knowledge are you centering in the language of assessments?
3. What is your plan for minimizing bias in grading?
4. How does your assessment strategy allow for students to play to their strengths while demonstrating their mastery of the learning outcomes?
5. What technologies are you assuming students can access to complete these assessments?

These questions are designed to prompt instructors to reflect on whether there is an equitable playing field when it comes to graded assessments. In the workshop, participants shared occasions when they allowed students the flexibility to choose a written or oral assignment based on their preferences and strengths and ways to hide students' identities during the grading process to minimize bias. Instructors discussed both the difficulty that added flexibility can create in their practice and the helpfulness for engaging students.

Students recommended that instructors recognize that not all students have access to the same learning resources. When designing assignments, it may be helpful for instructors to explicitly indicate the resources they are expecting students to leverage and consider how and when that access might be restricted:

> I remember I heard one student say, "I have to buy a tutor," – she had to buy a tutor for the class and then – I mean, there's a free tutoring session here but I kind of wanted a one-on-one session because I knew my professor wasn't available, and when I went to that tutoring session

on campus sometimes they would have multiple students trying to teach all at once. So it was really hard trying to, like, have someone that could kind of be here for me, and I couldn't really afford a tutor, nor could my parents. ... I think that would've been great to have tutors for low-income, first-generation students because they need more help compared to other students.

(Black woman, first-generation, Pell Grant–eligible sociology and communications student)

Students also noted that a growing percentage of students have extra demands on their time outside of academics. Although it is reasonable to expect students to spend meaningful time on a class, the reality is that students who need to work, parent, or fulfill other responsibilities are also more likely to have fewer resources with respect to time and money. Access to resources could facilitate or impede a sense of belonging. Being sensitive to and appropriately acknowledging social class–related dynamics among students is likely to foster increased awareness for those with class privilege and create support for others:

One of my employers asked me to submit my transcript. [And they asked] Why do you have a C in finance, but it's an introduction course? ... and I was like, it was a hard summer, it was a really hard semester, I was working three jobs, there was no way I could have concentrated.

(Asian woman, Pell Grant–eligible business student)

Overall, our conversation pertaining to assessment in the workshop asks instructors to consider ways to create assignments that allow students to demonstrate their mastery of the learning outcome and consider who their students are. We suggest reflecting on ways to create an even playing field, such as allowing students to choose from different assessment modalities and being mindful of students' time and access to resources.

Conclusion

We typically close the workshop with a discussion on considerations for receiving feedback from students related to unbelonging or exclusion. For example, using a mid-semester evaluation to gather anonymous feedback or inviting student comments can help students share what is and is not working for them. However, it is important to note that with formal course evaluations, instructors with visible minoritized and marginalized identities (e.g., women, men of color) may receive more critical feedback (Bavishi et al., 2010), especially when diversity is emphasized in a course. Participants are encouraged to consider their emotional state, remain open and nondefensive, and use the feedback to grow in their practice. We normalize for participants that receiving feedback pertaining to inclusion or belonging in a course where they are the subject matter expert could actually prompt a defensive response in them. Participants are encouraged to name for themselves how their emotional and behavioral reactions may manifest (e.g., fight, flight, freeze). More specifically, we highlight that receiving student feedback indicating that an instructor has been microaggressive, disrespectful, or unresponsive – which can all compromise a sense of belonging – the instructor is likely to experience strong human reactions. For instance, a defensive reaction could evidence itself as anger, resulting in the instructor becoming argumentative with or hostile toward students. An instructor who is embarrassed or hurt by the feedback could experience anxiety, feel helpless, lose confidence, and become overly accommodating. Understanding our emotional and behavioral tendencies when we perceive that our competence is being attacked or we have disappointed or harmed our students is critical to maintaining our identity as an inclusive practitioner committed to fostering a sense of belonging. Instructors are encouraged to develop a practice of actively reflecting on how their own professional and social identities, as well as perceptions thereof, may influence interactions with students and perceptions of student feedback. This could involve journaling in preparation for and while teaching the course, engaging trusted colleagues or communities in exploring identity-based classroom dynamics, and participating in continuing education that promotes mindfulness and critical consciousness (Hölzel et al., 2011; Kernahan, 2019).

We offer these reflection questions and stories informed by the components of the fearless teaching framework to help instructors understand that their classrooms are not islands. Instead, they exist within the context of a discipline, campus, city, nation, and world. Students do not leave their identities behind when they enter a learning space, and it is important to actively include students from backgrounds who have been actively excluded in the past, such that all students feel accepted, respected, and supported.

References

Ambrose, S. A., Bridges, M. W., & DiPietro, M. (2010). *How learning works: Seven research based principles for smart teaching.* Jossey-Bass.

Baumeister, R. F., & Leary, M. R. (1995). The need to belong: Desire for interpersonal attachments as a fundamental human motivation. *Psychological Bulletin,* 117(3), 497–529.

Bavishi, A., Madera, J. M., & Hebl, M. R. (2010). The effect of professor ethnicity and gender on student evaluations: Judged before met. *Journal of Diversity in Higher Education,* 3(4), 245–256.

Byrne, V. L., & Donlan, A. E. (2020). A mid-semester evaluation of college teaching to improve online teaching effectiveness. *Online Learning Journal,* 24(2), 94–110. doi:10.24059/olj.v24i2.2126

Davis, G. M., Hanzsek-Brill, M. B., Petzold, M. C., & Robinson, D. H. (2019). Students' sense of belonging: The development of a predictive retention model. *Journal of the Scholarship of Teaching and Learning*, 19(1). doi:10.14434/josotl. v19i1.26787

Donlan, A. E., & Byrne, V. L. (2020). Confirming the factor structure of a research-based mid-semester evaluation for college teaching. *Journal of Psychoeducational Assessment*, 38(7), 866–881. doi:10.1177/0734282920903165

Donlan, A. E., Loughlin, S., & Byrne, V. L. (2019). The fearless teaching framework: A model to synthesize foundational education research for university instructors. *To Improve the Academy: A Journal of Educational Development*, 38(1), 33–49. doi:10.1002/tia2.20087

Freeman, S., Eddy, S. L., McDonough, M., Smith, M., Okoroafor, N., Jordt, H., & Wenderoth, M. P. (2014). Active learning increases student performance in science, engineering, and mathematics. *Proceedings of the National Academy of Sciences*, 111(23), 8410–8415.

Freeman, T. M., Anderman, L. H., & Jensen, J. M. (2010). Sense of belonging in college freshmen at the classroom and campus levels. *The Journal of Experimental Education*, 75(3), 203–220.

Frymier, A. B., & Shulman, G. M. (1995). "What's in it for me?": Increasing content relevance to enhance students' motivation. *Communication Education*, 44(1), 40–50.

Geiger, R. (2014). *The history of American higher education: Learning and culture from the founding to World War II*. Princeton University Press.

Goodenow, C. (1993). Classroom belonging among early adolescent students: Relationships to motivation and achievement. *The Journal of Early Adolescence*, 13(1), 21–43.

Hatfield, N., Brown, N., & Topaz, C. M. (2022). Do introductory courses disproportionately drive minoritized students out of STEM pathways? *PNAS Nexus*, 1(4), pgac167.

Hattie, J., & Timperley, H. (2007). The power of feedback. *Review of Educational Research*, 77(1), 81–112. doi:10.3102/003465430298487

Hölzel, B. K., Lazar, S. W., Gard, T., Schuman-Olivier, Z., Vago, D. R., & Ott, U. (2011). How does mindfulness meditation work? Proposing mechanisms of action from a conceptual and neural perspective. *Perspectives on Psychological Science*, 6(6), 537–559.

Howard, T. C. (2001). Telling their side of the story: African-American students' perceptions of culturally relevant teaching. *The Urban Review*, 33(2), 131–149.

Kernahan, C. (2019). *Teaching about race and racism in the college classroom: Notes from a White professor*. West Virginia University Press.

Museus, S. D., Ledesma, M. C., & Parker, T. L. (2015). Racism and racial equity in higher education: Racism and racial equity in higher education. *Ashe Higher Education Report*, 42(1), 1–112. doi:10.1002/aehe.20067

Pellegrino, J. W., DiBello, L. V., & Goldman, S. R. (2016). A framework for conceptualizing and evaluating the validity of instructionally relevant assessments. *Educational Psychologist*, 51(1), 59–81. doi:10.1080/00461520.2016.1145550

Stein, S., & Andreotti, V. D. O. (2016). Decolonization and higher education. In M. Peters (Ed.), *Encyclopedia of educational philosophy and theory*. Springer Science + Business Media. doi:10.1007/978-981-287-532-7_479-471.

Thelin, J. R., & Gasman, M. (2017). Historical overview of American higher education. In J. H. Schuh, S. R. Jones, & V. Torres (Eds.), *Student services: A handbook for the profession* (6th ed., pp. 3–19). John Wiley & Sons.

Wentzel, K., & Brophy, J. (2014). *Motivating students to learn*. Routledge.

Zubrunn, S., McKim, C., Buhs, E., & Hawley, L. R. (2014). Support, belonging, motivation, and engagement in the college classroom: A mixed method study. *Instructional Science*, 42, 661–684.

3

WHAT WOMEN WANT

Pedagogical approaches for promoting female students' sense of belonging in undergraduate calculus

Casey Griffin and Dawn Berk

About 10 years ago, our math department initiated a serious campaign to improve student success in our introductory undergraduate mathematics courses. The DFW rate (the percentage of students earning a D, F, or withdrawing) in these courses was high, and students' satisfaction with these courses and retention into the next math course was low. The data were especially concerning when we zoomed in on the experience of students from underrepresented groups. In response, a task force was created and charged to investigate potential solutions. Several changes arose from this group's work, including the creation of a unit in the department that would develop and implement a new model of teaching and learning based on best practices and research. The second author of this chapter became the founding director of the new unit, known as the Mathematical Sciences Learning Laboratory (MSLL).

To improve student success in the introductory courses, the MSLL team developed a model consisting of two key principles. First, the courses would move to a higher level of coordination beyond common textbooks and exams. Instructors for each course would collaboratively develop and teach from a shared curriculum consisting of classroom activities and lesson plans. The curriculum would specify exactly what problems and activities students work on in each class session and provide a pacing guide for instructors. Second, the courses would provide consistent and regular opportunities for students to engage in *active learning*. Specifically, instructors would implement a teaching cycle beginning with a brief lecture, followed by students working on problems in pairs or small groups, followed by a whole class discussion. This cycle would be repeated two to three times in each class session. All instructors teaching courses in MSLL were expected to teach from the shared curriculum and engage in

DOI: 10.4324/9781003443735-4

the active learning model of instruction. In these ways, we could ensure that all students received high-quality and consistent learning opportunities across different sections of a given course. (For more details about the model used in MSLL, see Berk & Hiebert, 2009, and Cirillo et al., 2022.)

MSLL was charged with studying and improving three introductory mathematics courses – Intermediate Algebra, Pre-calculus, and Integrated Calculus. This chapter focuses on Integrated Calculus, an experimental, two-semester course sequence. This course is an alternative pathway for students who intend to major in science, technology, engineering, or mathematics (STEM) and thus need calculus but place into pre-calculus. The existing pathway consisted of a standard pre-calculus course followed by a standard calculus course, with both courses taught primarily via lecture. In contrast, the two-semester Integrated Calculus course weaves the pre-calculus and calculus content together throughout the year. Students who pass both semesters of the course receive credit for the standard calculus course. Bringing the course into MSLL resulted in the development of a shared curriculum and the implementation of the pedagogy cycle involving regular opportunities for active learning.

Unlike many educational reforms, the changes we began implementing 10 years ago have persisted and have resulted in improved student success. For example, the DFW rate has decreased by about 8% in the pre-calculus course and is about 13% lower in the Integrated Calculus pathway when compared to the standard pathway. Retention from pre-calculus to calculus has increased from about 53% in the standard pathway to about 78% in the Integrated Calculus pathway. Based on these results, the experimental Integrated Calculus course has since become a permanent course. However, one issue that needs further investigation is the effect of these changes on the experiences of students from underrepresented groups. Specifically, how are the active learning opportunities being received and experienced by these students?

This brings us to the 2019–2020 academic year, when the first author (Griffin) began her doctoral program in mathematics education and was assigned to work with the second author (Berk) as a teaching assistant in Integrated Calculus. By this time, the course curriculum had become stable and the DFW rates were already much lower than in the existing pathway. Griffin had never seen an undergraduate mathematics course taught in the way that Integrated Calculus was being taught and began to wonder whether active learning opportunities might influence women's retention in calculus and, ultimately, STEM. As one of the core designers and instructors of the Integrated Calculus course, Berk became intrigued as well. The existence of two competing pathways – one that involved active learning opportunities and one that did not – offered a rich site in which to explore these questions. After much reading and discussion, Griffin took the lead in designing a set of studies to investigate these questions. This chapter highlights what we have learned from one of these studies.

In this chapter, we make the case that providing more active learning opportunities – especially *interactive* opportunities – may support undergraduate women's sense of belonging and contribute to their retention in STEM. We share data from a study investigating women's sense of belonging in the two different calculus courses. While women in both courses identified ways in which learning opportunities in the course influenced their sense of belonging, women enrolled in the active learning calculus course reported a greater sense of belonging than women enrolled in the standard calculus course. Moreover, drawing on the findings, we identify several implications and recommendations for instructors of calculus and other introductory STEM courses.

The gender diversity problem in STEM

Diversity is critical to excellence in any field (Gibbs, 2014). Research is more typically conducted in teams rather than individually, and with more perspectives come more and different approaches to solving problems. A more diverse workforce increases the potential for identifying and tackling new types of problems that might not be identified by a more homogenous workforce. Moreover, diverse groups exhibit better problem-solving behaviors and hold more complex discussions than homogenous groups (Antonio et al., 2004; Hong & Page, 2004).

Unfortunately, women continue to be underrepresented in STEM fields, resulting in a lack of diversity that limits these fields of inquiry. The STEM gender gap is due at least in part to students' college major decisions (Carmichael, 2017; Chamberlain, 2017). Fewer women than men enter into undergraduate STEM majors (Eagan et al., 2015), and more women than men leave STEM. In fact, only about half of STEM-intending students complete a STEM degree, and of this already small proportion, women are 1.5 times as likely as men to switch out of STEM (Chen, 2013; Ellis et al., 2016). As a result, far more men persist and graduate with STEM degrees than women, leading to a homogenous STEM workforce.

Calculus can be an especially critical leak in the STEM pipeline and thus is a good site for investigation. Calculus is not only a required course for STEM majors but also often a prerequisite or corequisite for other STEM coursework, and so students who perform poorly in calculus may be prevented from taking other courses for their major. Consequently, calculus is a key junction at which students, especially women, decide whether to persist in STEM (Ellis et al., 2016; Rasmussen et al., 2019; Seymour & Hunter, 2019). The next natural question is – why?

Why undergraduate women students leave STEM

Students' sense of belonging in STEM plays a major role in their decisions to leave STEM, especially for women (Seymour & Hunter, 2019; Shapiro & Sax, 2011). Sense of belonging can be conceptualized as "one's personal belief that one is an accepted member of an academic community whose presence and contributions are valued" (Good et al., 2012, p. 701). One feels a sense of belonging when they feel connected to a particular environment or feel accepted and appreciated by others in that environment (Rosenberg & McCullough, 1981). Strayhorn (2012) argued that a sense of belonging can be so essential that one cannot engage in a space without feeling a sense of belonging in that space.

Research indicates that students with a stronger sense of belonging are more likely to persist in STEM and that women are less likely to develop a strong sense of belonging than men (Rainey et al., 2018; Seymour & Hunter, 2019; Shapiro & Sax, 2011). As Donlan et al. argue in Chapter 2, the U.S. system of education, particularly secondary and postsecondary institutions, was originally created by men, for the sole purpose of educating men. As a result, there is a masculine bias at the heart of most academic disciplines, methodologies, and theories (Gilligan, 1979, 1982). This is especially true for science and mathematics, in which discourse positions the field as a source of rational thought and objective truth – qualities associated with masculinity (Mendick, 2006). It is not surprising, then, that the ways in which science and mathematics classes have historically been taught reflect masculine values, which can be alienating for women and deter them from persisting in such spaces (Leyva et al., 2020).

So the question becomes "What can STEM faculty do to support their students' sense of belonging?" To explore this, first we need to identify factors that contribute to a sense of belonging. Here we focus on two key factors: (a) learning environment and (b) social and academic integration.

There is support within STEM education research that the learning environment might influence students' sense of belonging (Lahdenperä & Nieminen, 2020; Rainey et al., 2019). Based on their analysis of students' descriptions of positive and negative contributors to their sense of belonging in mathematics, Lahdenperä and Nieminen (2020) reported that students' perceptions of the learning environment contributed to their sense of belonging. For example, one student explained, "Lectures and small group sessions support my feeling of belonging in the mathematics community. Without these I would hardly participate in interactive learning of mathematics" (Lahdenperä & Nieminen, 2020, p. 484). Additionally, Rainey et al. (2019) found that students who experienced a more active learning environment (i.e., contrasting lecture) had greater perceptions of instructor care, which in turn related to a greater sense of belonging. In fact, the women in their study who had left STEM reported experiencing a more traditional learning environment (i.e., lecture), while preferring more active learning environments.

Other factors that contribute to students' sense of belonging are social and academic integration or fit (Hausmann et al., 2009; Hoffman et al., 2003; Lewis & Hodges, 2015; Tinto, 1975). Tinto (1975) described social integration as occurring primarily through peer group associations and interactions with faculty. Other studies confirmed that social connectedness supports students' sense of belonging. In their interview study with 201 college seniors who were STEM majors, Rainey et al. (2018) found that the most frequently cited contributor to sense of belonging in STEM was students' interpersonal relationships. Further, the students who left STEM reported a low sense of belonging and attributed it primarily to a lack of interpersonal relationships. Additionally, Hausmann et al. (2009) revealed a link between social integration, sense of belonging, and intention to persist.

Tinto (1975) described academic integration as students' intellectual and academic development and the faculty concern for students' development. Hausmann et al. (2007) found that while students in their study experienced a decrease in their sense of belonging as a group, instances of individual increases were associated with higher academic integration compared with those who showed decreases. Further, students' own perceptions of their academic integration seem to influence their sense of belonging as well. In Rainey et al.'s (2018) interview study, perceived competence was the second most frequently reported contributor to sense of belonging, and students who left STEM attributed their low sense of belonging to their low perceived competence in addition to their lack of relationships. Lewis and Hodges (2015) referred to this low perceived competence as "ability uncertainty," or "the experience of feeling unsure of one's status as an able and competent member in a domain" (p. 198).

Returning to our question of what STEM instructors can do to support their students' sense of belonging, we have a few hypotheses about how incorporating opportunities for students to engage in active learning might allow for a learning environment that supports students' social and academic integration and, in turn, their sense of belonging.

Active learning as a potential lever for change

Broadly speaking, active learning opportunities engage students in the learning process (Prince, 2004). More specifically, active learning is "the process of learning through activities and/or discussion in class, as opposed to passively listening to an expert" (Bonwell & Eison, 1991, p. iii). Examples of active learning opportunities include having students work on problems in groups or individually during class, engaging students in class discussions, using student response systems (e.g., clicker polls), and soliciting student questions – essentially anything that is not strictly listening to a lecture. Note that some of these learning opportunities are solo activities (e.g., working on problems individually or responding to a clicker poll), whereas others involve interactions with others (e.g., group work or engaging in class discussions). The President's Council of Advisors on Science and Technology's 2012 report recommended implementing active learning opportunities as a way to retain more undergraduate STEM students.

Active learning aligns with what some scholars refer to as feminist pedagogies. Feminist pedagogies aim to position not just the instructor but all students as sources of knowledge (E. Freeman, 2019). With the intention of deconstructing the power dynamic between the teacher and students and redistributing the power to students, feminist pedagogies incorporate collaboration, cooperation, and interactivity as a way to give agency to the learners rather than solely to the teacher. One might argue that adopting feminist pedagogies might deter men; however, active learning has been shown to benefit *all* students, not just women. Research indicates that students who are given opportunities to engage in active learning show higher levels of achievement, sense of mastery, and persistence than students who are not provided these opportunities (S. Freeman et al., 2014; Lahdenperä et al., 2019; Rasmussen et al., 2019).

Since the category of active learning is so broad, there lacks a consensus on the specific types of active learning opportunities that are most beneficial to students, especially when we compare student groups. Whereas Kogan and Laursen (2014) found that inquiry-based learning in a college mathematics course leveled the playing field in terms of men's and women's self-efficacy levels, Johnson et al. (2020) found that men continued to outperform women in inquiry-oriented abstract algebra. We are interested in investigating which types of active learning opportunities might best support women's sense of belonging in their calculus course. An earlier phase of this study inspired us to consider active learning opportunities on a continuum (Figure 3.1), with individual active learning opportunities on one end and interactive learning opportunities on the other. So, for example, individually working on problems and responding to clicker polls might fall more toward the individual end of the continuum, whereas group work and whole-class discussion fall toward the

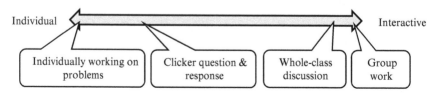

FIGURE 3.1 Continuum of active learning opportunities.

interactive end. We hypothesized that having opportunities to engage in active learning, especially interactive learning opportunities, might support women's sense of belonging in calculus.

As mentioned before, students who experienced active learning opportunities showed greater perceptions of instructor care and, in turn, a greater sense of belonging in STEM. Additionally, active learning environments that are student centered and allow for positive interactions with peers and with instructors support students' sense of belonging (Hoffman et al., 2003; Lahdenperä & Nieminen, 2020). Further, certain types of active learning opportunities (i.e., those toward the interactive end of the continuum) can offer opportunities for students to interact with each other and with their instructor and thus support their social and academic integration. Finally, Rainey et al. (2019) found that women tend to prefer active learning to lecture. Since active learning opportunities have the potential to target the contributors to students' sense of belonging, we think the presence of these opportunities, especially the more interactive types, could potentially support women's sense of belonging in calculus.

Studying women's sense of belonging in calculus

The study that we draw on in this chapter was designed to investigate the following research questions: (a) How does women's sense of belonging compare in the standard calculus course and the active learning calculus course? (b) To what do women in the two calculus courses attribute their sense of belonging? The study was conducted at the University of Delaware during the fall 2020 semester. Due to the COVID-19 pandemic, courses were taught online this semester. Eight sections of the standard calculus (C-S) course were offered, taught by a mix of permanent and temporary faculty, with each section capped at 100 students. The course was taught in a synchronous virtual format over Zoom. Two sections of the active learning calculus (C-A) course were offered, taught by two permanent faculty members, with each section capped at 50 students. (The second author, Berk, was one of the instructors.) This course was also taught synchronously via Zoom. To maintain opportunities for group work, instructors used Zoom's breakout room functionality.

Participants were students enrolled in one of two sections of C-S taught by the same instructor and students enrolled in either section of C-A. All three instructors were women and were permanent faculty who had taught their respective course several times. Students received an email inviting them to participate by completing a survey about their experience in the course. In C-S, 77% ($N = 158$) of 198 students completed the survey, and in C-A, 88% ($N = 80$) of 91 students completed the survey. For this study, only first-year students who self-identified as women were considered, resulting in a final sample size of 44 C-S students and 37 C-A students.

Data collection and analysis

To measure women's sense of belonging, a survey was designed and distributed electronically during the 3rd and 11th weeks of the 14-week semester. Good et al.'s (2012) Mathematical Sense of Belonging (MSoB) scale was incorporated into the survey. The MSoB portion of the survey consisted of 28 Likert scale items asking students to indicate the extent to which they agree or disagree with statements about their feelings of belonging in the course on a scale of 1 (*strongly disagree*) to 8 (*strongly agree*). To examine the extent to which students felt a sense of belonging (SB), we computed an average SB score for each student by taking the mean of the 28 Likert scale responses for each student. We grouped students by course and averaged their individual SB scores together to compute a composite score for each course at each time point (Week 3 and Week 11). We used analysis of variance to compare the averages across courses at each time point, and we used repeated measures analysis of variance to investigate change over time for each course.

In addition to the Likert scale items, we asked students to respond to the open-ended question, "What about the course and/or instructor has impacted your sense of belonging in calculus?" We analyzed the responses to this item using constant comparative analysis. We grouped students by course to investigate similarities and differences between the two courses. We individually coded the data and met to discuss emergent themes, resulting in a preliminary codebook. We then partook in an iterative process of recoding the data using the codebook, taking note of any questions that arose, and then meeting to reconcile and address any questions. Three cycles of this process led to the final codebook, which we used to individually code 10% of the data and reach 100% reliability. Often, individual responses contained multiple ideas, and thus a single student's response could be tagged with multiple codes. We computed frequencies of each code to identify salient aspects of the students' experiences that impacted their sense of belonging in calculus.

Results

We used students' responses to the MSoB portion of the survey to measure their sense of belonging in their calculus course. Women in C-A reported a significantly higher sense of belonging than women in C-S on both Survey 1 and Survey 2, with large effect sizes (Cohen, 1988; see Table 3.1.). Neither group showed significant change in their sense of belonging between Survey 1 (administered in Week 3) and Survey 2 (administered in Week 11), t_{C-A} (36) = 0.703, $t_{C-S}(43)$ = 0.458.

TABLE 3.1 Average scores (standard deviations) for sense of belonging for C-S and C-A women on Survey 1 and Survey 2.

	Survey 1				Survey 2			
	C-S	C-A	$t(79)$	d	C-S	C-A	$t(79)$	d
Sense of belonging	5.927 (1.27)	6.809 (0.99)	3.424*	0.76	5.965 (1.34)	6.945 (1.07)	3.581*	0.80

*$p < .001$.

These results left us wondering whether the C-A students experienced more opportunities to interact (e.g., consistent structured group work) than C-S students, which thus might have supported their social and academic integration and, in turn, their sense of belonging. However, rather than make assumptions or pigeonhole women into selecting items that contributed to their sense of belonging, we wanted to give women the opportunity to share in their own words what types of things influenced their sense of belonging. Next, we describe their responses to the question, "What about the course and/or instructor has impacted your sense of belonging?" Qualitative analyses of women's responses to the open-ended survey item produced two major themes that were particularly salient for both courses: learning environment and opportunities for interaction.

Learning environment

The category learning environment captured students' reports about their perceptions of the physical classroom environment (e.g., online format), as well as the classroom atmosphere and how they felt within that atmosphere. Students in both courses described the atmosphere as welcoming, inclusive, warm, comfortable, and fun:

> The instructor is super welcoming and creates a friendly environment in the class.
>
> *(C-A Student 1)*

> Talking to us before lecture starts and joking around with us during lecture helps to make the class seem less robotic.
>
> *(C-S Student 1)*

Students in both courses described the environment as safe, but "safe" seemed to have different meanings across the two courses. C-A women described how their instructor promotes a safe environment in which it is okay to be wrong, whereas C-S women described feeling safe in that they did not feel pressured to participate:

> If you answer a question wrong, [my instructor] doesn't make you feel bad or embarrassed which is really important.
>
> *(C-A Student 2)*

> [My instructor] makes it clear that she wants to help us learn and that it is more than okay if we aren't understanding a concept. She makes it feel comfortable to be wrong.
>
> *(C-A Student 3)*

> [My instructor] never singles anyone out and always offers help.
>
> *(C-S Student 2)*

> That I don't feel pressured to talk. Not pushing me to speak and feel anxious.
>
> *(C-S Student 3)*

Additionally, many C-A women reported having an instructor who made sure that all students understood a concept before moving on. For example, one student described how her instructor addresses confusion during class:

> [My instructor] always checks in to make sure no one is lost or has questions and if someone is confused, she makes sure she goes over the problem and doesn't move on until the confusion is resolved.
>
> *(C-A Student 4)*

A welcoming atmosphere where students felt safe to engage with the material created a learning environment in which students felt that they belonged.

However, whereas women in C-A reported only positive experiences with the learning environment, women in C-S reported mixed experiences. Women in C-S who reported positive experiences noted the instructor's efforts to bond with the students before beginning class, as C-S Student 1 described previously. Others reported negative experiences and that the virtual format negatively impacted their sense of belonging ($n = 5$):

> I mean, the class is online, so there is no way to feel like you belong.
>
> *(C-S Student 4)*

> It feels so cold and distant, nothing keeps me immersed in the class or the content.
>
> *(C-S Student 5)*

Interestingly, no C-A students reported feeling negatively impacted by the virtual format of the course.

Opportunities for interaction

The category opportunities for interaction captured students' reports about the various types of interactions they experienced during class. Some students provided specific details about the types of interactions that supported their sense of belonging, including both academic and social interactions. Academically, students described their experiences with interactive learning opportunities such as group work. It should be noted that times in which C-A students mention "being able to work with their peers" refer to times they engaged in group work. Here, two C-A students and one C-S student describe the academic interactions that impacted their sense of belonging:

> Being able to work with my peers every class has helped me feel more comfortable communicating with my peers and the professor.
>
> *(C-A Student 5)*

> I get to engage with other people who are learning the material.
>
> *(C-A Student 6)*

> Interactions and feedback between students and [the] teacher (questions, working on problems, etc.).
>
> *(C-S Student 6)*

Students also described opportunities to interact in a more social way with their instructor and classmates. Students in this study did not identify and talk about forming relationships as much as the participants in Rainey et al.'s (2018) study. However, some students did mention that forming connections with classmates within the context of group work and other interactions supported their feelings of belonging:

> I like how we always work in groups and it allows us to easily meet more people.
>
> *(C-A Student 7)*

> Working in groups has allowed me to build friendships as well as understand the material better.
>
> *(C-A Student 8)*

> Working in groups during class has helped me connect with other students more than in the large class Zooms.
>
> *(C-S Student 7)*

> When [the instructor] has us answer questions [in Zoom's chat functionality] because sometimes in the chat people will privately message you encouragement or questions and that is how I made some friends.
>
> *(C-S Student 8)*

Some students did not expand on the type of interaction and only responded to the open-ended item with something like "the ability to interact." Though these types of responses are not as specific as those previously mentioned, they do still indicate that students place value on the opportunity to interact and that it impacts their sense of belonging.

Summary and recommendations for practice

Women continue to switch out of STEM majors because they feel a low sense of belonging in STEM. Earlier we argued that there is a critical leak in the STEM pipeline after Calculus I and that calculus instructors could play a crucial role in patching that leak. We hypothesized that calculus instructors might be able to better support students' sense of belonging, especially women's sense of belonging, by incorporating opportunities for students to engage in active learning, particularly *inter*active learning.

This study addressed two research questions: (a) How do women's sense of belonging compare in a standard calculus course and an active learning calculus course? (b) To what do women attribute their sense of belonging in a standard calculus course and an active learning calculus course? To answer our first question, we first compared women's sense of belonging in both courses. Women in C-A reported a significantly higher sense of belonging than women in C-S at both Week 3 and Week 11 of the semester, and neither group showed significant change in sense of belonging between Week 3 and Week 11. These results led us to wonder whether perhaps the C-A students experienced more opportunities to interact (e.g., consistent structured group work) than C-S students, which might have supported their feelings of social connectedness and/or perceived competence, and in turn their sense of belonging.

We then analyzed the students' open-ended responses to the question, "What about the course and/or instructor impacted your sense of belonging in calculus?" We found that women in both courses attributed their sense of belonging to the learning environment the instructor established and to the opportunities to interact with their classmates and instructor in various ways. We conclude by discussing what calculus instructors can do with this information and providing a few recommendations for supporting women's sense of belonging that align with the findings of this study.

Learning environment

Women students attributed their sense of belonging in calculus to the learning environment established by their instructor. They described their calculus learning environment as a welcoming space in which they felt comfortable, safe, and supported. It is worth noting that both of these courses were taken in a virtual format due to the COVID-19 pandemic and that a handful of C-S students reported this negatively impacting their sense of belonging. However, the fact that this number was so small and that so many students voiced feeling welcomed and supported in a Zoom class speaks to the instructors' dedication to establishing a positive virtual learning environment.

Tip #1: Convey explicitly that it is okay to be wrong and ask questions

The instructors of both courses made their students feel safe in two ways. C-A students reported feeling safe to ask questions and be wrong because of the way the instructor responded to questions and wrong answers. C-A instructors explicitly communicated to students that wrong answers are welcome and not embarrassing; rather, they become learning opportunities for everyone. They established a mindset in the students that being confused and having questions are expected and normal. Not only were questions and confusion okay but the instructors were dedicated to resolving them before moving onto a new topic. This made students feel comfortable being wrong because they could trust that they would receive support from their instructor.

Tip #2: Encourage participation, but do not pressure students to participate

The C-S instructor also encouraged students to ask questions when they were confused or unsure of something and provided opportunities to have their questions resolved. She made students feel safe by respecting their comfort levels when it came to participating. While her students appreciated opportunities to participate during class, they reported that she never singled anyone out or pressured anyone to participate, which seemed to make them feel safe to learn on their own terms.

Opportunities to interact

Women students also attributed their sense of belonging to opportunities to interact with their classmates and instructor. This supports our hypothesis that interactive learning opportunities might support women's sense of belonging by attending to students' feelings of social connectedness and/or perceived competence. Interaction occurred in various ways for social and academic purposes.

Tip #3: Incorporate opportunities for students to engage with mathematics together

The C-A instructors incorporated consistent group work into the class structure, which provided students with frequent opportunities to work on math problems with classmates. C-A students reported that they appreciated these opportunities because they were able to form social connections with classmates and better understand the content. The instructors also visited groups to check in on their progress, which allowed for students to have one-on-one interactions with the instructor.

C-S students also occasionally engaged in group work, which made it easier for them to connect with others in their large Zoom class. This group reported that interactions among classmates also occurred via the Zoom chat functionality. They appreciated that the instructor did not block this functionality because they were able to ask and answer questions among themselves and form social connections.

Conclusion

The current study suggests ways in which instructors might target two factors that contribute to women's sense of belonging in STEM – the learning environment and social and academic integration. Specifically, the women in this study articulated the value of opportunities to interact with their classmates and the instructor and feeling safe to engage in such interactions. The safe and welcoming learning environment in which they could engage in these interactions allowed them to integrate both academically and socially integrate, and this in turn seemed to foster a sense of belonging. Further research is needed to identify clearer links between these constructs, as well as other ways in which instructors can support their students' sense of belonging in STEM.

References

Antonio, A. L., Chang, M. J., Hakuta, K., Kenny, D., Levin, S., & Milem, J. F. (2004). Effects of racial diversity on complex thinking in college students. *Psychological Science*, 15(8), 507–510. doi:10.1111/j.0956-7976.2004.00710.x

Berk, D., & Hiebert, J. (2009). Improving the mathematics preparation of elementary teachers, one lesson at a time. *Teachers and Teaching: Theory and Practice*, 15 (3), 337–356. doi:10.1080/13540600903056692

Bonwell, C. C., & Eison, J. A. (1991). *Active learning: Creating excitement in the classroom.* School of Education and Human Development, George Washington University.

Carmichael, S. G. (2017, April 19). *Women dominate college majors that lead to lower-paying work. Harvard Business Review.* https://hbr.org/2017/04/women-dominate-college-majors-that-lead-to-lower-paying-work

Chamberlain, A. (2017). *The pipeline problem: How college majors contribute to the gender pay gap.* Glassdoor. https://www.glassdoor.com/research/app/uploads/sites/2/2017/04/FULL-STUDY-PDF-Gender-Pay-Gap2FCollege-Major-1.pd

Chen, X. (2013). *STEM attrition: College students' paths into and out of STEM fields* (NCES 2014-001). National Center for Education Statistics, Institute of Education Sciences, U.S. Department of Education.

Cirillo, M., Berk, D., LaRochelle, R., Bieda, K. N., & Arbaugh, F. (2022). Undergraduate students' perceptions of features of active learning models for teaching and learning to teach mathematics. *International Journal of Research in Undergraduate Mathematics Education.* Advance online publication. doi:10.1007/s40753-022-00191-y

Cohen, J. (1988). *Statistical power analysis for the behavioral sciences* (2nd ed.). Lawrence Erlbaum. doi:10.4324/9780203771587

Eagan, K., Stolzenberg, E. B., Bates, A. K., Aragon, M. C., Suchard, M. R., & Rios-Aguilar, C. (2015). *American freshman: National norms fall 2015.* Higher Education Research Institute, UCLA.

Ellis, J., Fosdick, B. K., & Rasmussen, C. (2016). Women 1.5 times more likely to leave stem pipeline after calculus compared to men: Lack of mathematical confidence a potential culprit. *PLoS ONE, 11*(7), 1–14. doi:10.1371/journal.pone.0157447

Freeman, E. (2019, August). Feminist theory and its use in qualitative research in education. *Oxford Research Encyclopedia of Education,* 1–22. doi:10.1093/acrefore/9780190264093.013.1193

Freeman, S., Eddy, S. L., McDonough, M., Smith, M. K., Okoroafor, N., Jordt, H., & Wenderoth, M. P. (2014). Active learning increases student performance in science, engineering, and mathematics. *Proceedings of the National Academy of Sciences of the United States of America, 111*(23), 8410–8415. doi:10.1073/pnas.1319030111

Gibbs, K. (2014, September). Diversity in STEM: What it is and why it matters. *Scientific American.* https://blogs.scientificamerican.com/voices/diversity-in-stem-what-it-is-and-why-it-matters/

Gilligan, C. (1979). Woman's place in a man's life cycle. *Harvard Educational Review, 47,* 481–517. doi:10.17763/haer.49.4.h13657354l13g463

Gilligan, C. (1982). *In a different voice: Psychological theory and women's development.* Harvard University Press.

Good, C., Rattan, A., & Dweck, C. S. (2012). Why do women opt out? Sense of belonging and women's representation in mathematics. *Journal of Personality and Social Psychology, 102*(4), 700–717. doi:10.1037/a0026659

Hausmann, L. R. M., Schofield, J. W., & Woods, R. L. (2007). Sense of belonging as a predictor of intentions to persist among African American and White first-year college students. *Research in Higher Education, 48*(7), 803–839. doi:10.1007/s11162-007-9052-9

Hausmann, L. R. M., Ye, F., Schofield, J. W., & Woods, R. L. (2009). Sense of belonging and persistence in White and African American first-year students. *Research in Higher Education, 50*(7), 649–669. doi:10.1007/s11162-009-9137-8

Hoffman, M., Richmond, J., Morrow, J., & Salomone, K. (2003). Investigating "sense of belonging" in first-year college students. *Journal of College Student Retention, 4,* 227–256. doi:10.2190/DRYC-CXQ9-JQ8V-HT4V

Hong, L., & Page, S. E. (2004). Groups of diverse problem solvers can outperform groups of high-ability problem solvers. *Proceedings of the National Academy of Sciences of the United States of America*, 101(46), 16385–16389. doi:10.1073/pnas.0403723101

Johnson, E., Andrews-Larson, C., Keene, K., Melhuish, K., Keller, R., & Fortune, N. (2020). Inquiry and gender inequity in the undergraduate mathematics classroom. *Journal for Research in Mathematics Education*, 51(4), 504–516. doi:10.5951/jresemathduc-2020-0043

Kogan, M., & Laursen, S. L. (2014). Assessing long-term effects of inquiry-based learning: A case study from college mathematics. *Innovative Higher Education*, 39 (3), 183–199. doi:10.1007/s10755-013-9269-9

Lahdenperä, J., & Nieminen, J. H. (2020). How does a mathematician fit in? A mixed-methods analysis of university students' sense of belonging in mathematics. *International Journal of Research in Undergraduate Mathematics Education*, 6(3), 475–494. doi:10.1007/s40753-020-00118-5

Lahdenperä, J., Postareff, L., & Rämö, J. (2019). Supporting quality of learning in university mathematics: A comparison of two instructional designs. *International Journal of Research in Undergraduate Mathematics Education*, 5(1), 75–96. doi:10.1007/s40753-018-0080-y

Lewis, K. L., & Hodges, S. D. (2015). Expanding the concept of belonging in academic domains: Development and validation of the Ability Uncertainty Scale. *Learning and Individual Differences*, 37, 197–202. doi:10.1016/j.lindif.2014.12.002

Leyva, L. A., Quea, R., Weber, K., Battey, D., & López, D. (2020). Detailing racialized and gendered mechanisms of undergraduate precalculus and calculus classroom instruction. *Cognition and Instruction*, 39(1), 1–34. doi:10.1080/07370008.2020.1849218

Mendick, H. (2006). *Masculinities in mathematics*. Open University Press.

President's Council of Advisors on Science and Technology. (2012). *Engage to excel: Producing one million additional college graduates with degrees in science, technology, engineering, and mathematics*. The White House.

Prince, M. (2004, July). Does active learning work? A review of the research. *Journal of Engineering Education*, 93, 223–231. doi:10.1002/j.2168-9830.2004.tb00809.x

Rainey, K., Dancy, M., Mickelson, R., Stearns, E., & Moller, S. (2018). Race and gender differences in how sense of belonging influences decisions to major in STEM. *International Journal of STEM Education*, 5(10). doi:10.1186/s40594-018-0115-6

Rainey, K., Dancy, M., Mickelson, R., Stearns, E., & Moller, S. (2019). A descriptive study of race and gender differences in how instructional style and perceived professor care influence decisions to major in STEM. *International Journal of STEM Education*, 6(1). doi:10.1186/s40594-019-0159-2

Rasmussen, C., Apkarian, N., Hagman, J. E., Johnson, E., Larsen, S., & Bressoud, D. (2019). Characteristics of precalculus through Calculus 2 programs: Insights from a national census survey. *Journal for Research in Mathematics Education*, 50 (1), 98–111. doi:10.5951/jresemathduc.50.1.0098

Rosenberg, M., & McCullough, B. C. (1981). Mattering: Inferred significance and mental health among adolescents. *Research in Community & Mental Health*, 2, 163–182.

Seymour, E., & Hunter, A.-B. (Eds.). (2019). *Talking about leaving revisited: Persistence, relocation, and loss in undergraduate STEM education*. Center for STEM Learning. doi:10.1007/978-3-030-25304-2

Shapiro, C. A., & Sax, L. J. (2011). Major selection and persistence for women in STEM. *New Directions for Institutional Research*, 14(7), 5–18. doi:10.1002/ir

Strayhorn, T. L. (2012). *College students' sense of belonging: A key to educational success for all students*. Routledge. doi:10.4324/9780203118924

Tinto, V. (1975). Dropout from higher education: A theoretical synthesis of recent research. *Review of Educational Research*, 45(1), 89–125. doi:10.3102/00346543045001089

4

"WE'RE ALL IN"

Fostering inclusion and belonging through culturally sustaining and anti-racist pedagogy

Martha Alonzo-Johnsen, Anna Kurhajec, Patricia L. Maddox, Sarah McCann, Amir Z. Mohamed and Jennifer Trost[1]

On a student's first day of college amid the excitement, they likely desire two outcomes: to belong or "fit in" and to achieve academic success. For many students, the two are entangled. This is especially true for first-generation and BIPOC college students, who, by merely setting foot on campus, buck a system that from kindergarten through college is designed to exclude them academically and socially. Compounding this challenge is that, often, first-generation and community college students lack social networks and guides to help navigate potential opportunities and obstacles to college belonging and performance and feel that success is "all on them" (Moschetti & Hudley, 2015, p. 244). Conversely, many economically advantaged college students have "college concierge" parents who serve as a guide for their students and even "hoard" opportunities, while they "work in concert with schools to shape educational contexts around their children's needs and interests" (Hamilton et al., 2018, p. 116).

Higher education is catching on to this inequity and increasingly welcoming historically underserved students with research-based interventions that promote matriculation, belonging, and persistence: bridge programs, scholarships, and an array of other supports from tutoring to affinity groups, food shelves, and clothes closets (e.g., Nunn, 2021; Weiss & Bloom, 2022). The authors of this chapter teach at or in collaboration with Dougherty Family College (DFC), a 2-year associate degree–granting institution that emphasizes these kinds of holistic supports. Aimed at increasing bachelor's degree attainment, DFC is housed within the wider University of St. Thomas (UST) in Minnesota but is designed for students experiencing economic hardship and who may not be ready or able to access a 4-year college immediately after high school. DFC opened its doors in fall 2017 and serves

DOI: 10.4324/9781003443735-5

primarily BIPOC and first-generation students. By design, DFC utilizes best practices providing holistic, wraparound services to foster belonging and enable college persistence. These include intensive mentoring, a cohort educational model, significant tutoring opportunities, therapeutic interventions, and funding supports. As educators, we rely on these out-of-classroom interventions while fostering academic belonging.

At the same time, we know that what happens *in classrooms* can derail even the most intentional plans and supports for inclusion. Classroom environments can contribute to first-generation and nonmajority students feeling like outsiders, "not belonging, being viewed as different or less than, being misunderstood, excluded or invalidated, or being disadvantaged in comparison to the majority – experiences often unwittingly invoked by the comments or actions of their non [first-generation] peers and instructors" (Havlik et al., 2020). To boot, faculty may not see their own exclusionary and disempowering classist, White supremacist content and policies that can alienate students and impede their persistence. Even policies and practices aimed at supporting diversity and inclusion often lapse and should be revisited (Ahmed, 2012). With that in mind, we (faculty at DFC) adopted culturally sustaining pedagogy (CSP) as our instructional framework to help bolster academic belonging, shape our curriculum and policies, and provide significant classroom interventions to empower students.

The origin of CSP can be traced back to Gloria Ladson-Billings' (1995) seminal work. Ladson-Billings's conceptualization of culturally relevant pedagogy (CRP) laid the foundation for Paris and Alim's (2017) CSP. Not surprising, CRP and CSP both promote several key understandings: Students and their communities are not deficient but come with unlimited assets, including cultural wealth; education needs to include students in the co-creation of pedagogy and practice; and critiques of dominant power structures (including institutions and our own cultural practices) must happen in the classroom (Ladson-Billings, 1995; Paris & Alim, 2017).

Despite the numerous commitments shared by CRP and CSP, key differences exist between the pedagogies: First, CRP was developed with African American students in mind. CSP, on the other hand, extends its focus beyond African American students and recognizes the intersectional nature of identities as well as the fluidity of culture and cultural groups. Second, CSP seeks to provide a stronger and more explicit political commitment against the centering of White middle-class norms in the education system. The rhetorical shift from "relevant" to "sustaining" is representative of this commitment, as CSP seeks more than mere relevance and insists on educational processes and outcomes that incorporate and sustain BIPOC ways of knowing and being. Third, CRP does not meaningfully engage the possibility that communities of color can generate and reproduce harm through their cultural practices. CSP, on the other hand, tackles the issue head on and emphasizes the need to interrogate and problematize all pedagogies and practices that perpetuate injustice. Fourth, CRP has been widely accepted and frequently misappropriated. As a result, it has lost some of its ability to meaningfully change educational processes and outcomes in ways that benefit all learners but especially learners of color. The same cannot be said about CSP.

Our firm and universal belief is that when CSP is holistically enacted and embodied, students experience greater academic belonging, engage more deeply in academics, see themselves as scholars, and accelerate not only their academic skills but also their commitment to social justice as they move into a bachelor's program. In the sections that follow, we present five examples of how each of us have embraced CSP through high-impact instructional practices to facilitate academic belonging and growth in our DFC courses. Because we highlight course interventions, we believe that faculty at any college or university, with any level of institutional support, can replicate our work.

Constructing curriculum with student collaborators

What happens inside college classrooms matters – and CSP demands that we honor students' cultures and empower them to co-create classroom experiences. CSP warns us against fostering a superficial classroom "belonging" where students comport to exclusionary and harmful norms to fit in and maintains that inclusion requires real power sharing, particularly regarding policies, content, and co-creating an environment that honors students and their communities. In 2020, I (Sarah McCann) worked with former students to deconstruct, and then re-create, a theology course for first-year students titled Foundations of the Christian Tradition. The "syllabus project" centered on the academic belonging of these and future students, exemplified in the course changes highlighted below.

Background and the syllabus project

In May 2020, the DFC community was rocked both by COVID-19 and the murder of George Floyd, and we struggled to combat the message that some lives matter more than others.

My response was to seek to amplify DFC student power and voice in the spirit of CSP – the impetus for the syllabus project. I intended to maximize student belonging for the "interns" reworking the course as well as future students, who I hoped would engage more with content and skill building.

The group of seven interns (previous students) was diverse: women and men; African American, Latinx, and White; Atheists, Muslims, and Christians; LGBTQIA+ folks. We met five afternoons for 2 hours and worked independently between meetings. I paid them $20 per hour, honoring their expertise and labor, and in return students committed to producing curriculum changes – significant, resume-building work. I knew that with training and support, interns could identify and dismantle racist, classist, and ageist content and policies and integrate CSP-supported readings and tasks that would help students grow academically, while skillfully promoting social justice.

Interns read selections on high-impact teaching practices, CSP, and K–12 CSP examples. We agreed that for our work, departmental requirements, the CSP focus, and writing development were nonnegotiables. Everything else could be retained, altered, or replaced.

We structured each of our meetings around a central topic and goal: (a) syllabus welcome and course purpose, (b) course policies, (c) readings, (d) essential questions and objectives, and (e) assignments. We discussed best practices aligning with each topic and wrestled with questions: What is the purpose of essential questions, and how can CSP shape them? How do we know that students learned? Are policies fair? What is missing, and what needs to go?

Interns replaced readings, altered course policies, and rewrote tasks and essential questions (e.g., "What do we do when scriptures foster anti-Blackness?"). They also included their bios in the syllabus, desirous of future students tapping them for support.

Three changes represent global course shifts:

1. Interns developed the course theme – Theology From the Margins – and highlighted innovations driven by African American, Latinx, women, low-income, and LGBTQIA+ folks. Current students see their cultures reflected and develop deeper capacity for internal and external theological critique.
2. Interns created a "capstone" group project on social justice movements. Students prepare and teach a class on a movement they choose (BLM, #MeToo, immigration, etc.), focusing on course liberation ideas. These classes provide a strong synthesis of learning, center community assets, and inspire student activism.
3. I no longer deduct points for absences and reduced late work deductions from 20% to 10%. Changes reflect student climate and deeper opportunity for their discernment around competing responsibilities. Today, attendance and assignment completion rates are strong.

Power and networks

The syllabus project also sparked conversations about power and social networks. The project rested considerable power with interns – a challenging but valuable process. When interns reduced the late work deduction, I was scared. But interns flipped my perspective, arguing for reduction as a carrot –

that students could now better weigh competing priorities and turn in higher quality work rather than rush to submit a subpar paper. Today there is more energy around learning – a positive outcome for current students. How to share *power* with current students remains a question.

Interns included their bios to signal support to current students and later served as informal mentors. In this capacity *and* in their ability to center student cultures and contexts in the course, interns reflect the "college concierge" parent network outlined by Hamilton et al. (2018). DFC has a school-wide mentorship program, but how important is "course mentorship" to student engagement and achievement, and what could that look like? How might we leverage social networks (families, communities, employers) more broadly to enable courses to reflect the needs and interests of our first-generation, BIPOC students?

The syllabus project offers one pathway to interrogate our courses while incorporating CSP. Hiring former students offers us pedagogical partners who are both intimately aware of the course as is and empowers collaborators capable of envisioning it anew.

Say our names: An invitation into classroom belonging on day 1

My name is Amir Mohamed. I know firsthand the significance of being able to speak students' names. Throughout my K–12 education, teachers would always get my name wrong. I came to dread the first day of class when teachers would bewilderingly look at their paper and try to pronounce my name. When I got to college, things did not improve. Some professors were not interested in who I was. Others continued the pattern of mispronouncing my name. Consequently, I rarely felt known at school. Instead, ascribed social markers defined me as "alien," "other," and "deficient." My experiences in educational spaces have profoundly shaped me and are still with me today.

On the first day of each semester, I recount those experiences to the second-year students in my Public Speaking course. I do so in the most genuine and unfiltered way I know how. When I look around the room, I usually see eyes interested in hearing more and heads nodding in affirmation. The honesty with which I speak draws students in. In those moments, I'm a real person: someone with a story that resonates with their own experiences of hurt, hardship, and struggle.

The students in the learning communities I am a part of come from a variety of cultural backgrounds. They, too, move through the world in racialized bodies marked as *other*. Many are immigrants, or children of immigrants. Nearly all of them have high financial need and navigate higher education as first-generation college students. They also share something else in common, though few will admit it on the first day of class: They desire to be seen and heard. They desire to belong.

Recognizing that, I pause and take time to talk about the importance of feeling known. I discuss the power and beauty of solidarity, and I stress the impact that a loving learning community can have on their trajectory as students and people. My words are never forced. I believe what I'm saying with every fiber of my being. As they sit in their seats, they usually sense that and know it to be true. By the time my brief reflection ends, most of us want to go a little deeper with each other.

We continue building the foundation of our learning community by sharing our preferred names with one another and creating space for unstructured and impromptu dialogue. Through this simple act, students have felt empowered to speak their truths. In one of my classes, students chose to recall their own stories of feeling invisible while at school. As a part of that conversation, two students informed the class that they desired to be addressed by different names than the ones listed in the college roster.

One of the students explained that the roster listed him as "James," but his Hmong name was Kub.[2] Kub never chose to mention his Hmong name during orientation because he didn't want to inconvenience anyone. After engaging in our class exercise that morning, Kub felt inspired to express his full cultural self. He no longer wanted to check his name and culture at the door. He then taught us that his name means "gold." When he told us that, I responded by saying "I bet your parents must think you are pretty valuable to have named you Kub." My words were well received. Kub held my gaze, smiled, and nodded his head in agreement. Surrounded by the strength, love, and affirmation of a community, Kub was no longer invisible. In that space, he felt known.

When Kub was done sharing, a classmate named Diego lauded Kub for his courage and authenticity. Diego informed the class that he, too, would like to be called something different. He explained that he has two first names, Diego and Manuel. He added that when he is at home his family calls him Manuel, or Meme, not Diego. Noticing some of his peers were confused, Manuel helped us unpack some of the culturally embedded knowledge his words carried. He taught us that many Latinx families bestow two first names upon their children and that it is not uncommon in many Latinx cultures for children to be referred to by their second names. Inviting us deeper into his story, Manuel pointed out that throughout his education his teachers never demonstrated an interest in understanding his many names. They simply defaulted to calling him by the first name on the page. Manuel's message to us that morning culminated when he powerfully stated that many Latinx students are forced to live fragmented lives.

Our students should not have to live fragmented lives. They should not have to exchange their rich ways of knowing and beautiful cultural traditions for an education that cannot see them or empower them. Incorporating culturally sustaining practices like inviting students to share their preferred names, creating space for them to reflect on their respective identities, discussing the importance of community, acknowledging the ways in which hegemony in education can shape a person's experience, and reminding students they are not alone can help us engender a greater sense of academic belonging in our classes. Although the practices noted above may seem insignificant, against the fierce, violent, and unrelenting force of White supremacy, they are revolutionary.

Academic belonging in the science classroom

When I (Martha Alonzo-Johnsen) signed up for AP Physics in high school, I believed it was going to be the class that helped me uncover the secrets of the universe. I was excited and curious before I entered that physical space, only to find I was one of two women and the only person of color. My classmates were surprised I was there since I had stumbled audibly in previous AP classes, and some asked if I could "handle" AP Physics. According to them, I did not belong. Over the semester, the lack of belonging wore on me, and my questions about the universe were dismissed as I had to stick to the script. I felt like I had nothing to contribute to this classroom, and my questions and insights were not valued. Because of that experience, as I entered college, I wanted nothing to do with Physics and leaned toward Biology.

In college, science courses can be weed-out courses where only a select few persist if they follow the guidelines and leave their personal questions behind. Additionally, many underrepresented students do not see themselves reflected in scientific spaces, which adds a barrier to academic belonging (National Science Board, National Science Foundation, 2022; Seymour et al., 2019). Finally, content is presented in isolation without connection to community, so why would students care if it is not relevant to their lives?

In my General Biology classroom, I create a space that promotes academic belonging: where my students can see themselves reflected in the content and they help to shape it. If they have personal curious questions, I welcome them. I bridge their interests in biology with the content of our course by promoting projects that they would like to see happen in their community.

Traditionally in the science classroom we focus on the findings of the scientific community and spend little time on how those discoveries were made. Our students are aware of the scientific method as it is taught in high school, but the opportunity to practice the scientific method is limited. Additionally, students are not aware that scientists compete for funding, which is a process like the show *Shark Tank*. Scientists develop a testable hypothesis and show proof of concept by already having done part of the experiment. Many rely on their reputation and previous success to obtain the funding. Ultimately, scientists prepare a grant proposal to ask for funding, which I ask my students to do for their final project. Instead of writing a grant, they make a pitch, like the show *Shark Tank*, where they become the experts and must convince a panel of "sharks" to fund their research.

To prepare students to identify a viable proposal, I remind them they are already experts in their families and community. I ask them to keep that in mind as we start to investigate biological topics important to them. In the class, I ask them to dig deeper into the research being done in the scientific community and note what is missing or cannot be easily found in scientific literature. For example, we discussed new literature on weight loss when covering the musculoskeletal system. The research concluded that exercising in the afternoon was more beneficial than exercising in the morning. However, upon examination, there were gaps in the research as they only tested middle-aged men. Some of my students were curious because they did not fall into this demographic, but news articles written about it implied that this could apply to anyone. A group of students wanted to know why they did not study other types of people, and I asked them how they would address it. This launched their investigation into the musculoskeletal system and their proposal for addressing this gap in knowledge.

When they finally present to the "sharks," who are invited teachers and students, they have become experts in their field. Students have engaged in preliminary research and practiced developing hypotheses. As a group, they present their proposal and defend their methodology to obtain funding. My goal is that they recognize the scientists they are and how important it is to participate in the generation of knowledge.

Our students are weary of scientific research because the communities they come from have been historically ignored or taken advantage of. They do not see themselves reflected in the scientific community. There is a skepticism that accompanies them to the science classroom, and rightly so. Engaging in this process can bring up these harms and cause them to further question their belonging in science. CSP has led me to address these concerns by centering their biology questions and presenting them to the wider DFC community. Through this project we also examine and challenge the ways in which scientific research is done. As a group we seek to purposefully include all peoples to gain knowledge and reduce harm. I stress that science is never static and always changing, which can both encourage and frustrate them. I also stress that their voices are needed and that the full story of science cannot develop without them.

Students as historians

Teaching within a discipline that has been designed to exclude, I (Anna Kurhajec) emphasize agency as a pathway toward academic belonging by allowing students to take control of course content in my introductory

World History course. Barriers to belonging in history are built into the discipline: power, truth, whose stories are told, whose are not, and who gets to decide. Our students often struggle with the sense that history is not for them. They've encountered a history that marginalizes certain voices, perpetuates certain stereotypes – some people are included as always victims and/or villains; some people are remembered only for their suffering, never for their joy. This reminds us that history has a lot of power: the act of writing, recording, and recounting historical narratives can be (and has been) a kind of violence. Here, we see the stakes of belonging. Whose stories and experiences belong in history and whose do not? Whose have been excluded and whose have been centered? Which experiences, struggles, and lives are documented and analyzed, and which are not? Who does history belong to and who belongs in history? My hope is that in my class students learn that history belongs to them.

To address this, I emphasize agency and academic belonging in my world history course using approaches rooted in CSP. First, students hone their critical engagement skills by interrogating the discipline itself. Students are assigned a series of quotes about history, written by historians and other prominent figures. Students select a quote to help them "unpack" the discipline of history and the work historians do. We explore questions about how historical narratives have developed, whose stories get told, and what makes a source trustworthy. It invites students into the question of belonging: who gets to belong? Who decides? And why? We use these questions to explore the relationship between history, truth, and violence, emphasizing that history is always constructed through arguments, and those arguments are always incomplete. This beginning acknowledges that history is necessarily biased, but it also gives students a path toward making their own arguments about what history matters and what needs to be remembered.

We build on this critique over the course of the semester with students taking on the role of historians. I ask students to bring their own expertise to bear in the class. Early in the semester, I ask students to write a brief story: a history of the world from their own perspective, no research allowed. Students must emphasize and leave out what they choose; their own histories are fair game. The explicit message here is *you* get to decide who belongs and what stories matter. During the bulk of the semester, students hone their historian skills through collaborative research: picking historical topics and framing good historical questions that they want to explore together, conducting research to learn more, and, ultimately, developing strong, evidence-based arguments that answer their questions. This process is rigorous, but students are up to the challenge because they have buy-in on the questions we engage. The course culminates with an opportunity for students to be historians in a way that is familiar to them: as teachers. In small groups, the students teach the class for the day. They choose the topic, prepare a 2-

hour lesson, assign the reading, develop discussion questions, and even assign homework. Some students are initially terrified by this prospect, but each semester they end up shining in the role.

Framing the class around the student as historian builds a sense of academic belonging by encouraging students to see themselves as historical agents, which fosters confidence: they have the power to decide what history matters. It also gives them an opportunity to tell their own stories and narratives so that they are literally putting themselves into history. In this way, they see themselves belonging in history as both subject and creator. In line with the CSP framework, when students become historians, they also get the opportunity to do the hard work of applying their critiques reflexively: their own assumptions and biases are opened for examination.

By centering the students as historians and drawing on the importance of critique, complexity, and reflexivity called for by CSP, we take on a range of traditional barriers to academic belonging that show up in the history classroom. While students in my course build their historical confidence, this approach also raises important pedagogical questions. For example, what are the implications when students dictate so much of course content? What about the traditional expectations and benchmarks in the field of history outside of my class? Do my students suffer because they chose to learn about Korean pop band BTS rather than World War II? It's possible. Yet, I contend that giving content over to students demands a level of active learning that makes for a *more* rigorous course in which students develop transferable skills and are even better equipped to dive into World War II (or whatever part of history they seek to understand). Does this hold true for students who are considering a degree in history? I hope so. And while we face a host of other questions about how belonging in my class translates into belonging outside of it, when my students are historians, we are all learning something new together.

Creating academic belonging while bridging two colleges

DFC and the College of Arts and Sciences (CAS) occupy two distinct spaces within UST. DFC students take courses on the Minneapolis campus, which has a corporate feel largely populated by graduate students. CAS students take courses in St. Paul, the campus with a traditional college feel. In addition to the campus segregation, the diversity of identities adds to separation and isolation. Most CAS students identified as predominantly White and affluent, lacking experiences with difference in this segregated metropolitan area, which creates tension, stress, and violence for students from marginalized identities. DFC's first entering class remarked on a lack of inclusion with the larger UST community and felt no compulsion to visit the main campus. This raised concerns because the main purpose of DFC is to build a pathway to a bachelor's degree, and many DFC graduates will continue at UST. In 2018, segregation and isolation between the two colleges meant that the natural creation of informal student relationships that bolster belonging and persistence failed, a problem we attempted to mitigate through an intentional academic partnership.

Our partnership (Jennifer Trost and Patricia Maddox) began by chance in a faculty seminar where we discussed DFC students' struggle with campus community belonging (Nunn, 2021). We decided to bring our Introduction to Sociology courses together through a doubly engaged, co-taught course. *Evicted* (Desmond, 2016), the common read for sociology students, meant we focused on housing insecurity and homelessness as our themes, which were ripe for discussion on bias, assumptions, and life experiences. We anticipated that this theme would allow students to confide, grow, and bond; a theme and a space provided a base, but we needed intention for it to grow. In this section, we share how over seven semesters we created, evolved, and engaged students to increase academic and campus community belonging through a culturally sustaining, community-engaged project focused on students' growth and development.

Our initial course

In our first iteration of the course, we believed that creating shared experiences through parallel engagement with a family shelter would build student relationships across the colleges. Our initial partnership included two classes together, an orientation, and a closing reflection. Additionally, students provided youth activities on Saturdays at the shelter. The groups for these activities remained within their colleges; while physically together at the shelter, we did not provide shared time or space for additional connection. Although this model got us moving forward, the intentional connections and trust needed to build more academic and campus community belonging was lacking.

The evolution

Academic and campus community belonging required more intentional engagement with our class partnerships. We moved from two to six classes together, four of these classes in intentionally created groups with members from both DFC and CAS. This required continuous conversations and reflection with one another to determine whether we had any issues within groups and where they needed more support. Moreover, because DFC students identified as first-year students, Dr. Maddox limited her course enrollment to first-year students, providing a space where all students, new to the university and new to identifying as college students, could interact. Moving into assigned groups meant students could get to know those in their group more deeply. We consistently reflected on group makeup, matching the personalities and strengths of students from both colleges and facilitating an environment where students felt comfortable to share their authentic selves. These blended groups allowed students to build lasting connections. One student shared in their community engagement wrap-up reflection,

> I have seen some of them in the gym and started up conversations with them about certain things we've done in class, or just small talk, which I know would have never happened if it wasn't for our blended course.

Each class, the activities and readings provided more depth and layers to the thorny issue of housing insecurity in America, while attempting to dismantle the segregation of the two colleges. Students came from different backgrounds, but most had limited exposure and experiences with housing insecurity. The common assumptions and biases regarding this population crossed identity lines and was an area for all students to learn about housing insecurity and how to engage with each other. One student explained,

> It was not always the easiest to find equal ground on some of the material we were learning about in class, but that is from having different backgrounds. … Talking with them gave me [an] understanding that everyone comes from a different path, because I know without this class, I probably would not have talked to most, if not all, of the kids in the class.

Building trust and familiarity fostered spaces for students to find connection and belonging. On several occasions, students revealed their own journey with housing insecurity to the larger class, adding to the knowledge base and depth of our learning on the topic. The creation of a sense of belonging is imperative for this kind of disclosure.

Students' experience and reflections on the activities, groups, and youth engagement shaped the course. Nearly half of the course grade centered on the students' reflections of our time in the paired classes and dictated the continuous evolution of the partnership. This partnership allowed DFC and CAS students to create a stronger sense of familiarity with the larger community and a better sense of belonging on the main campus and strengthened their academic belonging in the discipline of sociology. Bringing together first-year students on any campus can create powerful connections and build students' academic belonging.

Ideas for implementation

Creating a sense of belonging is the responsibility of the entire campus community (Nunn, 2021). Faculty play a key role in shaping academic spaces where students can show up as their authentic, curious, knowledgeable, and academic selves. Throughout the examples in this chapter, we highlighted ways in which faculty can bring students' experiences, identities, and knowledge into the center of a course. While DFC is a niche institution, the approaches here are useful in most classroom environments. Some can be implemented in a day. Others may take a semester or two to refine. Here are our suggestions for your use:

- Build relationships with students and know them holistically; know their name, where they arrived from, and what they hope to do with your course or their degree.
- Create assignments that allow students to create knowledge and become experts in an area, tapping into their knowledge, strengths, and lived experiences.
- Cross-pollinate with others in your field, college, or university, especially those whose experience may be different than yours.
- Develop feedback systems for students to engage with the syllabus, assignments, policies, and practices and ensure that you consider, reflect on, and implement their suggestions.
- Allow space for students to bring in their own interests, the outside world, and past learning and provide space for unconventional or non-traditional learning.
- Identify the barriers to success within your field, name them, and find ways to mitigate them. Assist students in bridging these barriers.

Future growth

CSP calls on us to be critically reflexive; thus, we must reflect on our teaching and learning and continue to examine how centering White supremacy and other systems of power can impede academic belonging for our students. This calls on us as educators to address our own biases largely, work that happens in conjunction with addressing larger systems of oppression. Dismantling these systems begins with an act of trust on the part of faculty that extends to students. When we believe our students know what matters and empower them to lead us, our collective learning expands exponentially, and we are all better for it.

As faculty, we continue to wrestle with the following issues: How do we measure the success of CSP in the classroom? What about persistence? Can we see belonging translate to academic success in our courses and beyond? What happens to the academic belonging that we foster in the classroom and community at DFC when students move into less intentional spaces? What are the bigger stakes of working to develop belonging in a system/structure that is exclusionary by design and in implementation? Does building belonging in higher education actually translate to liberation? To more freedom, support, and care for our students? How can we go about finding these answers?

For students to feel a sense of academic belonging, they need to feel comfortable in bringing their whole selves into these spaces. This requires us as educators to be "all in." We have shown some of the ways in which we foster classroom environments, where students can begin to grow and feel pride in their educational journey.

Note

1 This chapter has six first authors who made equal contributions to the design and development of the chapter.
2 Names have been changed to pseudonyms.

References

Ahmed, S. (2012). *Racism and diversity in institutional life.* Duke University Press.

Desmond, M. (2016). *Evicted: Poverty and profit in the American city.* Penguin Books.

Hamilton, L., Roska, J., & Nielsen, K. (2018). Providing a "leg up": Parental involvement and opportunity hoarding in college. *Sociology of Education,* 9(2), 111–131.

Havlik, S., Pulliam, N., Malott, K., & Steen, S. (2020). Strengths and struggles: First-generation college-goers persisting at one predominantly White institution. *Journal of College Student Retention, Theory and Practice,* 22(1), 118–140.

Ladson-Billings, G. (1995). Toward a theory of culturally relevant pedagogy. *American Educational Research Journal,* 32(3), 465–491. doi:10.2307/1163320

Moschetti, R., & Hudley, C. (2015). Social capital and academic motivation among first-generation community college students. *Community College Journal of Research and Practice,* 39(3), 235–251.

National Science Board, National Science Foundation. (2022). *Higher Education in Science and Engineering. Science and Engineering Indicators 2022* (NSB-2022–2023).

Nunn, L. M. (2021). *College belonging: How first-year and first-generation students navigate campus life.* Rutgers University Press.

Paris, D., & Alim, S. (2017). *Culturally sustaining pedagogies: Teaching and learning for justice in a changing world.* Teachers College Press.

Seymour, E., Hunter, A. B., & Thiry, H. (2019). *Talking about leaving revisited: Persistence, relocation, and loss in undergraduate Stem Education.* Springer.

Weiss, M., & Bloom, J. (2022). *"What works" for community college students? A brief synthesis of 20 years of MDRC's randomized controlled trials.* MDRC.

PART II

Promoting academic belonging via the first-year seminar and department-wide interventions

5

THE FIRST-YEAR SEMINAR AS A VEHICLE FOR BELONGING AND INCLUSION FOR UNDERREPRESENTED COLLEGE STUDENTS

Keisha C. Paxton, Yesenia Fernández and Joanna B. Perez

In this chapter, we focus on how we use the first-year seminar to facilitate belonging and inclusion to support students in their transition to college. California State University, Dominguez Hills is a Hispanic-serving institution and a minority-serving institution; thus, we are uniquely poised to discuss the use of the first-year seminar with first-generation college students and underrepresented minority students. We adopted this particular high-impact practice (Kuh, 2008) because of its effectiveness with underrepresented minority (Martin, 2017) and first-generation students (Martin, 2017; Smith & Zhang, 2010). The first-year seminar is an ideal vehicle to support our institution's standing commitment to support belonging among its student population.

The first-year seminar is unique among high-impact practices in that it seeks to capture students upon entry to college and positively impact their first year and beyond (Padgett et al., 2013). This distinct intervention provides a gateway for incoming students to aid in the transition to college using a college entry course as the mechanism to do so. The goal of the first-year seminar is to have a radiating effect on each student's college experience by providing support early on and teaching them how to maintain that momentum as they continue their educational journeys. The first-year seminar is one way our institution can intentionally structure opportunities to support students' integration into campus life instead of putting the onus of cultivating belonging solely on the students themselves.

The first-year seminar provides the opportunity for students to acclimate to college life and to develop their identity in higher education by having small seminars where students can engage with both the professor and students in meaningful ways while learning about and practicing college success

DOI: 10.4324/9781003443735-7

skills. Research on the impact of first-year seminars has been mixed, with some studies showing it to be an intervention effective in increasing retention, persistence, and graduation rates (e.g., Das et al., 2021; Jenkins-Guarnieri et al., 2015). However, other studies do not support these findings (e.g., Hendel, 2007). One reason why we may see differences in these results is the variety of forms the first-year seminar or first-year experience take. Furthermore, the mere presence of a first-year seminar program does not necessarily mean that participants will feel a sense of belonging at the university (Strayhorn, 2009); rather, we believe that an intentional goal to cultivate belonging among students is key. Below, we describe our dynamic first-year seminar format and highlight how we value and cultivate belonging among our incoming first-year students.

The first-year seminar at California State University, Dominguez Hills

Our first-year seminar began with its first cohort in fall 2015. The impetus for this new program was to improve retention and graduation rates by providing a robust intervention for students as they first enter college. This effort was one intervention of many instituted to address the "Graduation Initiative 2025," which was a challenge posed to all CSU campuses by the California State University Office of the Chancellor to increase 4-year graduation rates to 40% and 6-year graduation rates to 70%.

Our program is based on three foundational tenets: supporting student success, helping students acclimate to college and see themselves as scholars, and guiding students to develop both a present and future orientation. Like other first-year seminars, we have the goal of helping students acclimate to college life by fostering a sense of community in the seminars. Additionally, we want to develop students' academic belonging by aiding them in developing their scholar identity and seeing themselves as lifelong learners. To that end, we focus on supporting students in creating goals for college, for their career, and for life beyond college.

We know that underrepresented students may lack a sense of belonging (Gopalan & Brady, 2020; Parr, 2020), be unfamiliar with the hidden curriculum (Laiduc & Covarrubias, 2022), and struggle with imposter syndrome in college due to structural inequalities. Hence, we strive to create positive experiences upon entry to college so that students persist to year 2 and ultimately to graduation. There are nearly 14,000 undergraduate students at CSU Dominguez Hills. Of these, nearly half (47.5%) of the student population are first-generation college students, nearly 80% (78.8%) are from ethnic backgrounds that are underrepresented in higher education, and two-thirds are Pell Grant eligible (66.5%). One-third (33.2%) of our students are in all three of these groups. Thus, our mission to help our students acclimate to college and develop their scholar identity fueled by a sense of belonging is necessary for our student population. Our first-year seminar is one of the primary vehicles we use to do this.

The first-year seminar at CSU Dominguez Hills has the moniker the Dream Seminar because it is a dream course for the students to take upon entering college, but it is also a dream course for our faculty to teach. The synergy of incoming students and engaged faculty creates the essential elements for an exciting semester together. The course is an academic, disciplinary-focused, 3-credit seminar instilling college knowledge via the faculty member's discipline using belonging as a tactic for building community inside and outside of the classroom, as well as for promoting the development of a scholar identity. Our first-year seminar is offered as UNV 101 and is capped at 20 students to create a small class environment. While this course fulfills a General Education requirement, it is not a required course for all incoming students. On average, there are approximately 30 sections offered during the year. First-year students can take the seminar during any term of their first year (i.e., summer prior to their first year, fall, or spring).

An important and unique element of our first-year seminar is the focus on faculty development. Faculty who teach our first-year seminar (known as "preceptors") undergo a competitive process where their course proposals are reviewed and deemed appropriate for engaging first-year students. Most semesters, we have preceptors from each of our five colleges. However, the College of Arts and Humanities and the College of Natural and Behavioral Sciences typically comprise the lion's share of first-year seminar preceptors. The majority of preceptors return to teach their seminar the following year or in the future.

Faculty preceptors receive ample support in creating a seminar that is indeed a Dream Seminar. Intentional faculty development in the area of teaching first-year students has been shown to be effective in improving the experience of first-generation college students (Tobolowsky et al., 2020). In the creation of their seminar, faculty engage in a multi-day training session led by the director of the first-year seminar program. These faculty receive a great deal of professional development that helps them create a course tailored to the developmental needs of incoming students and grounded in cultivating belonging in an academically safe environment. All faculty preceptors participate in training sessions throughout the academic year, specifically in May, August, and December and as needed if special circumstances arise (e.g., transitioning to online instruction during the COVID-19 pandemic) for as long as they teach in the program. These training sessions focus on such topics as creating transparent assignments; teaching Generation Z; developing learning outcomes and assessment; creating relevant, often scaffolded, writing assignments for first-year students; developing engaging course activities for new college students; and cultivating a sense of belonging and community in the classroom.

Upon starting in the first-year seminar program, new preceptors are brought together with other faculty preceptors who have taught the first-year seminar. In creating this community among the faculty, an environment is cultivated where faculty share ideas for student engagement strategies and lessons learned. Faculty who have taught their seminar a few times serve as quasi mentors for the incoming preceptors. This helps reduce the learning curve for newer preceptors as they gain the benefit of the experience of our more seasoned preceptors. This also serves to create a sense of belonging among faculty preceptors. We know that the culture of academia is to work in independent silos; however, this culture can foster a sense of isolation among faculty (Shulman, 1993). The faculty preceptors who teach our Dream Seminar relish the opportunity to gather, check in, and exchange ideas. This builds a sense of belonging among them. Notably, many of our faculty preceptors are faculty of color and/or the first in their families to attend college. This sense of belonging enhances their experiences of academia and allows a parallel process to be created such that the faculty then cultivate this positive sense of belonging in their classes.

One unique part of our first-year seminar is that we strongly encourage a co-curricular activity for each seminar. We define a co-curricular activity as one that engages students outside of the traditional classroom, provides the opportunity for students to engage with one another differently than they would inside the classroom, and provides the opportunity for the faculty preceptor to engage with the student differently outside of the classroom. This provides another opportunity for the faculty preceptor to be creatively engaged in the creation of their course. The co-curricular activity is intentionally designed to cultivate belonging and build community. Taking students outside of the traditional classroom provides additional opportunities for students to get to know one another without the goal of completing an assignment. It also gives them time to practice social skills and collectively experience something unique that they would not get to experience in any other classes.

Academic belonging and the Dream Seminar

Our first-year seminar is designed to facilitate academic belonging, such as feeling competent, confident, and accepted in academic settings (Nunn, 2021). A key goal is to help students develop their scholar identity, first by selecting a major or solidifying the major they identified upon entering college. Identifying a major contributes to a sense of belonging in higher education as students feel in step with their peers, whom they perceive as knowing exactly what they want to do in and after college. Furthermore, it provides confirmation of why they are in college. Since many of our students attended K–12 public schools and are also first-generation college students, they are less likely to experience academic belonging immediately upon entering college than their peers who attended private schools and who are not first-generation college students (Nunn, 2021). Our first-year seminar seeks to temper any differences in K–12 preparation and even the playing field for students to create an atmosphere where each student feels as if they belong in higher education. One way in which we do this is by acknowledging and affirming the cultural wealth that students bring with them to college and fostering a sense of community.

Highlighting two seminars that are effective in cultivating belonging and inclusion

In the examples that follow, Dr. Yesenia Fernandez and Dr. Joanna Perez, respectively, share how they developed and delivered their unique first-year seminars. They describe how they proactively created their seminars to cultivate belonging within the classroom and within the university. Each preceptor has taught their seminar multiple times, so the resulting description provides the development of a strong seminar.

Abriendo Caminos/Paving the Way: Our experiences as first-generation college students

I developed a first-year seminar focused on the experiences of first-generation college students because after more than 20 years of being a high school and district administrator, I realized that the same systems that affected my trajectory as a first-generation student continue to affect students today. That "first-gen" identity is carried into all spaces not meant for me or those like me, particularly in White spaces or those that operate as White spaces as a result of systematized racism and lack of culturally affirming practices (Williams et al., 2022). While this campus is considered a Hispanic-serving institution, it continues to serve and operate culturally as a predominantly White institution. Through this class, I wanted to teach students about the field of education but to do it in a way that we were thinking critically about these academic spaces and how they serve to replicate the systemic oppression we experience as minoritized groups in society. The goal for the course is to learn about these oppressive forces and the hidden curriculum of academia (Laiduc & Covarrubias, 2022) but also to learn how to thrive in these spaces while honoring and affirming our cultural and community assets through culturally affirming practices.

Through course content, students learn about the K–16 educational trajectories of first-generation college students. We delve into multiple aspects of the college pathway, particularly the barriers minoritized students experience. Students learn what researchers say about the trajectory of first-generation students, read first-person narratives from first-generation college students, and eventually write their own narratives in an effort to cultivate a sense of belonging in academia. Students read first-person first-generation narratives, report briefs, research articles, and book chapters to learn what the literature says but also to begin to develop their scholar identity (Quiñonez & Olivas, 2020), engage in academic inquiry (Hunter & Linder, 2005), and cultivate academic belonging. We end the semester focusing on best practices that articulate both what students can do and what institutions do to improve college persistence and graduation rates. Through these conversations of institutional support (Stanton-Salazar, 2011), students gain a better understanding of the programs they are a part of, the emails they receive offering services, and how they can leverage campus offices, which they visit, to help them succeed, therefore unpacking some of the hidden curriculum (Jackson, 1990; Laiduc & Covarrubias, 2022). At the end of the course, students reflect on their educational journeys within the context of the literature they have read and write testimonios (first-person narratives) that help them understand their own trajectories and those of their families (Delgado Bernal et al., 2012).

Although we spend much of the time immersed in what the research says about first-generation student persistence and what institutions do to support us, it's the way we spend the time together to have these conversations that truly engenders community, a sense of belonging, and a strong sense of self, which are critical to persistence (Dueñas & Gloria, 2020; Museus & Chang, 2021). To begin, the class is organized as a series of circulos, or "talking circles," which is an approach borrowed from First Nations pedagogy-in-action (Kovach, 2009; Tachine et al., 2016). Circulos are intended to create a space where students see each other's humanity and connect to one another and the land (Cisneros, 2022). Each class opens with circulo time, during which, as a class, we see each other literally and figuratively by engaging in conversations about our experiences while sitting facing each other in a circle. Dialogue ranges from topics related to their educational experiences in K–12, to their experiences and challenges as college students, to personal topics unpacking familial, cultural, community assets, rituals, and knowledges (Yosso, 2005). Students might be asked to talk about programs they were a part of in high school or resources they are taking advantage of on campus or to bring a plant that is part of their family narrative or talk about a ritual that is meaningful to their family. Building shared experiences and honoring their family's assets, seeing them for the fullness of their identities, and incorporating culturally affirming practices collectively are as critical to developing a sense of belonging on campus as engaging them with peers and other campus resources (Garcia, 2019; Museus, 2014). Students are also intentionally taught how to work with a study group, to learn from one another and unpack hidden curriculum, which also fosters belonging and inclusion (Jehangir, 2010; Museus & Chang, 2021). Students collaborate on several assignments in these groups, which helps them foster a sense of academic belonging and develop critical peer networks (Stanton-Salazar, 2011).

Intentionally connecting students to campus resources and co-curricular experiences is central to the first-year seminar to bridge academic and student services and foster a sense of belonging. By bringing the offices into the classroom, the community they create in class includes these campus resources and institutional agents. Students begin to see their classroom experience extend to the entire school community. Aside from the library, other offices and co-curricular activities in this seminar course center on culturally affirming practices, honor students' diversity, and create a system of support for students to learn skills necessary to navigate White spaces. For example, a member from Student Psychological Services is invited to be a guest lecturer. During that session, students not only learn about the services that are available for them but also learn about mental health and being a college student. Part of this discussion is a conversation on microaggressions, implicit bias, and imposter syndrome (Yosso et al., 2009). As a class, we read research on these topics as they relate to first-generation and minoritized college students and discuss how these experiences have been part of their K–16 academic journeys. The guest lecturer builds on class discussions and provides students with ways to manage these experiences so that they maintain their mental health. Similarly, cultural centers such as the Women's Resource Center and Queer Center discuss how their centers and other cultural centers on campus are safe spaces for students and also foster a sense of belonging.

Attending a co-curricular activity as a group is also a requirement for the first-year seminar and aims to further develop students' sense of belonging and engagement. For this course, the co-curricular activity focuses on students' cultural identities as students are asked to attend an event put on by one of the campus cultural centers or off-campus event that is culturally connected to them or engages an aspect of their identity. So often school campuses, curricula, and culturally White spaces ignore and erase students' identities. Thus, the goal for this course is to honor students' identities and knowledges through culturally affirming and humanizing pedagogies (Garcia, 2019; Williams et al., 2021).

The last two assignments in this seminar are aimed at centering students' family assets and knowledges and decentering assimilationist aspects of academia. Students write a testimonio in which they select an aspect of their identities as first-generation/minoritized students and write about their experiences in K–16. Some students have written about being English learners or about their family's journey as undocumented or mixed-status families, and others have written about the low expectations that come with being a student of color. End-of-course student surveys always reflect how much students appreciate this assignment as it centers the student voice and their knowledge while allowing them to reflect on their experiences. Our journeys as first-generation students and our interactions in culturally White spaces are complex. Similarly, the journeys of their families are intertwined with those of the elders in their families and, as such, students' final projects are to conduct structured elder interviews, reflect on their "findings" in groups, and present the findings to the class. Students record audio or video of their family members discussing how they've learned what they know, through formal education or otherwise. These assignments allow us to engage in discussions of whose knowledge matters and why (Jehangir, 2010; Yosso, 2005), particularly in academia, and how we can change the perception that only knowledge from postsecondary institutions matters.

While the course content is research and writing heavy, much of the work is done with the support of study groups, which ultimately also serve to create community and a sense of belonging. Students select their own study groups after the second week of spending time in circulos during class sessions. The course assignments and activities are meant to intentionally engage families, integrate culturally affirming practices, and humanize the student experience by centering student voice. My hope is to have a balance of activities to help students develop their academic identity and gain practical skills to assist them in other classes but also ensure that students feel seen and that their intersectional identities valued and for them to see the power of community across campus.

Undocumented and unafraid

As a proud daughter of Guatemalan immigrants and first-generation scholar, I am committed to approaching my scholarship, teaching, and community engagement with a social justice lens. In my research, I examine how systems of power and inequality shape the social conditions of immigrant communities. As an educator, I seek to facilitate student-centered learning environments that draw on students' experiences, strengths, and resilience. In the process, I participate in efforts that center the voices and address the needs of underserved communities. It is not often that I can combine all of my passions in one space. However, through the first-year seminar, I bridge my research expertise, passion for teaching, and dedication to the community.

UNV 101: Undocumented and Unafraid is a course that introduces students to sociological concepts, theories, and research methods to analyze immigration in the United States. Beyond covering course content and enhancing individual as well as professional development, the goal of the class is to provide a space where students apply what they learn outside of the classroom. To do so, the curriculum, assignments, class activities, discussions, and co-curricular engagement are tailored to validate, affirm, and uplift students' lived experiences and role as agents of social change. Key to this process is building community by incorporating time to reflect and share. Hence, throughout the semester, students utilize their sociological imagination, which refers to the connection between history and biography, to critically analyze their own social worlds.

Part of ensuring that students gain a sense of belonging is having them work on assignments that center their voices, knowledge, and interests. For instance, their final project, known as the "Immigration Visual Sociology Portfolio," is scaffolded into a series of processing assignments that lead up to a final research photo essay and presentation. The purpose of the assignment is for students to critically understand the unique experiences of diverse immigrant communities, recognize the power of narrative, and honor their journeys throughout the process. In other words, the project is meant to develop their critical thinking skills while also increasing their sense of belonging not just to campus but in academia overall, by centering the voices and stories.

Key to the process and strategies to support students along the way is to break down the project into smaller steps. Students begin with reflecting on the perception of undocumented immigrants in the larger society by writing a poem. Once all students complete the poem, we discuss the social construction of immigration, particularly with regards to the lives of undocumented immigrants. This includes carving out time in class to understand the meaning and significance of intersectionality in shaping our own social position. To better understand the lived experiences of immigrants in the United States, students then interview an immigrant whom they admire. Students often decide to interview a family member, neighbor, friend, or someone they have recently met on campus. Through this interview, students learn about the migration journey, school and/or work experiences, as well as the sacrifices, challenges, and/or changes that their interviewee has undergone upon arrival to the United States. By the end, students learn about the immigrant's past, their experience while living in the United States, and personal thoughts about today's political climate.

After gaining insight from an immigrant, students use the interview transcription to select a topic for their final project (i.e., family, education, language, etc.). To make sense of the data and organize the flow of their project, students complete a brainstorming worksheet. This includes delineating the topic, three subthemes, and social position of the interviewee and thinking about the implications for the larger society, including historical as well structural forces that impact the interviewee's lived experiences. Next, students become familiar with the use of scholarly literature to contextualize each subtheme by attending a library session and submitting an annotated bibliography. Utilizing a template, students then bridge what they learned through the interview and academic sources by completing a final paper outline. Throughout the semester, students take photographs of their interviewee to provide a visual context of their lives. The photos and final paper outline are then used to create a poster (collage format), where they orally present their research findings based on primary data (interview) and sociological research (academic sources), as well as what they have learned through this project.

In addition to presenting in class through an art gallery format, students organize a photo exhibit that is open to the campus community and their families. During this campus presentation, all posters are displayed, and each student has an opportunity to briefly share about their projects in front of all those in attendance. While the event centers the photo exhibit, it provides students with a transformational experience. For instance, given that most of my students are undocumented or part of a mixed-status family, as well as first-generation and low-income students of color, they often feel as though their voices are not valid and that they are not legitimate knowledge bearers in academia. As such, the project provides them with an opportunity to understand the power they hold in producing knowledge in academia, while also acknowledging the resiliency of immigrants in our society. At the same time, their families feel part of the CSU Dominguez Hills community and recognize the important role they play in the educational aspirations and achievements of their students. This event also showcases the power of promoting college-going within their communities (Luedke, 2020). The sense of community and family among us all is deeply moving and has demonstrated the power of applying what one learns outside of the classroom and claiming safe space to welcome those who do not have the opportunity to regularly come to the CSU Dominguez Hills campus.

For first-year students, their ability to survive and thrive in academia is tied to the support, resources, and networks that they have access to throughout their journey. Within the classroom, this can be accomplished through engaged pedagogy, which bell hooks (1994) described as empowering if both the educators and students are open to being vulnerable, exchanging knowledge, and changing institutional practices that value community rather than individuality. This can be accomplished through first-year seminars. In Undocumented and Unafraid, student feedback, both informal and formal, reveals that engaging in the final project, seeing their families on campus, and building strong connections to both faculty/staff and peers have a positive impact on their sense of belonging and goals beyond CSU Dominguez Hills. For many, it is the first time they see themselves reflected in curriculum, acknowledge the power of community narratives, and share an academic space with their loved ones. In this process, rather than being ashamed or diminishing their social positions and lived experiences as integral parts of their higher education trajectories, first-year students embrace, utilize, and expand on their foundational knowledge and experiences as motivation to press forward and support others along the way. In other words, when historically underserved student populations have the academic, professional, and personal support to grow, they not only increase their capacity to succeed but also gain the tools to uplift those around them. Ultimately, first-year seminars are spaces that are transforming academia and the lives of students as well as their loved ones.

Lessons learned

Through the 8 years during which this version of our first-year seminar has been offered, we have amassed several lessons learned that we have used to continually improve the program. These lessons comprise ways to enhance developing belonging among students in the classroom. By designing curricula and incorporating class activities that are student centered, first-year students begin to recognize themselves as intellectually capable and confident. Beyond fostering academic belonging in the classroom, the first-year seminars provide opportunities for students to gain a sense of belonging within the larger CSU Dominguez Hills community through co-curricular activities and the integration of expertise of diverse campus partners.

One essential key to the success of our first-year seminar is the faculty. First, recruiting highly motivated faculty has proven to impact the engagement, preparation, and enthusiasm of both faculty and students. On one hand, faculty are eager to cultivate a space of learning that is grounded on their passion and desire to foster a sense of belonging for first-year students. On the other hand, students are motivated in the classroom as they can feel that their professors care about their well-being and success. This matters because it offers faculty and students spaces where they co-learn and build a strong sense of community. For faculty, the continuous training adds to their effectiveness in the classroom and serves to develop a sense of belonging for them. In fact, as faculty point out, this feeling of belonging to something bigger than yourself influences how they teach their seminars because they know firsthand the importance of intentionally building community with their colleagues. Hence, they teach their courses with the same goal of cultivating a sense of belonging and community for students in their first-year seminars.

Integral to fostering a sense of academic belonging is developing a sense of campus community belonging. Hence, a key element of our first-year seminar is getting students engaged in the larger campus community. Each preceptor designs assignments and activities requiring students to explore opportunities on campus where they can find their place. One lesson is to include speakers who talk about the disciplinary focus of the course but also share their college journeys. Preceptors are encouraged to ask all speakers to talk about their college experiences and how they found their place in college. This provides multiple perspectives to the students on the college experience and reminds them that there is no single way to experience college. In addition, we encourage students to engage in the campus community in pairs or small groups (e.g., campus sporting events, club meetings, cultural events, etc.); this provides the support needed to try something new and continues to cultivate a sense of belonging (i.e., "we're in this together").

We have also learned that having regular small-group exercises helps build group cohesion among the students. As first-year students, having opportunities to connect with peers is an integral part of learning how to acclimate to a college campus. Within our first-year seminars, small-group exercises include course content and peer engagement activities, assignments, and co-curricular activities. In addition to centering student voices, small-group engagements enhance students' critical thinking, interpersonal skills, and sense of belonging. For instance, they learn how to communicate, engage in active listening, work alongside diverse groups of people, and build community. When first-year students become comfortable with a small group of peers, it gives them the ability to build stronger connections that may become long term. In many cases, students who first meet through the first-year seminar support each other throughout their higher education journeys. It is important to note that in addition to completing the class requirements, our students form strong bonds due to their shared experiences and positionalities.

Many of our faculty preceptors were first-generation college students or have spent a large part of their career supporting first-generation college students. To this end, they have a keen understanding of the importance of family in the educational journeys of students of color and first-generation college students. These faculty recognize that to enhance belonging is to embrace the whole person, not just their student identity. As demonstrated earlier, both Dr. Perez and Dr. Fernandez provide examples of how they incorporate family into their courses. This provides a space for students to feel like whole beings without the need to compartmentalize their identities as scholar vs. family member.

Conclusion

A sense of belonging is crucial to thriving as a college student and even more so for underrepresented and first-generation students. We cannot assume that belonging is automatic simply because an institution is a minority-serving institution such as ours. As such, we work diligently to cultivate a sense of belonging as well as academic identity development for our incoming first-year students. We recognize that most universities, including ours, are entrenched in a historical milieu of the traditional academy and espouse, intentionally or not, academic perspectives that may not be conducive to both the academic belonging and social belonging of underrepresented students and their families. We seek to give students the support they need to thrive in academia and beyond while recognizing our role in providing an atmosphere necessary for them to feel like they belong, as an individual and as a scholar, and that the campus is a welcoming place to their families as well. Key to this is cultivating a sense of community in a seminar that acknowledges their experiences, cultures, families, and voices. In doing so, we help to mitigate the development of fragmented identities as we provide a safe environment where they can feel like they belong in higher education.

References

Cisneros, N. A. (2022). Indigenous girls write, right!? Unsettling urban literacies with indigenous writing pedagogies. *Urban Education*, 57(10), 1757–1783. doi:10.1177/00420859211003933

Das, R., Schmitt, E., & Stephenson, M. T. (2021). A quasiexperimental analysis of first-year seminar outcomes at a large university. *Journal of College Student Retention, Research, Theory, & Practice*, 0(0), 1–15. doi:10.1177/15210251211038591

Delgado Bernal, D., Burciaga, R., & Flores Carmona, J. (2012). Chicana/Latina testimonios: Mapping the methodological, pedagogical, and political. *Equity & Excellence in Education*, 45(3), 363–372.

Dueñas, M., & Gloria, A. M. (2020). ¡Pertenecemos y tenemos importancia aquí! Exploring sense of belonging and mattering for first-generation and continuing-generation Latinx undergraduates. *Hispanic Journal of Behavioral Sciences*, 42(1), 95–116.

Garcia, G. A. (2019). *Defining "servingness" at Hispanic-serving institutions (HSIs): practical implications for HSI leaders*. American Council on Education.

Gopalan, M., & Brady, S. T. (2020). College students' sense of belonging: A national perspective. *Educational Researcher*, 49(2), 134–137. doi:10.3102/0013189X19897622

Hendel, D. D. (2007). Efficacy of participating in a first-year seminar on student satisfaction and retention. *Journal of College Student Retention: Research, Theory & Practice*, 8(4), 413–423.

hooks, b. (1994). *Teaching to transgress: Education as the practice of freedom*. Routledge.

Hunter, M. S., & Linder, C. W. (2005). First-year seminars. In M. L. Upcraft, J. N. Gardner, & B. O. Barefoot (Eds.), *Challenging and supporting the first-year student: A handbook for improving the first year of college* (pp. 275–291). Jossey-Bass.

Jackson, P. W. (1990). *Life in classrooms*. Teachers College Press.

Jehangir, R. (2010). *Higher education and first-generation students: Cultivating community, voice, and place for the new majority*. Springer.

Jenkins-Guarnieri, M. A., Horne, M. M., Wallis, A. L., Rings, J. A., & Vaughan, A. L. (2015). Quantitative evaluation of a first year seminar program: Relationships to persistence and academic success. *Journal of College Student Retention*, 16(4), 593–606.

Kovach, M. (2009). *Indigenous methodologies: Characteristics, conversations, and contexts*. University of Toronto Press.

Kuh, G. D. (2008). *High-impact educational practices: What they are, who has access to them, and why they matter*. Association of American Colleges and Universities.

Laiduc, G., & Covarrubias, R. (2022). Making meaning of the hidden curriculum: Translating wise interventions to usher university change. *Translational Issues in Psychological Science*, 8(2), 221–233. doi:10.1037/tps0000309

Luedke, C. L. (2020). Lifting while we climb: Undergraduate students of color communal uplift and promotion of college-going within their communities. *The Review of Higher Education*, 43(4), 1167–1192.

Martin, J. M. (2017). It just didn't work out. *Journal of College Student Retention: Research, Theory & Practice*, 19(2), 176–198.

Museus, S. D. (2014). The culturally engaging campus environments (CECE) model: A new theory of success among racially diverse college student populations. In M. Paulsen (Ed.), *Higher education: Handbook of theory and research* (Vol. 29, pp. 189–227). Springer. doi:10.1007/978-94-017-8005-6_5

Museus, S. D., & Chang, T. H. (2021). The impact of campus environments on sense of belonging for first-generation college students. *Journal of College Student Development*, 62(3), 367–372.

Nunn, L. M. (2021). *College belonging how first-year and first-generation students navigate campus life*. Rutgers University Press.

Padgett, R. D., Keup, J. R., & Pascarella, E. T. (2013). The impact of first-year seminars on college students' life-long learning orientations. *Journal of Student Affairs Research and Practice*, 50(2), 133–151. doi:10.1515/jsarp-2013-0011

Parr, N. J. (2020). Differences in the age – Varying association of school belonging with socioemotional flourishing among minority and non-minority college and university students. *Journal of American College Health*, 70(5), 1336–1340. doi:10.1080/07448481.2020.1808662

Quiñonez, T. L., & Olivas, A. P. (2020). Validation theory and culturally relevant curriculum in the information literacy classroom. *Urban Library Journal*, 26(1), 2.

Shulman, L. S. (1993). Teaching as community property: Putting an end to pedagogical solitude. *Change*, 25(6), 6–7.

Smith, W., & Zhang, P. (2010). The impact of key factors on the transition from high school to college among first-and second-generation students. *Journal of The First-Year Experience & Students in Transition*, 22(2), 49–70.

Stanton-Salazar, R. D. (2011). A social capital framework for the study of institutional agents and their role in the empowerment of low-status students and youth. *Youth & Society*, 43(3), 1066–1109.

Strayhorn, T. (2009). An examination of the impact of first-year seminars on correlates of college student retention. *Journal of the First-Year Experience & Students in Transition*, 21(1), 9–27.

Tachine, A. R., Bird, E. Y., & Cabrera, N. L. (2016). Sharing circles: An Indigenous methodological approach for researching with groups of Indigenous peoples. *International Review of Qualitative Research*, 9(3), 277–295.

Tobolowsky, B. F., Cox, B. E., & Chunoo, V. S. (2020). Bridging the cultural gap: Relationships between programmatic offerings and first-generation student benchmarks. *Journal of College Student Retention: Research, Theory & Practice*, 22(2), 273–297.

Williams, K. L., Mobley, S. D., Jr., Campbell, E., & Jowers, R. (2022). Meeting at the margins: Culturally affirming practices at HBCUs for underserved populations. *Higher Education*, 84(5), 1067–1087. doi:10.1007/s10734-022-00816-w

Williams, K. L., Russell, A., & Summerville, K. (2021). Centering Blackness: An examination of culturally-affirming pedagogy and practices enacted by HBCU administrators and faculty members. *Innovative Higher Education*, 46, 733–757.

Yosso, T. J. (2005). Whose culture has capital? A critical race theory discussion of community cultural wealth. *Race Ethnicity and Education*, 8(1), 69–91, doi:10.1080/1361332052000341006

Yosso, T. J., Smith, W., Ceja, M., & Solórzano, D. (2009). Critical race theory, racial microaggressions, and campus racial climate for Latina/o undergraduates. *Harvard Educational Review*, 79(4), 659–691.

6

STRENGTHENING LEARNING COMMUNITIES

Belonging in a UK physics department

Camille B. Kandiko Howson, Amy Smith, Jessie Durk, Michael F. J. Fox, Vijay Tymms and Mark Richards

In this chapter, we provide insight into academic sense of belonging in the UK and describe how, through multiple subprojects that make up the Strengthening Learning Communities (SLC) project, we are exploring the role of sense of belonging in a physics department in a research-intensive, mid-size urban institution. We provide background on the context of underrepresentation in physics in the UK, followed by a discussion of our theoretical framing and approach. Finally, we detail five projects that are part of the SLC project and how they are directed at building a community of practice that is knowledgeable and proactive around increasing equity, diversity, and inclusion in physics by thinking about these issues from a sense of belonging perspective.

Sense of belonging is hard to quantify and measure (Robertson et al., 2019). It can be challenging to engage faculty in highly quantitative science, technology, engineering, and math (STEM) fields, particularly in research-intensive institutions, with the qualitative methods that can provide insight into how to address inequalities in the student experience. However, drawing on a discipline-based educational research (DBER) perspective and using the more familiar language of grades and statistical methods to analyze data can provide a more accessible route for faculty in subjects, such as physics, to engage in educational research and work to create an inclusive educational community. In this chapter, we present an approach for exploring sense of belonging with faculty in a physics department for the purpose of addressing attainment differences across student characteristics and ultimately informing decisions about the curriculum.

The SLC project was initiated in 2020 with institutional funding, after noticing significant gaps in outcomes between certain demographic groups.

DOI: 10.4324/9781003443735-8

We use the phrase *awarding gaps* to focus the cause of the gaps on structural factors rather than a student deficit model. There is existing evidence that awarding gaps, in both gender and other demographic groups, are – at least in part – related to different attitudes, identity, and a lack of sense of belonging (Lewis et al., 2016) in minority groups. The broad aims of the SLC project are to investigate the extent of awarding gaps between demographic groups, plus those students with protected characteristics; research the causes of any such gaps; and implement targeted strategies in pedagogical and pastoral practices within the institution to improve the university experience for all students to ensure parity for all.

This collaborative partnership, working across an institution but initially focused on a single department, represents a significant institutional commitment to tackling awarding gaps across student groups, supporting research and practice to improve belonging across a diverse student body and investing in a growing community of physics education research, a nascent field in the UK. In this chapter, we draw on selected aspects of this project to demonstrate a departmental approach to fostering academic belonging.

Understanding belonging

Much of the foundational literature on sense of belonging from the past 50 years has been focused on the United States and has explored links between student sense of belonging and student retention. More recently, sense of belonging has been reexplored in the context of an increased and more diverse student body, focusing on student success in addition to retention (Testa & Egan, 2014; Yorke & Longden, 2004). Research on belonging in the context of UK higher education has been closely linked with research on student engagement and the positive link with student success. The shift from retention to a more holistic approach to student engagement has come with a corresponding shift in the onus of responsibility from students to institutions (Tight, 2020).

The relationship between engagement and belonging is complex. Belonging, as an affective measure, has been seen as a counterpoint to behavioralist notions underpinning the student engagement discourse. Engagement focuses on what students do, whereas belonging focuses on students' perceptions rather than actual behaviors. However, seminal research in the UK argues that belonging emerges from engagement (Thomas, 2012). Belonging is also linked with the environment, in which social and cognitive attributes form connectedness (Kift, 2004). "Sensibilities of belonging are formed in relation to constructions of capability: to belong in a field such as higher education, the student must be recognized as having the capability to belong" (Burke et al., 2016, p. 19).

Quantifying belonging

In higher education research, sense of belonging is measured as a metaconstruct rather than being measured through direct empirical measurement; measures tend to be of experience or engagement (Kane et al., 2014). In the UK, belonging emerged as a metaconstruct in research trying to broaden measures of higher education that have focused on satisfaction and a customer mentality. Research on belonging draws on several different areas. One area focuses on how belonging varies across student characteristics, particularly among underrepresented and minority students, and how addressing this can mediate awarding gaps seen widely across the sector (Cureton & Gravestock, 2019; Thomas et al., 2017). Another area focuses on institutionally based research projects, exploring belonging within specific institutional contexts (Ahn & Davis, 2020; Wilcox et al., 2005). Both are linked with social agendas addressing student mental health and well-being.

There have been national efforts in the UK exploring belonging as part of wider research into the student experience. The What Works? Student Retention & Success program consisted of seven projects that collected data from several thousand students across 22 higher education institutions. Included was Yorke's (2016) Belongingness Survey, which measures belongingness via three subscales: Engagement, Belonging to Faculty or Department, and Academic-Related Self-Confidence. Thomas's (2012) analysis of the overall program singled out promoting students' sense of belonging as its number one recommended strategy for increasing student retention and overall success. In another project, Robertson et al. (2019) found sense of belonging to be a key "intangible asset" (p. 14) in higher education – something highly valued but hard to quantify. It is subjective and multifaceted and changes over time.

Belonging as relational and situated

UK-based research has explored the impact of the institutional habitus on students' sense of belonging (Reay et al., 2010). This research links the context of an institution to students' engagement with it (Read et al., 2003). More recent research has highlighted belonging as a construct and experience that is situated and relational (Ahn & Davis, 2020; Gravett & Ajjawi, 2022), noting that sense of belonging in educational contexts is promoted by social connections across academic and professional staff, peers, friends, and one's surroundings (Richardson, 2018; Watson et al., 2010). In this research, we note how belonging reinforces relationships for staff and students – and that this happens both positively and negatively.

> Belonging is fundamentally *contextual*, not just in the sense that people develop and experience belonging differently in different contexts but that students' understandings of what constitutes and contributes to belonging is partly informed by their perception of the context that they belong *to*.
>
> *(Cohen & Viola, 2022, p. 14)*

In this vein, we acknowledge that some students do not relate to dominant belonging discourses in their departmental and institutional contexts and note that belonging is "not inherently positive," particularly for underrepresented students (Guyotte et al., 2019, p. 14). For example, for women in physics, there can be a perceived choice between "fitting in or opting out" (Lewis et al., 2016). Research on belonging across underrepresented student characteristics is gaining attention due to the higher education regulatory environment in England, led by the Office for Students (OfS).

Underrepresented students in the UK

The Equality Act (2010) legally protects people from discrimination in the workplace and wider society. It replaced previous antidiscrimination laws with a single act and outlines the parameters of what constitutes unlawful behavior. It covers the following protected characteristics:

1. age
2. disability
3. gender reassignment
4. marriage or civil partnership (in employment only)
5. pregnancy and maternity
6. race
7. religion or belief
8. sex
9. sexual orientation

In relation to higher education, students cannot be discriminated against, including in admissions, based on these characteristics. In terms of the regulatory agenda, the OfS (2022a) identifies the following underrepresented groups:

- students from areas of low higher education participation, low household income, or low socioeconomic status
- Black, Asian, and ethnic minority students
- mature students (over 21 years of age)
- disabled students
- care leavers (i.e., students who have spent time in foster care)
- carers (i.e., students with responsibility for caring for others)

- people estranged from their families
- people from Gypsy, Roma, and Traveler communities
- refugees
- children from military families

To address unequal access and participation in higher education, the OfS (2022b) has set the following key performance indicators to focus its activity. The first is the gap in higher education participation between most and least represented groups across local areas. Second is the gap in participation at highly selective institutions between the most and least represented groups. Next is the gap in noncontinuation between most and least represented groups. The last two address the gap in degree outcomes between White students and Black students and between students with disabilities and nondisabled students.

To support delivery of these key performance indicators, higher education institutions are required to complete access and participation plans, which set out how they will improve equality of opportunity for underrepresented groups to access, succeed in, and progress from higher education. Access and participation plans have been updated over time and criteria have changed in relation to OfS priorities. The research reported here is in this broader regulatory context, with specific institutional metrics around access by socioeconomic disadvantage and the recruitment of Black students. However, the extent to which these institutional targets can "trickle down" to the academic departments may be limited in institutions with department-based admissions practices and high degrees of departmental autonomy (Kandiko Howson et al., 2022).

Theoretical frames and approaches

Grounding this chapter are three theoretical frames. The first is research on belonging and engagement (discussed above) and applying largely institutionally based research to a departmental context. This is supported by the second frame of DBER, which has emerged within STEM disciplines to investigate and improve undergraduate learning and development and inform teaching reform efforts. DBER links "expert knowledge of a science or engineering discipline, of the challenges of learning and teaching in that discipline, and of the science of learning and teaching generally" (Singer et al., 2012, p. 2). The third frame informing this chapter is the approach of embedded and situational action research (McNiff & Whitehead, 2006). This acknowledges that the research is done in a specific departmental context by active agents within the department, which itself is situated in a specific institutional context.

Research-intensive physics department context

This study was conducted in an institution several years into an ambitious program of change, supported by a top-down, policy-driven, 9-year investment plan. The institutional change program is based on four pillars focusing on (a) reforming assessment, (b) embedding active learning, (c) fostering an inclusive and diverse culture and sense of belonging, and (d) supporting digital and technology enhanced learning. The strategy included a series of competitive calls for funding for departments and other units to address the pillars in local contexts. This chapter reports on a project funded through this scheme.

The project is situated in the Department of Physics, one of the largest in institution. There are approximately 250 undergraduate students per year, they have high grades on entry, and the culture is competitive. Most commute to campus across London. About half are from outside the UK and only a quarter are women. This field has long-standing gender gaps and a lack of recruitment, retention, and progression of women students (in contrast to higher education nationally, where women students outnumber men).

Gender participation gaps also exist in the Department of Physics for faculty members. There are only 14 women faculty members within the department, compared with 112 men. Across the UK there is a similar underrepresentation in physics – a recent report found that only 12% of professors and 21% of senior lecturers were women (Institute of Physics [IOP], 2017). In the department, the paucity of women faculty means that an undergraduate could progress through their degree and not have been lectured by a single woman physicist.

The Department of Physics gathered a comprehensive database of module-level attainment over the past 5 years together with demographic characteristics such as gender, school type, school results, country of origin, ethnicity, and socioeconomic background. In a summer project, a master's-level student used this database to create a statistical model to investigate to what degree student attainment in our physics undergraduate degree programs is correlated with gender, school type, and school results. The results indicate that there is a persistent gender awarding gap in overall degree outcome. However, how the gap varies by course unit has been less clear. Further, how this gap differs across wider sociodemographic characteristics, and intersections of these, is of concern. Addressing these gaps became a significant institutional concern to ensure a supportive environment for all students, building on a positive sense of academic belonging.

The Strengthening Learning Communities project

The SLC project builds on the preexisting detailed knowledge of awarding gaps in physics. It aims to investigate the underlying cause(s) behind the awarding gaps and pilot targeted interventions to alleviate it. Drawing on the idea of belonging as a metaconstruct, the SLC project draws together different subprojects through thematic areas. This cross-departmental effort engages undergraduate student partners, a dedicated PhD student, a postdoctoral researcher, faculty across all levels in physics, as well as partners in higher education studies and other interdisciplinary areas. The project strands involve (a) exploring undergraduate student attitudes, behavior, engagement, belonging, and attainment; (b) an analytical methodology to explore awarding gaps across a decade of cohorts; (c) research on the effects of pedagogical innovation and assessment reform on attainment, particularly for historically underrepresented groups; and (d) student-led projects on topics such as transition to university and assessment. This is supported by a seminar series open to undergraduates, postgraduate students, and staff with invited international guest speakers and a cross-institutional journal club exploring physics education research papers.

While there has been considerable speculation on why awarding gaps might be present, there has not yet been a concerted effort to fully understand their prevalence, reasons for existence, and methods to reduce or eliminate them. The SLC project has supported and been involved with several staff–student partnership projects looking at assessment, the curriculum, and the experiences of underrepresented faculty. These projects explore different aspects of the curriculum and academic student experience to help understand the prevalence, reasons for existence, and methods to reduce or eliminate awarding gaps and support students' sense of belonging. We highlight five projects, each covering a different aspect of students' academic experience, all involving students as researchers or active research participants, to draw out how to create a supportive and inclusive academic environment and foster students' sense of belonging.

Doctoral research project on sense of belonging

Research shows that pervasive stereotypes about physics act as a barrier to belonging for underrepresented groups, yet social norms within the context of studying physics, which have the power to influence behavioral decisions, are underresearched. This doctoral research project focuses on students' experiences and belonging through three questions:

1. What are faculty and students' behavioral beliefs related to studying physics?
2. What are faculty and students' normative beliefs related to studying physics?
3. How do these beliefs influence student behavior and authenticity when becoming a physicist?

The study uses mixed methods and utilizes focus groups and questionnaires with undergraduate students and faculty to determine what social norms are present in an undergraduate physics department and how these norms influence student behavior. This approach lends itself well to studies on sense of belonging within STEM as quantitative findings can be used as a hook to engage with those from more positivist backgrounds. This acts as a starting point from which to discuss more in-depth qualitative findings, which will often get to the *why* of research questions on sense of belonging.

Research has found that the influence of sense of belonging on other constructs such as identity and self-efficacy is stronger for physics students later in their studies (Hazari et al., 2020; Lewis et al., 2016). This study uses a longitudinal approach and tracks a first-year undergraduate cohort through the first 3 years of their undergraduate physics degree to illuminate the changes that occur for physics students as they interact more with their department and physics communities.

One key finding from this doctoral research is that students and staff see transferable social skills such as "cross-cultural awareness" and the "ability to contribute to discussions" as less valuable for a physics student than dis-cipline-based skills such as "problem solving." Importantly, students see these social skills as significantly less valuable for a physics student after 1 year of instruction. This may suggest that students (and faculty) value the skills that contribute to success in the most frequently used traditional assessment methods such as written exams, as opposed to the skills beneficial in less frequently used group-based assessments. Students' devaluing of social communication skills was reinforced in how they described an often "unhealthy" decision to prioritize academic work over socializing. Curricu-lum design therefore can influence how students value community in their degree studies, which ultimately has implications for sense of belonging.

Laboratory project

We found that academic sense of belonging is fostered through academic-based social interactions. Undergraduate teaching laboratories are one of the few places where students spend extended time interacting with their peers, teaching assistants, and faculty instructors. Labs are also considered an essential part of a physics degree and are therefore a formative part of all physicists' identities (whether positive or negative). To understand student views on experimental physics, we used the Colorado Learning Attitudes about Science Survey for Experimental Physics (Zwickl et al., 2013) in all 3 years of teaching labs. The activity is being used as a means for students to reflect on the purpose of experimental physics, while also allowing us to measure whether the lab courses affect student views on experimental phy-sics and the impact of changes to the teaching lab courses.

As an extension, and in collaboration with an undergraduate research student, we also developed a new measure related to self-efficacy using the Colorado Learning Attitudes about Science Survey for Experimental Physics. We hope this measure will help us better understand how our students position themselves relative to experts and provide insight into students' academic sense of belonging to the discipline of physics. Furthermore, by partnering with a student for this project, we established students as stakeholders in the evaluation of their teaching and learning and encouraged student awareness of educational research in a STEM-focused research university. This project has also been an opportunity to engage physics faculty with educational research through publishing initial results and expectations in the *Physics Education Research Conference Proceedings* (Fox et al., 2022).

Exam experience among first-year physics students

We found that a key aspect of students developing a positive academic sense of belonging is being able to engage with their course and progress through assignments. Our findings suggest that the exam experience is a key component in creating a sense of academic belonging for students. High-stakes exams are a feature of many STEM courses, with performance on initial assessments impacting students' feelings regarding whether their course was the "right" choice for them.

This mixed methods student partnership project explored the cancellation of A-level school examinations (the typical upper-secondary school leaving qualification in the UK), due to the COVID-19 pandemic, and students' subsequent experiences of first-year university physics exams. Student co-researchers co-designed a quantitative questionnaire that explored first-year students' self-efficacy and test anxiety in university physics exams and how these were impacted by the cancellation of school exams. Self-efficacy has been shown to correlate with sense of belonging for undergraduate physics students and as a preexisting and well-researched concept can be used as a proxy measure to gain initial insights into sense of belonging. Follow-up qualitative focus groups explored students' exam experiences and how these related to their sense of belonging at university.

Students who felt more negatively impacted by the cancellation of school exams reported lower self-efficacy and higher test anxiety in their university physics exams compared with students who felt more positively impacted. This is both in terms of the students having a chance to prove themselves and therefore earn and deserve their place at university through good grades and in terms of mastery experiences of sitting exams. These findings suggest that a lack of "mastery experiences" can impact students in future examinations in terms of their self-efficacy and test anxiety.

The findings of the study were used to inform the design and creation of a *Welcome Booklet* (Rahman et al., 2021) for future students, which has since been rolled out to subsequent cohorts of first-year students. The *Welcome Booklet* focuses on tackling feelings of imposter syndrome and promoting a sense of belonging by introducing the first-year modules and the relevant staff, signposting students to where they can get support, and listing the specific communities in the Physics Department, such as the Blackett Lab Family (for students of Black heritage), women and non-binary in physics, and the Physics LGBT+ committee. These resources aim to support students' self-efficacy in relation to exam taking.

Toward an inclusive physics curriculum

Going beyond the departmental context, this student partnership project was undertaken with support from the national accrediting body, the IOP. The current narrative surrounding physics is that it is objective, based on a fixed set of laws and formulae, and uninfluenced by subjective lived experiences (Bruun et al., 2018). The IOP (2022) recently announced their new accreditation framework for physics undergraduate courses. The new accreditation moves away from the transfer of knowledge and toward the teaching of transferable skills. It is summarized in five key principles. Of relevance to this project is the new focus on equality, diversity, and inclusion, which is covered by Principle 4: Universities and physics departments must have a clear commitment to equality, diversity, and inclusion and this should be evident within the university and departmental culture, environment, and physics curriculum.

This project, led and undertaken by students, examines the current state of physics curricula across the UK in IOP-accredited institutions through detailed analysis of syllabuses, lecture notes, and assessment methods. Through this study, students acted as co-researchers to identify how, if at all, universities are currently highlighting marginalized physicists – or the historical context surrounding discoveries – in their teaching material and whether this is included in assessment. In addition to providing a paid research opportunity for four undergraduate students, this study includes outputs that aim to tackle inclusivity in the curriculum, including resources for practitioners with details on physicists from marginalized backgrounds for use across the sector (Inclusive Physics, 2023).

Women physics faculty members' teaching choices and decisions

The final project we highlight focuses on demographic gaps in the faculty body and the impact of these gaps on students' sense of belonging to the academic environment. As mentioned previously, there is a significant underrepresentation of women faculty in the Physics Department. This issue has been raised by the undergraduate students at staff–student committee meetings, highlighting its significance for students, and therefore a student partnership project seemed particularly valuable. This is important to address as role models have been shown to be significant both for a student's ability to see themselves as a "physics person" and to form a sense of belonging in physics; that is, "you cannot be what you cannot see." For context, academic staff in the department are eligible to lecture and can opt to lecture a range of courses – from core courses in the first and second years to optional courses in the third and fourth years.

This staff–student project investigated this gender disparity in faculty delivering teaching by having students co-conduct semistructured interviews with 7 of the 14 academic women faculty in the department (out of 126 faculty). We investigated their teaching motivations, decisions, and choices through the lens of expectancy–value theory (Eccles & Wigfield, 2002). Students led on the analysis, finding lecturing to be highly valued by the academic women faculty, particularly the interaction with students, as they stated that lecturing was exciting and interesting. However, a key factor in their decision to lecture was their own expertise – they felt that lecturing a course within their specialism reduced the cost of having to learn new material and allowed them to feel confident that they could demonstrate interest and in-depth knowledge and link the course to current research.

A perceived high cost was found for administrative and pastoral roles and for lecture courses outside of the academic women's specialism. The women in our study mentioned time and workload and that they would not feel as confident taking on these roles, suggesting an area where physics departments should endeavor to offer support. This work increases the department's understanding of the needs of women faculty, which will inform how to increase and normalize their visibility during the undergraduate degree, without "forcing" them to take on specific teaching duties as a "token" gesture (Viefers et al., 2006). This project shows the importance of sense of belonging for faculty, which is necessary to help support students' engagement and belonging. Students co-presented the findings at institutional conferences, further amplifying their voices.

Research-led approach to supporting staff and student belonging in Physics

The five projects detailed above highlight how every aspect of the student experience can influence their academic sense of belonging. The doctoral research project highlights how intertwined students' academic sense of belonging is with their disciplinary context. Students can overly focus on "doing" physics independently, to the detriment of collaborating with others and building an inclusive community – key factors for developing a sense of belonging. The labs project shows the importance of students engaging in the collaborative activities of the discipline to develop their sense of belonging to the discipline and to raise their self-efficacy.

The three student partnership projects – on first-year exams, an inclusive curriculum, and supporting women faculty – each provide further insight into how different aspects of students' academic experience can contribute (or not) to their sense of belonging. Supporting students in assessments is relevant for all students and key to students feeling part of the course. An inclusive curriculum can support diverse students to be able to identify with their course and can broaden the educational experience for the entire cohort. The project on women faculty highlights how important those who design and deliver the curriculum are, especially as role models.

Reflecting more broadly, themes from the partnership projects draw out the importance of integrating activities of students and faculty. Students have given very positive feedback on being in the role of a researcher exploring belonging, rather than as a passive recipient of the outcomes of others' ideas. Students were able to draw on their departmental context as well as their disciplinary skills in the projects – such as modelling and machine learning analytical skills. This further integrates students as researchers in a research-led institutional environment.

Student voices have been central to the projects – from students selecting topics, engaging as researchers and participants, and disseminating and developing outputs for use across the institution. Students have continued to engage with research seminars and journal clubs on physics education research, and some are considering pursuing the topic in further study.

The undergraduate students who took part in the partnership projects have all gained experience in conducting education research, from the initial ethics review stage through to data collection and analysis and dissemination of results at institutional conferences and an online physics education research conference. Student feedback confirmed that these experiences have been central in allowing these student partners to feel both part of a research team and agents for positive change within the department through their contributions and unique insights and perspectives.

Lessons learned: Supporting academic belonging in Physics

It is essential to integrate the disciplinary context in efforts to support students' academic sense of belonging. This chapter highlights how this can happen in a physics department, and findings may be applicable to other STEM departments. Specific ways of engaging students may look different across social science and humanities fields, but promoting students' active engagement within their field of study is key.

The student partnership projects are examples of an "action-oriented approach" to educational research that not only aims to gather insight into a problem but immediately works on tackling it. This helps students – those as co-researchers and the student body as a whole – see the impact of educational research. We received favorable feedback on the *Welcome Booklet* from both students and faculty.

A key enabler for engaging staff widely across the department has been bringing in faculty's disciplinary expertise and using this to explore key issues around the student experience. This provides a way in for many staff not accustomed to engaging with educational or student partnership research.

We also identify the key role of faculty on teaching-intensive contracts to lead and drive change in the department. Many of these staff have time committed to conducting research on aspects of teaching and learning and the student experience. Investment in such student-oriented roles pays off.

Conclusion: Building an inclusive community

This project aims to develop demonstrably effective measures to support students' sense of belonging and reduce the awarding gap for demographic minority students. We hope these lines of research will have a wide impact, not just for the department but across the institution and beyond. Attempts to enhance minority groups' sense of belonging feed into building a strong and inclusive community throughout the department and can be rolled out across departments.

References

Ahn, M. Y., & Davis, H. H. (2020). Four domains of students' sense of belonging to university. *Studies in Higher Education*, 45(3), 622–634. doi:10.1080/03075079.2018.1564902

Bruun, M., Willoughby, S., & Smith, J. L. (2018). Identifying the stereotypical who, what, and why of physics and biology. *Physical Review Physics Education Research*, 14(2), 020125.

Burke, P., Bennett, A., Burgess, C., Gray, K., & Southgate, E. (2016). *Capability, belonging and equity in higher education: Developing inclusive approach.* Centre of Excellence for Equity in Higher Education, University of Newcastle.

Cohen, E., & Viola, J. (2022). The role of pedagogy and the curriculum in university students' sense of belonging. *Journal of University Teaching & Learning Practice*, 19(4), 6–17.

Cureton, D., & Gravestock, P. (2019). We belong: Differential sense of belonging and its meaning for different ethnicity groups in higher education. *Compass: Journal of Learning and Teaching*, 12(1). doi:10.21100/compass.v12i1.942

Eccles, J. S., & Wigfield, A. (2002). Motivational beliefs, values, and goals. *Annual Review of Psychology*, 53(1), 109–132.

Equality Act. (2010). https://www.gov.uk/guidance/equality-act-2010-guidance

Fox, M. F. J., Bland, S., Mangles, S., & McGinty, J. (2022). Expectations of how student views on experimental physics develop during an undergraduate degree. *Physics Education Research Conference Proceedings* (pp. 182–187). doi:10.1119/perc.2022.pr.Fox

Gravett, K., & Ajjawi, R. (2022). Belonging as situated practice. *Studies in Higher Education*, 47(7), 1386–1396. doi:10.1080/03075079.2021.1894118

Guyotte, K. W., Flint, M. A., & Latopolski, K. S. (2019). Cartographies of belonging: Mapping nomadic narratives of first-year students. *Critical Studies in Education*, 62(5), 543–558. doi:10.1080/17508487.2019.1657160

Hazari, Z., Chari, D., Potvin, G., & Brewe, E. (2020). The context dependence of physics identity: Examining the role of performance/competence, recognition, interest, and sense of belonging for lower and upper female physics undergraduates. *Journal of Research in Science Teaching*, 57(10), 1583–1607.

Inclusive Physics. (2023). *Towards an inclusive physics curriculum*. https://www.inclusivephysics.co.uk/

Institute of Physics. (2017). *Academic staff in UK physics departments*. https://www.iop.org/sites/default/files/2020-07/Staff-characteristics-2017-18.pdf

Institute of Physics. (2022). *Degree accreditation framework*. https://www.iop.org/sites/default/files/2022-09/IOP-Degree-Accreditation-Framework-July-2022.pdf

Kandiko Howson, C., Cohen, E., & Viola, J. K. (2022). Inertia in elite STEM widening participation: the use of contextual data in admissions. *British Journal of Sociology of Education*, 43(6), 950–969.

Kane, S., Chalcraft, D., & Volpe, G. (2014). Notions of belonging: First year, first semester higher education students enrolled on business or economics degree programmes. *The International Journal of Management Education*, 12(2), 193–201.

Kift, S. (2004, July 14–16). *Organising first year engagement around learning: Formal and informal curriculum intervention* [Paper presentation]. 8th Pacific Rim First Year in Higher Education Conference, Dealing with Diversity. Melbourne, VIC, Australia.

Lewis, K. L., Stout, J. G., Pollock, S. J., Finkelstein, N. D., & Ito, T. A. (2016). Fitting in or opting out: A review of key social–psychological factors influencing a sense of belonging for women in physics. *Physical Review Physics Education Research*, 12(2), 020110.

McNiff, J., & Whitehead, J. (2006). *All you need to know about action research*. Sage.

Office for Students. (2022a). *Our approach to access and participation*. https://www.officeforstudents.org.uk/advice-and-guidance/promoting-equal-opportunities/our-approach-to-access-and-participation/

Office for Students. (2022b). *Participation performance measures*. https://www.officeforstudents.org.uk/about/measures-of-our-success/participation-performance-measures/

Rahman, N., Christie, R., Smith, A., & Durk, J. (2021). *Welcome Booklet*. Imperial College London Department of Physics. https://www.imperial.ac.uk/media/imperial-college/faculty-of-natural-sciences/department-of-physics/internal/physics-education-group/Amy-Smith-Booklet.pdf

Read, B., Archer, L., & Leathwood, C. (2003). Challenging cultures? Student conceptions of "belonging" and "isolation" at a post-1992 university. *Studies in Higher Education*, 28(3), 261–277. doi:10.1080/03075070309290

Reay, D., Crozier, G., & Clayton, J. (2010). "Fitting in" or "standing out": Working-class students in UK higher education. *British Educational Research Journal*, 36(1), 107–124.

Richardson, J. (2018). *Place and identity: The performance of home*. Routledge.

Robertson, A., Cleaver, E., & Smart, F. (2019). *Beyond the metrics: Identifying, evidencing and enhancing the less tangible assets of higher education*. QAA Scotland Enhancement Themes. https://www.enhancementthemes.ac.uk/docs/ethemes/ evidence-for-enhancement/beyond-the-metrics-identifying-evidencing-and-enha ncing-the-less-tangible-assets-of-higher-education.pdf?sfvrsn=ca37c681_8

Singer, S. R., Nielsen, N. R., & Schweingruber, H. A. (Eds.). (2012). *Discipline-based education research: Understanding and improving learning in undergraduate science and engineering*. National Academies Press. https://www.nap.edu/cata log/13362/discipline-based-education-research-understanding-and-improving-lea rning-in-undergraduate

Testa, D., & Egan, R. (2014). Finding voice: The higher education experiences of students from diverse backgrounds. *Teaching in Higher Education*, 19(3), 229–241. doi:10.1080/13562517.2013.860102

Thomas, L. (2012). *Building student engagement and belonging in higher education at a time of change*. Paul Hamlyn Foundation. https://www.phf.org.uk/wp-con tent/uploads/2014/10/What-Works-report-final.pdf

Thomas, L., Hill, M., O'Mahony, J., & Yorke, M. (2017) *Supporting student success: strategies for institutional change: What works? Student retention and success programme final report*. Paul Hamlyn Foundation. https://www.advance-he.ac.uk/ knowledge-hub/supporting-student-success-strategies-institutional-change

Tight, M. (2020). Student retention and engagement in higher education. *Journal of Further and Higher Education*, 44(5), 689–704.

Viefers, S. F., Christie, M. F., & Ferdos, F. (2006). Gender equity in higher education: Why and how? A case study of gender issues in a science faculty. *European Journal of Engineering Education*, 31(1), 15–22.

Watson, S., Miller, T., Davis, L., & Carter, P. (2010). Teachers' perceptions of the effective teacher. *Research in the Schools*, 17(2), 11–22.

Wilcox, P., Winn, S., & Fyvie-Gauld, M. (2005). "It was nothing to do with the university, it was just the people": the role of social support in the first-year experience of higher education. *Studies in Higher Education*, 30(6), 707–722.

Yorke, M. (2016). The development and initial use of a survey of student "belongingness", engagement and self-confidence in UK higher education. *Assessment & Evaluation in Higher Education*, 41(1), 154–166. doi:10.1080/02602938.2014.990415

Yorke, M., & Longden, B. (2004). *Retention and student success in higher education*. McGraw-Hill International.

Zwickl, B. M., Finkelstein, N., & Lewandowski, H. J. (2013). Development and validation of the Colorado learning attitudes about science survey for experimental physics. *AIP Conference Proceedings*, 1513(1), 442–445.

7

"WHAT'S YOUR MAJOR?"

How one department addressed belonging and equity through a curriculum overhaul

Denise Kennedy, Giselle Navarro-Cruz, Soon Young Jang, Eden Haywood-Bird and Nancy Hurlbut

The Early Childhood Studies (ECS) Department at California State Polytechnic University, Pomona (CPP), has grown substantially since its conception. In 2014, a diverse group of 13 professionals, including faculty from different disciplines, 2- and 4-year campuses across California, and local employers met for 3 days to conceptualize a new early childhood degree program. In this spirit of collaboration and a focus on community needs, the ECS Department has cultivated a commitment to anti-racist, inclusive, and equity-driven pedagogy. In 2020, the department embarked on a curriculum revision project guided by the voices of our students. The first goal of this project was to foster students' sense of belonging and inclusion by learning about their ongoing interests and diverse needs and simultaneously supporting students' efforts to be successful in their academic and career objectives. A second goal was strengthening the department's commitment to anti-racist practices by infusing this perspective into all of our courses.

The curriculum revision project involved a fivefold process. First, the department met with early childhood studies majors to hear their voices and learn what they wanted from the program and their career of choice. Second, the department obtained feedback from the workforce community and school districts to better understand the needs of graduates. Third, the department hired an expert anti-racist consultant who provided our entire faculty with targeted anti-racist training that informed our redesign of the entire ECS curriculum. Fourth, we became involved in California's early childhood policies and advocacy work that impacts the lives of children, families, and our students. Lastly, we spent many hours in discourse to help us more clearly reflect on what we had heard, our process, and our desired outcomes. Building student belonging is crucial for retention and success in

DOI: 10.4324/9781003443735-9

higher education (Masika & Jones, 2015). This chapter showcases how a department underwent a curriculum revision process to increase student sense of belonging and community by ensuring that students developed a sense of competence and self-efficacy and a connection to working with children. Research has shown that the lack of self-efficacy among minority students in higher education and lack of a sense of belonging have been linked to lower GPAs, diminished persistence, and decreased retention rates (Smith et al., 2014). In addition, a study by D'Amico et al. (2014) identified that commitment, support, and positive university experiences (i.e., academic, social, and socio-academic) are factors that have a significant impact on transfer students' performance.

The curricular revision was centered on the voices of our students and community stakeholders to meet their needs and to integrate linguistically and culturally responsive pedagogies and anti-racism throughout our curriculum. We tried to ensure that student and community needs were reflected in our program's curricular changes to increase academic belonging. Our changes highlight the inextricable links between student and community stakeholder needs. For example, our conversations with local school district representatives led to the realization that two early childhood special education courses, rather than one, would better prepare our students for the job market. We therefore developed one special education course based on development and another focused on curriculum. Adding the second course strengthened our students' preparation by addressing the school district's needs. Our curriculum revision project was grounded in student voices and strengthened through an anti-racism training, community feedback, and an understanding of fast-developing state policies in early childhood education, all of which increased student belonging in our program.

In this chapter, we provide an overview of processes and approaches the ECS Department took to revise our curriculum scope and sequence. Additionally, we discuss how the faculty came to understand the needs of our majors and how we utilized the voices of students to guide our work. Finally, this chapter's cross-cutting narrative is a snapshot of the effort to understand how a department can center students' needs alongside academic requirements to address belonging.

Background context

Initially, the ECS Department was not a department but a pilot degree program under the umbrella of the Education Department in the College of Education and Integrative Studies. When the major began accepting students, the only permanent early childhood faculty member was working as the interim dean of the college; therefore, all courses were taught by part-time, temporary faculty. The Education Department advised students during this time as a pilot degree. It was only after graduation of the first cohort, in spring 2018, that the ECS Department became a stand-alone department while remaining a pilot degree program. Starting in fall 2018, the department boasted around 160 majors total, two full-time tenure-line faculty, and a department chair who worked half-time. Most courses in the department continued to be taught by part-time, temporary faculty, most of whom had been with the department since 2016. The department continued to add one new tenure-track faculty every year until the pandemic, when no new faculty were hired university-wide during the 2020–2021 academic year.

This history is important for context, as it demonstrates the department's early challenges in affirming its identity, let alone understanding the identities of the students who had chosen early childhood studies as their undergraduate major. Transfer students from community colleges were the only students admitted to the program for the first 6 years and transitioned from a 2-year college to a 4-year university. While the temporary, part-time faculty were excellent teachers and were devoted to the field of early childhood, for many of them this was not their primary professional obligation, making it difficult for the department to learn about the needs of our students. It was not until a significant number of courses were taught by permanent, tenure-line faculty who dedicated their time to analyzing the entire course sequence that it became clear that the department's curriculum was not aligned with what students needed/wanted or with the specific gifts and funds of knowledge that each of them brought to the table. Funds of knowledge are the skills, resources, knowledge, practices, and ideologies we accumulate through our past and present experiences (González et al., 2006). We wanted to highlight the richness of our students' culture, experiences, and practices. A funds of knowledge framework is used as a culturally responsive pedagogy that highlights the knowledge every individual brings with them to teaching and learning spaces by utilizing this knowledge in their learning.

Since the ECS program only accepted transfer students, fostering belonging has been crucial for our students, who transferred from many different community colleges. Therefore, the ECS Department has been committed to a transfer-receptive culture, defined as an "institutional commitment by a four-year college or university to provide the support needed for students to transfer successfully" (Jain et al., 2011, p. 257). Because of students' reduced time with us, the department must target our approaches to fostering belonging. Based on the research on student belongingness and transfer-receptive culture, ECS has pre- and posttransfer efforts in place to increase student success and a sense of belonging. First, collaborative relationships with feeder community colleges and the 4-year university created a statewide transfer model curriculum to improve the timely graduation rate of transfer students. ECS's lower division courses were aligned among most community colleges to make the transition for transfer students seamless. Next, a new student orientation was implemented to assist in the transition and ensure academic success. A large body of research has specifically documented the detrimental effects of feelings of belonging uncertainty on the academic performance of minority students in higher education (Smith et al., 2014; Walton & Cohen, 2011), linking belonging uncertainty to lower GPAs, diminished persistence, and a lessened chance of graduation. The ECS Department has increased the academic performance of transfer students and reduced equity gaps by enhancing transfer students' sense of belonging through various curricular activities that reflect the students' funds of knowledge, options to follow a curriculum pathway aligned with their professional goals, and opportunities to participate in research with faculty members. ECS students can engage in several activities, such as participating in the ECS club, meeting with faculty to work on research projects, presenting their research, and creating community with existing ECS students to increase social adjustment and support in academic adjustment. Faculty members assist in mentoring transfer students in research projects and career goals.

Getting to know a student population

We have a diverse student population at our university, which is designated as a Hispanic-serving institution. In 2020, 49% of students identified themselves as Latino, 21% as Asian/Pacific Islander, 3% as Black, 15 % as White, 6% as other, and 5% as international. Fifty-eight percent of students are first-generation college students, and 76% receive federal financial aid, of whom 44% are Pell Grant recipients. In addition to the high need for financial aid, the university has identified growing food and housing insecurities as barriers to persistence and graduation in the student population. In 2018, the California State University (CSU) system, comprising 23 universities, released a basic needs study, which showed that 41.6% of CSU students experienced food insecurity and 10.9% experienced homelessness within the last year (Crutchfield & Maguire, 2018). Our department survey data mirror those of the university population.

While department data helped us understand our students' diversity, the faculty–student interactions provided a deeper understanding of who our students are. Over the years, faculty have built relationships with multiple students who have shared the many obstacles they must overcome while pursuing higher education. Many students have shared their dual identities of parent and student. Student parents are persistent as they navigate the complexities of accessing resources to support a family and manage their schedules (Adams et al., 2015; Navarro-Cruz et al., 2021). They are highly motivated, and their children often serve as their primary source of motivation (Brooks, 2012; Estes, 2011; Navarro-Cruz et al., 2021; Ricco et al.,

2009). Understanding and supporting student parents in our department is crucial as we strive to help students and enhance the lives of children and families. Students have also shared the financial burdens they experience. Students have shared the importance of having late-night and weekend courses so they can work and provide for their families. In addition, students shared the financial burdens they experience while pursuing higher education, with most working either part-time or full-time. Because of their various responsibilities, many of our students required diverse course schedules, which included evening and weekend times. We also found that most of our students preferred hybrid courses to accommodate their busy schedules.

To obtain greater feedback from our students, a series of convenings were held during the first 2 years of the program. The goal of these convenings was to better get to know our students and learn about their experiences in courses and how to strengthen the program. This was important as students who started with the program did not have full-time faculty as advisors, so they lacked a sense of belonging as they did not know whom to go to for support. Students themselves asked for a space for them to share their concerns. We provided a space where students were free to share their concerns, questions, and suggestions about the program. One of the key components they shared was obtaining more information and support on career pathways. Students shared their diverse expertise as family childcare owners, early childhood educators, parents, and babysitters. They emphasized the importance of being prepared for career goals beyond being a teacher. We organized a post-baccalaureate convening to which faculty from various graduate schools were invited. Students learned about various graduate pathways in which they can continue working with young children. The students' feedback was positive, and they appreciated hearing about different career paths. Students were especially interested in the teaching pathway and were happy to hear that Cal Poly Pomona offered a credential and master's in education. This approach highlights the need for academic departments to prioritize authentic student voices to foster their sense of belonging.

Fostering academic belonging

Academic belonging is a concept rooted in several theoretical frameworks. Wenger's (2009) social learning theory posits that the foundation of learning is rooted in social participation rather than an individual process. Therefore, learning must include the student's lived experience and engagement in the social world. There are four learning components in Wenger's theory: (a) community – learning as belonging, (b) practice – learning by doing, (c) meaning – learning by experience, and (d) identity – learning by becoming. The interconnectedness of these four components is created through relationships and shared experiences in the classroom and program. Fostering inclusion and belonging among all students, especially historically excluded and marginalized student populations, in higher education (e.g., students of color, low-income, first-generation college students, etc.) has been the focus of our department from the beginning. We identified our students' diverse backgrounds and experiences using university and department survey data.

Student voice and representation in curriculum revisions

For our students to feel a sense of belonging, they needed to be heard (Weiss, 2021). The surveys, personal interactions, and convenings informed us what students needed and wanted. First, students wanted to feel represented in the courses they took. Our student population is ethnically, racially, and linguistically diverse, and they wanted to see themselves represented in the courses. In addition, they wanted to be able to choose a pathway that would prepare them for their future career, not only teaching. Faculty in the department reflected on what changes needed to be made to strengthen student understanding of how to enhance the well-being of children and families and feel a sense of belonging in the ECS program. Collaboration with tenured and part-time faculty was essential in revising our entire curriculum. We revised 40 courses that included anti-racist components (including removing old courses and adding new courses) and revised road maps that considered students' diverse needs. Since we had 40 course outlines to revise, each faculty member involved took the lead on specific courses in which they had areas of knowledge or expertise and invited adjunct faculty teaching those courses to participate in course revisions. As a result, five full-time and six part-time faculty participated in revising the curriculum. We met regularly in addition to weekly department meetings and discussed what we learned and what steps to take. Ultimately, we developed six new options that allow students to choose a career path in early childhood that best aligns with their goals. These options were developed based on student feedback on their career aspirations and lived experiences.

Our student population is ethnically, racially, and linguistically diverse. This information was important to know in redesigning our courses. To create a sense of belonging in our department, it was crucial that we valued our students' diversity and funds of knowledge. It became evident that we had to redesign our courses to include the lived experiences of our students. Furthermore, our students were experiencing the racist rhetoric that was happening throughout the country. Black Lives Matter was picking up steam and shining a light on decades of police brutality and the killing of Black men, women, and children. Creating anti-racist, inclusive, and equity-driven pedagogy was necessary to bring students' lived experiences into the classroom. An essential goal of this project was to foster students' sense of belonging and inclusion by learning about their ongoing interests and diverse needs while helping students become successful in their academic and career objectives. Research has shown that positive academic outcomes are predicted by a sense of belonging (Lewis & Hodges, 2015).

We are committed to transforming the consequences of the legal and social formation of racism and intersecting forms of oppression through anti-racist and decolonial pedagogy and linguistically and culturally responsive approaches and advancing social justice and equity in early childhood education. During the 2020–2021 academic year, the ECS Department participated in an anti-racist training led by an early childhood anti-racist expert. This training aimed to support the ECS program's concepts of multilingualism and anti-racism throughout all of the required core courses while preparing faculty to teach to the diverse student population we served. While at Cal Poly Pomona, early childhood studies students learn processes important for early childhood development and identify theory implications in examining and applying principles and practices within diverse family, program, and community contexts.

Career options

During our various data-gathering efforts, we learned that reworking our curriculum needed to sufficiently address student academic belonging. We also needed to modify the career trajectories within our curriculum to meet students' needs. Students shared the importance of taking coursework that prepared them for various career opportunities for working with young children and families. Students were interested in becoming child therapists, social workers, speech therapists, child life specialists, childcare directors, elementary teachers, bilingual educators, infant educators, and preschool educators. They highlighted the importance of obtaining the competencies to work with diverse children in diverse settings.

In reenvisioning the scope and sequence of our curriculum and thinking about what students need regardless of their career path, we saw how students' feelings of belonging should be threaded throughout this process. In practice, we began by considering how students experience the ECS major. However, by the end of our 2-year redevelopment and redesign process, our thinking shifted to emphasizing student sense of belonging in the early childhood studies major. It was not until we reenvisioned both the scope and sequence through the different degree options, as well as how we integrated our students' overarching funds of knowledge into our curriculum through anti-racist and anti-colonialist pedagogy, that we came to the realization that curriculum can be a force for change. Our curricular revisions help students in that major understand themselves, their place in their field, and how they belong there. Most important, centering their input in our curriculum revisions communicates that they deserve to be part of the conversation.

Initially, the early childhood studies baccalaureate degree only accepted transfer students from community colleges because not enough faculty had been hired to support lower- and upper-division students. This initial degree program had four emphases:

1. Leadership in early childhood – for students interested in a teaching trajectory.
2. Childhood equity and program administration – for students interested in becoming directors of childcare centers
3. Infant–toddler program and practices – for students interested in working with children birth to age 2.9
4. General emphasis – for students interested in other early childhood career options

All but emphasis 4 were aligned to very specific career pathways. The purpose of emphasis 4 was to provide a pathway for the approximately 40% of early childhood studies majors who were not interested in the other three career pathways. This emphasis pathway would give students the coursework that would better align with their career goals. In practice, emphasis 4 became a default emphasis that students used any course to complete this emphasis's requirements. Emphasis 4 had become a way for students to include community college courses or GE credits that did not relate to a specific career goal. Being able to do so allowed them to graduate as quickly as possible. However, this meant that students did not obtain the depth and breadth of early childhood content that would prepare them for their careers of choice.

The original four emphases did not work as intended since the university did not allow them to be listed on the student's transcript or diploma. From a student's perspective, the emphasis they selected did not matter. Students shared that they needed clarification on which emphasis to take, when to take the elective courses, and the impact of choosing one emphasis over another. Furthermore, students shared that all four emphases focused on teaching since they had to complete 120 hours in a school setting. During the convening with students, it was clear that students did not feel they were being prepared for careers outside of teaching. Furthermore, because many of our students worked and raised children, completing 120 hours of practicum in schools when they were not planning to become teachers simply did not make sense.

Based on student feedback and the department's understanding of the changes in the field, the department embarked on a yearlong process of creating six new options in the major, including teaching and non-teaching options, to better help students meet their career goals. Because approximately 40% of early childhood studies majors do not go into teaching, it was apparent to the department that we needed to provide a concrete non-teaching pathway for those students whose final course did not require them to complete hours in an early childhood classroom. This would also provide information making it clear to employers and credential programs that students who graduated in the non-teaching option are not necessarily prepared to teach. Options, unlike emphases, do appear on the student transcripts and diplomas, so they have the advantage of aligning with the student's career choice. At the end of our year-long process, we produced the following six options:

1. Teaching – Early childhood education (0–8 years)
2. Non-teaching
3. Multilingual teaching (0–8 years)
4. Integrated teacher preparation program for special education in the mild/moderate range
5. Integrated teacher preparation program for special education in extensive support
6. P-3rd Grade Teaching

Options 1 through 5 are all aligned with community college early childhood education/child development associate degrees for transfer, whereas option 6 is aligned with the elementary education degree for transfer. One of the discoveries through this process was that a small but still substantial number of students transferred into our degree program with this elementary education associate degree. Because they did not have an early childhood education associate degree, it was difficult for students in this pathway to graduate in 2 years. We developed option 6 with the specific goal of addressing this barrier and thus created an appropriate pathway for these students to graduate in 2 years, as is possible with the other options. In all of our endeavors in this curriculum revision process, which resulted in six career pathway options, we centered students' voices to foster belonging.

Challenges

We experienced several challenges in this curriculum revision process. The department revised program learning outcomes and all ECS course learning outcomes, embedding anti-racist and linguistically and culturally responsive pedagogies as primary frameworks throughout the courses. At the center of these revisions was a focus on student belonging. We wanted to ensure that students felt connected and important (Strayhorn, 2019) as they prepared for their future careers. Research has indicated that a sense of belonging can influence a student's choice of study field (Reay, 2012). Furthermore, the department devised a sustainable recruitment plan to attract under-represented Native American and Black students to the major. One of the issues we faced was the extended course outlines (ECOs). All faculty were using the original ECOs created in 2014–2015 as part of the proposal for this new program. All ECOs needed to be updated to reflect the department's new orientation focused on anti-racist, anti-colonialist pedagogy, as well as to align with revised program learning outcomes (PLOs) and student learning outcomes (SLOs), which were centered on belongingness for students and community stakeholders.

An additional challenge was the new accreditation requirements. As the program had to align with higher education standards to maintain accreditation, the department also had to collect robust data on all students every semester. The National Association for the Education of Young Children (NAEYC) standards for higher education programs had to be aligned to the new PLOs and SLOs so that the data collected aligned with NAEYC accreditation. One of the main requirements for NAEYC accreditation is to collect data on specific key assessments that must be given to each student in the program. We have specific assessments that are in four different courses. Before starting the curriculum revision, the department collected data for 1 year and, through that process, learned that many students were either not completing the key assessment as written or that faculty were altering the key assessment, making the data unusable. Therefore, we needed to revise the ECOs to ensure that key assessments were incorporated into courses to substantiate that the revised PLOs and SLOs are met in the program, which will have implications for student success.

A secondary primary challenge has been aligning the program major with candidates' final career aspirations beyond teaching. Much of the originally required coursework did prepare students to teach in preschool or enter a postgraduate elementary multiple subjects credential. This multiple subjects credential with a BA in ECS enables students to be transitional kindergarten through Grade 6 credentialed teachers in California. However, upon analysis of student surveys and anecdotal conversations with students during advising sessions, the program has discovered that student aspirations are much more varied. As previously discussed, up to 40% of ECS candidates seek careers that are early childhood education adjacent. These candidates have no intention of being classroom teachers but instead hold aspirations to pursue various careers that, while not specifically in teaching, orbit children and families from birth through age 8. A nonexhaustive list of career pathways that students discussed includes pediatric occupational therapists, child life experts, child psychologists, social workers, speech–language pathologists, and pediatric nurses and doctors.

Our plan for improving the program of study for students with diverse interests included changing the course core and developing additional or different option pathways for students not interested in teaching or administration. Before this work, the core courses focused on teaching pedagogy and methods. This did not make sense for many of our graduates who had no intention of being classroom teachers. Though it seems simple on the surface, this work was one of the most challenging aspects of the department's transformation of the BA degree. It forced us to think about what theory and practice all professionals working with children must have. We were required to reflect on what competencies transcend being in the classroom for all individuals who work with young children and their families. This process was more painful and required more time than the department initially allotted. There were many discussions between faculty about what each core course imparted to students by way of values and competency related to early childhood and child development, as well as utilizing anti-racist and anti-colonialist practices while also intentionally centering student belonging in their career pathway. Including student voices in career pathways has fostered a sense of belonging in the program (Weiss, 2021). Initially, the department struggled with exactly how to do this work. Only when we thought about the rights of young children and their families regardless of who the professional was in their life could we nail down the specific competencies that all our graduates, regardless of the option, must gain through their coursework.

Centering student belonging

It was not until we dug into this work that we were able to see how reenvisioning the scope and sequence of our curriculum and thinking about what it is that students need regardless of their career path that we were able to see how students' feelings of belonging should be threaded throughout this process. While we began by asking how students experience the ECS major, by the end of our 2-year redevelopment and redesign process, it had morphed into more about students' belonging in the early childhood studies major. Faculty reenvisioned both the scope and sequence of courses through the options and integrated students' overarching funds of knowledge into our curriculum through anti-racist and anti-colonialist pedagogy, where we felt our curriculum became a force for change. This change enables students in their chosen option to have a clear career pathway as well as clarity on how they belong there in their chosen field of study. We listened to students' voices so they would feel a stronger sense of belongingness in the ECS program and university.

To safeguard student success, the program continues to integrate transfer students from local and regional community college child development/early childhood education programs by providing a pathway for the approved Early Childhood Education Transfer Model Curriculum and the approved Curriculum Alignment Project (eight lower division courses that faculty from across the state developed to provide consistent educational core transferrable courses throughout California's community college, Cal

State, and UC early childhood education/child development programs), as well as to serve CPP students. Transfer students who have completed the early childhood education transfer associate degree can graduate in 2 years by completing the 60 units of required coursework at California State Polytechnic University, Pomona. Students who start at CPP as first-year freshmen can graduate in 4 years by completing the 120 units of required coursework. The baccalaureate program includes 120 units, including articulated transfer courses. Students who meet the requirements for general admission to the university can elect ECS as their major with a specific option. Those students who have completed the lower-division core courses at Cal Poly Pomona or matriculated from another institution of higher education must have a C or better in each of these six lower-division core courses to enter the major. Students must earn a C or better in all major coursework to graduate. The ECS program faculty have worked tirelessly to advise students, ensuring that they complete the roadmap for their chosen option. Faculty in ECS are very hands-on with our students, thus continuing to increase the sense of belongingness for our students, which is positively associated with retention and success in higher education (Masika & Jones, 2015).

Conclusion

The goal of the department was to redesign a program that supports student belonging. First, due to NAEYC accreditation, we reduced the number of PLOs and SLOs required. Next, we engaged all faculty, tenure-line, and adjuncts who wanted to participate in revising the ECOs for the program. All tenure-line faculty participated, and six adjunct faculty participated. We planned to have a summer retreat to work on this, but due to the COVID pandemic, we had to work remotely and did it in pairs. We created 40 new ECOs through the university curriculum committee, and all were approved for fall 2022 implementation. We also created the six career-aligned options described above, which began in fall 2022. In these revisions, we also considered state initiatives impacting early childhood education, such as universal transition kindergarten. The Commission on Teacher Credentialing is proposing a new PK–3 early childhood education specialist instruction credential in California, so our option 6 is directly related to ensuring that children ages 3–8 years are taught by qualified teachers.

This experience has been arduous but rewarding. Faculty worked collaboratively and came together on this project. While this is the first year students have had to choose an option, our hope is that the new options will prepare students for their career choice, whether it is entering a preschool classroom as a teacher upon graduation, attending graduate school, or entering into a post-baccalaureate credential program. We do consider this iteration of our curriculum to be an entry point, and we expect that multiple tweaks and minor edits will be required before we find a sort of sweet spot. In addition, we have been able to hire three new tenure-line faculty, all of whom began in fall 2022. All three faculty searches were anchored in the revisions to our curriculum, and each call was aligned with anti-racist, anti-colonialist pedagogy and critical race theory. Their collective life experiences, individual funds of knowledge, and academic expertise will add to the richness of our revised courses and curriculum. We also expect that as we march into the future, our students' needs, as well as the needs of the field, will require us to reevaluate and reflect on our curriculum and courses to ensure that they continue to utilize and create a sense of academic belonging for our students. We anticipate that this process will be ever-evolving and never-ending, and our curriculum and courses may look entirely different in just a few short years. Being okay with the ever-present disequilibrium is one of the fundamental lessons the department has learned through this process. It helped us understand how our students felt as we intentionally sought to include their collective funds of knowledge in individual courses.

Acknowledgements

This work was funded by the Teagle Foundation, College Futures Foundation, and CSU Chancellor's Office for Curricular Design for Student Success.

References

Adams, G. C., Spaulding, S., & Heller, C. (2015). *Bridging the gap: Exploring the intersection of workforce development and child care*. Urban Institute. http://hdl.voced.edu.au/10707/378691

Brooks, R. (2012). Student-parents and higher education: A cross-national comparison. *Journal of Education Policy, 27*(3), 423–439. doi:10.1080/02680939.2011.613598

Crutchfield, R., & Maguire, J. (2018). *Study of student basic needs*. California State University. https://www.calstate.edu/impact-of-the-csu/student-success/basic-needs-initiative/Documents/BasicNeedsStudy_phaseII_withAccessibilityComments.pdf

D'Amico, M. M., Dika, S. L., Elling, T. W., Algozzine, B., & Ginn, D. J. (2014). Early integration and other outcomes for community college transfer students. *Research in Higher Education, 55*, 370–399.

Estes, D. K. (2011). Managing the student-parent dilemma: Mothers and fathers in higher education. *Symbolic Interaction, 34*(2), 198–219.

González, N., Moll, L. C., & Amanti, C. (Eds.). (2006). *Funds of knowledge: Theorizing practices in households, communities, and classrooms*. Routledge.

Jain, D., Herrera, A., Bernal, S., & Solorzano, D. (2011). Critical race theory and the transfer function: Introducing a transfer receptive culture. *Community College Journal of Research and Practice, 35*, 252–266.

Lewis, K. L., & Hodges, S. D. (2015). Expanding the concept of belonging in academic domains: Development and validation of the ability uncertainty scale. *Learning and Individual Differences, 37*, 197–202.

Masika, R., & Jones, J. (2015). Building student belonging and engagement: Insights into higher education students' experiences of participating and learning together. *Teaching in Higher Education*, 21(2), 138–150. doi:10.1080/13562517.2015.1122585

Navarro-Cruz, G. E., Dávila, B. A., & Kouyoumdjian, C. (2021). From teen parent to student parent: Latina mothers' persistence in higher education. *Journal of Hispanic Higher Education*, 20(4), 466–480. doi:10.1177/1538192720980308

Reay, D. (2012). *Researching class in higher education*. British Education Research Association. https://bera.ac.uk/wp-content/uploads/2014/03/Researching-Class-in-Higher-Education.pdf

Ricco, R., Sabet, S., & Clough, C. (2009). College mothers in the dual roles of student and parent: Implications for their children's attitudes toward school. *Merrill-Palmer Quarterly*, 55(1), 79–110. https://www.jstor.org/stable/23096278

Smith, J. L., Cech, E., Metz, A., Huntoon, M., & Moyer, C. (2014). Giving back or giving up: Native American student experiences in science and engineering. *Cultural Diversity and Ethnic Minority Psychology*, 20(3), 413–429.

Strayhorn, T. L. (2019). *College students' sense of belonging: A key to educational success for all students*. Routledge.

Walton, G. M., & Cohen, G. L. (2011). A brief social-belonging intervention improves academic and health outcomes of minority students. *Science*, 331, 1447–1451.

Weiss, S. (2021). Fostering a sense of belonging at universities. *European Journal of Education*, 56, 93–97.

Wenger, E. (2009). A social theory of learning. In K. Illeris (Ed.), *Contemporary theories of learning: Learning theorists in their own words* (pp. 209–218). Routledge.

PART III

Fostering academic belonging through integrative and supportive learning communities

8

BUILDING COMMUNITY FOR MEN OF COLOR THROUGH SENSE OF BELONGING

Theresa Ling Yeh, Joe Lott II and Kandi Bauman

Men of color in the United States face greater barriers in education and the workforce than almost any other demographic group. Educational spaces and institutional structures, particularly at predominantly White institutions, have created unique challenges for undergraduate men of color as they seek to find belonging. These obstacles create conditions that can negatively impact students' academic and psychosocial outcomes. Launched in 2016, the Brotherhood Initiative (BI) at the University of Washington (UW) is a cross-unit, collaborative effort that draws on design-based research practices to create networks of community and support for men of color (defined here as Black, Latino, Native American, Pacific Islander, and Southeast Asian students who identify as male) across campus. A core premise of the BI is that sense of belonging is a primary condition for success that increases the likelihood that men of color will attain their educational goals. Over the last 5 years, we have integrated theory-driven constructs with student and practitioner data to develop and refine a series of cohort-based seminars, student-led and staff-led activities, and support practices that strengthen the overall BI learning community. In this chapter, we will describe the theory of action that guides our work and explain how we conceptualize "sense of belonging" as a critical condition for success for undergraduate men of color. We will then illustrate how our theory of action informs the design of our seminar curricula as well as our pedagogy in ways that cultivate and expand their sense of belonging.

Sense of belonging for men of color

Extensive research indicates that sense of belonging has a positive impact on a wide range of postsecondary outcomes, including academic achievement,

DOI: 10.4324/9781003443735-11

self-efficacy, and motivation (Freeman et al., 2007), as well as college persistence, academic engagement, and mental health (Davis et al., 2019; Gopalan & Brady, 2020; Hausmann et al., 2007; Lewis et al., 2016). Students' feelings of acceptance and connectedness to their institution are critical to educational success because students function better in environments where they feel a strong sense of belonging. Conversely, when these feelings are absent, students tend to feel less motivated and their academic performance suffers (Strayhorn, 2019).

Although important for all students, the need for belonging is even more critical in contexts or settings that feel different or unfamiliar, as well as in environments where students are more likely to feel marginalized or unwelcome (Strayhorn, 2019). Yet students from underrepresented backgrounds often experience a lower sense of belonging than students from dominant groups, at least in part because encounters with racism and discrimination negatively impact belonging (Hurtado & Carter, 1997; Johnson et al., 2007; Murphy et al., 2020; Nuñez, 2009; Ribera et al., 2017; Tachine et al., 2017). For students of color – and particularly men of color – understanding their sense of belonging is important to understanding how particular forms of social and academic experiences may affect them (Brooms, 2018; Hurtado & Carter, 1997). Building a sense of belonging for men of color at predominantly White institutions is especially critical because they experience feelings of isolation, lack of support, and hostility from peers, staff, and faculty members at higher rates than other populations (Cole et al., 2020; Lee & Ransom, 2011).

Numerous studies highlight the importance of a welcoming campus climate, culturally relevant learning experiences, and positive interactions with peers and faculty in building a sense of belonging for students of color. Engaging in high-impact practices such as learning communities, undergraduate research, service learning, and leadership opportunities also promotes belonging (Ribera et al., 2017; see also Chapter 10). Interacting with people with similar backgrounds and experiences, as well as those with different racial backgrounds and experiences, can lead to greater feelings of connectedness for students of color (Museus & Chang, 2021; Strayhorn, 2008).

Academic belonging, defined as the perception that one is valued and accepted as a legitimate member in their academic domain (Lewis et al., 2016; see also Chapter 9), is particularly important for men of color as they continue to have the lowest levels of postsecondary persistence and degree attainment compared to other populations (Huerta et al., 2021). As the primary conduit to a student's academic major and department, our experience suggests that faculty can have an immense impact on the way that men of color experience academic belonging both in and out of the classroom. Faculty, through their advisory and mentoring roles, can bolster academic belonging by valuing student strengths and contributions or hinder belonging by creating an unwelcoming or hostile learning environment.

The UW Brotherhood Initiative

The Brotherhood Initiative is a design-based research project that seeks to improve postsecondary outcomes for students who identify as men of color from five underrepresented racial/ethnic groups at the University of Washington by providing multiple pathways to engage in academic, civic, and leadership opportunities and access resources that will advance their success. Several aspects of the program are intentionally designed to foster an academic sense of belonging for participants, most notably the cohort-based learning community. We define *sense of belonging* as a phenomenon that "captures the individual's view of whether he or she feels included in the college community" (Hurtado & Carter, 1997, p. 327) as well as the "the experience of mattering or feeling cared about, accepted, respected, valued by, and important to the campus community or others on campus" (Strayhorn, 2019, p. 4). To build this community, participants join a cohort as first-year students and enroll in a year-long academic seminar in both their first and second years of college. The formal curriculum, which ends after the second year, is coupled with intensive, individually tailored advising; support services; and co-curricular programming that students continue to receive until graduation.

A theory of action for course design, reflection, and equity

Recognizing the connection between sense of belonging and academic outcomes, particularly for historically marginalized students, faculty and instructional designers may seek ways to build a sense of belonging in the classroom. There is no shortage of practices to choose from to increase belonging in academic spaces, but which practices are most effective in certain classroom settings? Which interventions are most impactful within and across majors? How can practices be modified to meet the needs of students from particular demographics? Understanding, layering, sequencing, and evaluating the wide array of empirically grounded practices that promote belonging can be a daunting and complex process.

What is a theory of action?

In the BI, we use a theory of action to plan for, foster, and evaluate, among many outcomes, student belonging. We define a theory of action (ToA) as a connected set of propositions that explain how strategies are combined and prioritized to address clearly defined problems and produce desired outcomes. Although a ToA is often associated with the coordination of organizations, programs, and new initiatives, it also serves as a valuable tool in improving teaching and learning in a variety of contexts. A ToA can illuminate how various practices translate into student learning and success (Center for Educational Leadership, 2014; Cobb & Jackson, 2011).

A clear and well-defined ToA is important for three reasons. First, a clear ToA can make visible how actions are grounded in current research and demonstrate informed practice. A deep and personalized understanding of evidence-based pedagogies and pedagogical strategies can aid faculty in increasing retention and success rates for students; however, documenting the nature through which practice draws from research provides one mechanism for adapting practice as emerging research reveals more effective and innovative strategies. Second, a ToA provides the opportunity to integrate local knowledge and practices into generalized theories and frameworks. Academic interventions and strategies, regardless of how good they look on paper, need to meet the needs of students and function within the institutional context they are implemented in. A ToA should not only reflect which theories and frameworks are being utilized but also suggest how they are being combined, customized, and adapted. Lastly, a ToA offers a clear path for assessment and evaluation, creating insight and innovations that are more rigorous, timely, and useful.

A ToA that moves beyond a checklist of strategies can promote an understanding of the dynamic relationship between knowledge, practice, and outcomes. It can be a particularly useful tool for faculty and instructional leaders seeking ways to support men of color in the classroom and related academic spaces. While there has been a great deal of interest and effort in preparing men of color to navigate challenging academic spaces (i.e., changing what students do and assume), more must be done to develop teaching strategies and design learning environments that work best for men of color (i.e., changing what faculty do and assume). To support men of color, who are often overlooked and underserved in the classroom, we believe a ToA can help faculty identify deficit thinking, conceptualize how and what change is possible, and point to ways in which existing institutional supports can supplement the classroom to improve learning outcomes.

The Brotherhood Initiative ToA

The BI theory of action was developed in 2016, as part of the design-based research process that undergirds this project. During the formation phase of the BI, we drew on research on the individual and institutional factors that impact men of color and conducted interviews with men of color at UW to develop a theory of action to incorporate components we hypothesized to be critical to the design of this project. After working with five cohorts of students and carefully examining what we are learning, we have refined our model (see Figure 8.1). A core premise of our approach is that the BI should create the conditions for success that will increase the likelihood that men of color will attain their educational goals.

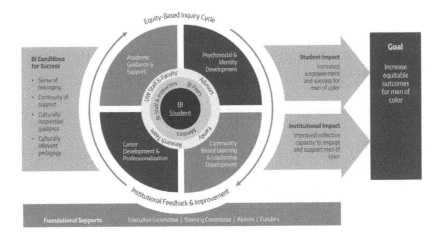

FIGURE 8.1 BI theory of action.
Source: Printed with permission from the Brotherhood Initiative.

The central structure of the BI ToA broadly reflects the complex set of interactions between individuals and their environments. Incorporating aspects of both Bronfenbrenner and Morris's (2006) bioecological model of human development and Rendon's (1994) validation theory, we acknowledge the lived experiences of undergraduate men of color to create a supportive community that mediates students' development and learning.

The conditions for success serve as guiding principles for all subsequent actions, relationships, and anticipated outcomes. As such, these conditions influence all other components and processes in the model. Conditions for success are optimal when (a) opportunities and structures that foster a sense of belonging are widely available, (b) support is continuous and not bound by structure or academic standing, (c) guidance and support are culturally responsive, and (d) the curriculum and pedagogical approaches are culturally relevant.

The layered circles surrounding the individual in the model represent students' multifaceted interpersonal relationships with various people, both on- and off-campus. Together, the conditions for success, in combination with these relationships, facilitate development around four major areas of enrichment that we determined to be crucial to the success of men of color: (a) academic guidance and support, (b) psychosocial and identity development, (c) community-based learning and leadership development, and (d) career development and professionalization. (For a more complete description of the BI ToA, see Lott et al., 2021.) As one of the most underrepresented and marginalized populations in college, it stands to reason that men of color need to experience some degree of belonging to thrive and succeed academically (Turner & Zepeda, 2021). For this reason, the BI theory of action situates sense of belonging as a prerequisite for all our work, from curriculum development to academic guidance to co-curricular programming.

Developing course practices and experiences that promote academic belonging

The BI model is rooted in the assumption that academic belonging can be achieved through theory-driven design at both the programmatic and course levels. In addition to the bioecological model (Bronfenbrenner & Morris, 2006) and validation theory (Rendon, 1994), the design and pedagogical approach of the BI are closely aligned with Museus et al.'s (2017) culturally engaging campus environments (CECE) model of college success. The CECE model has two main categories of culturally engaging campus environments: cultural relevance and cultural responsiveness. Within cultural relevance there are five indicators, including cultural familiarity, culturally relevant knowledge, cultural community service, meaningful cross-cultural engagement, and culturally validating environments. Indicators for cultural responsiveness include collectivist cultural orientations, humanized educational environments, proactive philosophies, and holistic support.

The model serves as a framework for postsecondary institutions to cultivate conditions for belonging for historically marginalized student populations. Although the BI was not designed with the CECE model explicitly in mind, the language of the framework is particularly useful in understanding why and how the BI serves men of color. Within the BI, we create conditions for belonging through our staff structure and composition, campus partnerships, planning practices, and inquiry-based assessment cycle.

Instructional team

A primary mechanism by which the BI fosters a sense of academic belonging is through the structure of our learning community. The BI instructional team, which is central to this community, comprises primarily faculty, staff, and graduate students of color. By adopting a team-teaching approach to our seminars, we maximize the varied expertise of each instructor while also offering the opportunity for students to develop deeper relationships with a consistent group of UW staff who value their experiences. Having a larger team also enables us to focus more individual attention on each student, making the classroom feel like a smaller and more welcoming community.

Networks and partnerships

In addition to the project team, the BI has developed a network of steering committee members and campus practitioners who are critical to creating a sense of institutional belonging for students. With a vast group of collaborators from minority affairs, the counseling center, the career center, student life, and various academic departments, the BI draws on their expertise to co-teach some seminars and serve as guest speakers. Many social identities are represented across these campus partners, including race, ethnicity, sexual orientation, nationality, and immigrant status. Inviting partners into the classroom helps students find others across campus whom they can identify with and seek support from.

Curriculum planning

Each year the BI team engages in an intensive course planning process, in which we evaluate, prioritize, and refine our learning objectives. We utilize the pillars of the ToA to guide our discussion about *what* we will teach, and we use the conditions of success to clarify *how* we will teach it. As an example, our ToA specifies that we will teach about health, wellness, and help-seeking behaviors, and our conditions of success help us decide who to bring in as guest speakers, what specific issues to focus on, and how to facilitate discussion. Ultimately, our ToA serves as both a guide and a rubric for content selection and delivery.

Equity-based inquiry process

Central to our ToA is the equity-based inquiry cycle, which describes the dynamic and ongoing nature of collecting and analyzing data to refine our understanding of how and why the initiative's outcomes are achieved. Each year, the BI utilizes student surveys, previous assignment submissions, and instructor observations to analyze the effectiveness of our course structure and design in achieving the learning and community objectives established in our ToA. We then take these data and use them to inform our curriculum planning process.

Course implementation

The BI was developed to address the retention and graduation disparities men of color face at a large, competitive, predominantly White institution. The learning community is designed to provide participants with culturally responsive instruction (see also Chapter 4) and holistic support through four program pillars. As a multiyear project, elements of the pillars are present throughout but most concentrated in the first 2 years of course-related instruction. Both the first-year and second-year courses are structured as active learning spaces where interaction with classmates is emphasized, and each course provides developmentally appropriate content to foster academic belonging.

First-year implementation

The first-year course is a three-quarter seminar offered for two credits each quarter. It is built around three main themes: community cultural wealth, sense of belonging, and self-authorship. The seminar focuses on providing BI students with the awareness, resources, skills, and tools necessary to succeed in their first year of college. To do this, the course prioritizes learning objectives related to two primary pillars in our theory of action: academic guidance and support and psychosocial identity development. The strength and quality of instruction related to these pillars are dependent on a sense of belonging. When classroom activities, assignments, guest presenters, and culminating projects are designed with belonging in mind, we theorize that the resulting self-efficacy will allow students to engage with the course content in more meaningful ways.

Cultivating academic familiarity, socialization, and agency

The first-year course emphasizes students finding belonging within the BI and throughout the institution. Simply familiarizing students with academic expectations and institutional resources is often not enough (Mata & Bobb, 2016). While many first-year success courses may introduce students to a variety of campus resources, the BI is intentional in introducing resources in ways that build cultural familiarity. *Cultural familiarity* can be understood as "the extent to which college students have opportunities to physically connect with faculty, staff, and peers who understand their backgrounds and experiences" (Museus et al., 2017, p. 192). The instructional team works with academic support partners to bring in guest speakers who either reflect some aspect of our class demographic or can offer a culturally responsive approach to discussing academic support services. We regularly supplement presentations from professional staff with student panels that speak to experiences that have led to greater feelings of belonging in particular support spaces. Our students have shared that our emphasis on cultural familiarity is particularly helpful in dispelling common misconceptions and fears about utilizing campus services like tutoring, counseling, and study centers.

Academic socialization experiences are also important for all students but particularly for men of color. The process of socialization helps students to develop a strong identity as capable learners, which we posit bolsters academic belonging even in the face of adversity. The BI class allocates time each quarter to address common academic challenges, including how to effectively understand and utilize a class syllabus, sending professional emails to faculty and staff, and what to do when falling behind in class or missing assignment deadlines. These sessions are important for students to become versed in academic expectations that are often left implied and, as a result, can lead to feelings of uncertainty. As one student recollected in their end-of-quarter course survey:

> The presentations about college information – that was something that was introduced to us in the first meeting, and that also continued to be presented in other sessions, which I found to be incredibly useful. Because especially for me, a first-generation student, no one tells us a lot of this stuff, so to have a space where I was told this information made acclimating to college so much easier and less stressful.

By teaching students about skills and behaviors that are often hidden and yet critical to academic success, our goal is to help them feel more confident in the classroom, essentially launching the process of academic socialization.

The BI is also a space where students learn to develop trusting relationships with faculty and staff. *Humanizing* as a pedagogical approach is not only about the "extent to which students felt like faculty and staff cared about them and were committed to their success" (Museus et al., 2017, p. 199) but it acknowledges the fact that "learning environments are not neutral" and are imbued with a particular worldview that privileges certain types of engagement and achievement (Pacansky-Brock et al., 2020, p. 2). In the BI, we seek to create a humanized educational environment through a variety of strategies. As a part of the first week introductions in the fall quarter, we introduce the teaching team by talking about our own backgrounds, values, and purpose in this work. Once the quarter commences, we continuously emphasize office hours as a place to connect with faculty about homework support but, more important, about course topics, academic goals, and transitioning to college life. We also convey care through the tone, clarity, and flexibility of each quarter's syllabus. Rather than solely focusing on course policies and assignments, the BI syllabi help students to identify when and how to reach out for support. This was particularly important during the COVID-19 pandemic when expectations concerning attendance, class engagement, and assignments required consistent and open communication between faculty and students.

Providing opportunities to demonstrate learning with cultural relevance

Each quarter of the first-year course sequence challenges students to apply the course concepts in culturally meaningful and relevant ways. Most notable, the winter quarter seminar introduces students directly to sense of belonging as theory and lived experience. The quarter begins with an in-class lecture and discussion introducing the theory behind sense of belonging and how belongingness has been shown to impact academic outcomes for marginalized students. Throughout the quarter, we ask students to reflect on what belonging looks, feels, and sounds like in their own lives through an online discussion board assignment. We strive to introduce belonging as multisensory and to challenge students to think of belonging more holistically. As a part of the assignment, students post pictures and sound recordings of spaces where they experience the greatest sense of belonging (see Chapter 12 for a closer examination of place and belonging). Student submissions have focused on images and sounds that reflect family, friends, sports teams, gaming communities, and places of worship. We also ask that students read and respond to each other's posts, which helps to build threads of cultural familiarity within the group. Through the assignment, students identify the interactions and environmental factors that resonate in their own attempts to find belongingness. As one student reflected in their online post:

> The first sound comes from my English 111 lecture, where my instructor is wrapping up and saying goodbye to the class. I chose this sound because learning is a big part of my life and I pride myself on being a good student. Though it is sometimes difficult to stay focused and on task during these online [Z]oom classes. My teacher in this class is very engaging and always has on a smile and attempts to pick up the energy of the class which I think helps create a better sense of belonging in the class.

These BI assignments provide opportunities for students to articulate the unique ways in which they see and experience belonging as undergraduate men of color while simultaneously discovering similarities and differences in experiences within the cohort.

The winter seminar also allows students to identify and discuss what it means not to belong. Through use of an online discussion board, we ask students to post an image and description of on- or off-campus spaces where they feel like they do not belong. Past students have identified campus social spaces (campus dining, dormitories, etc.) and academic spaces (classrooms, field trips, internships) as sites where they question their belonging. The posts help to normalize what many men of color experience in isolation and provide yet another way for students to build familiarity with each other. In one particularly poignant post, a student captured what so many students described as the mental isolation associated with larger lectures and courses, sharing:

> The picture that I decided to pick was the big lecture halls. I felt that this was an important picture because of how the big halls make me see

college as something that is scary and threatening just due to how many people the class will have. This made me feel that I was someone who didn't belong just because I felt like I couldn't ask for help which made me want to start keeping to myself in the bigger classes. This experience made me want to be more involved in smaller courses like the Brotherhood Initiative due to the belonging that I feel in this class. Eventually, I want to be able to grow and try to gain stronger confidence in myself in bigger courses so that one day I can feel a sense of belonging in bigger lecture halls.

As students begin to recognize and name the feeling of not belonging, they can identify strategies to actively seek places that do promote academic belonging, giving them greater agency over their educational experience.

In the spring quarter, students capstone their learning on the concept of self-authorship (Baxter-Magolda, 2001) by developing an e-portfolio curated with favorite BI assignments, reflection on first-year experiences, and visualization of future goals. Students are encouraged to personalize their e-portfolios to tell a unique and culturally relevant story about their first-year college journey. In the words of one student:

The most helpful assignment this quarter has to be the e-portfolio. I definitely discovered new parts of myself when doing this project. For example, I do so many assignments and projects in different classes, but never saw them as collective, but instead, as individual pieces that aren't related. So when seeing it all compiled into something beautiful that told my story throughout my first year, I was both proud and surprised. I will continue to add to my portfolio and grow it as I go through the rest of my college years.

As expressed in this comment, each quarter's culminating project not only serves as an opportunity for students to demonstrate their growth concerning the course learning objectives but also infuses the course concepts with their own experiences and cultural/community knowledge. Each project provides students with an opportunity to exchange "cultural knowledge" (Museus et al., 2017) and build cultural familiarity across intersecting identities. Each project positions students as learners – able to identify and apply course concepts – and knowers who can challenge and contextualize information reflecting their community history, wisdom, and experiences.

Second-year implementation

The second-year course is also structured as a three-quarter seminar. Building on the learning community that we established in the first year, the second year is dedicated to further deepening the sense of belonging within the community. While the first-year seminar places emphasis on the individual student and the first two pillars in our theory of action, the second-year seminar focuses more externally by centering the other two pillars: (a) community-based learning and leadership development and (b) career development and professionalization.

Connecting academic and professional development to community-focused projects

While the theme of the second-year course has evolved over time, it has always taken a community-centered approach. In the first few years, the culminating assignment was a "legacy project," where students developed a project to give back to the UW community. We ask them, "What do you want your legacy to be in terms of making this space more hospitable for men of color who come after you, your little brothers in the BI, but also the BI more broadly?" Often these projects addressed an aspect of belonging. For example, one group developed a guide for incoming men of color to find resources and community around campus, while another developed a workshop on getting engaged with student organizations.

Most recently, the course has been structured to focus on positive social change. By working in small groups to name a problem of interest that impacts their own communities and then developing a small-scale project to address that problem, students are uncovering common values and interests with their BI peers, which often strengthens their sense of belonging. This form of cross-cultural engagement provides students with meaningful opportunities to work closely with others in their cohort to solve real problems over an extended period of time.

At the same time, embedded in the sophomore course curriculum are multiple workshops and assignments about professional development, from exploring majors to refining one's resume and learning to network. The students are challenged to explore all of the opportunities at UW afforded to them, determine what they want to do, and take advantage of them before they graduate. These were often daunting concepts, particularly for students from first-generation, low-income, or immigrant backgrounds. However, the assignments are scaffolded to gradually weave in relevant skills and concepts. For example, over the course of a quarter, students create experiential learning plans to sketch out how they will explore their academic and professional interests.

Creating a welcoming and safe learning community

In teaching the course, we intentionally focus on creating a sense of belonging between the instructor and students, as well as among the students themselves.

By fostering an informal, comfortable atmosphere in the classroom, we provide a safe space for students to think critically, question, and make mistakes. For example, at the beginning of some classes the instructor often shares personal anecdotes that illustrate his own struggles or questions. This sets a tone of authenticity and openness, as described in a reflection from this instructor:

> I would talk about how I was struggling in structural equation modeling while they failed statistics too. ... And so through that first 10 to 15 minutes of class, it just sets the tone, in my experience, of the classroom being a completely different feel for the rest of it. There's a lot more real talk – questions are never situated as, like, stupid or what have you – people felt more comfortable ... it felt like a safe space ... like it was our space and we were allowed to be flawed together and then we would correct each other and grow together. That was kind of the shift to what I felt was like authenticity.

We also use free-writes at the beginning of class to introduce a topic or question and to set the tone for class. By playing music for several minutes while students write, we create an atmosphere where students feel more relaxed and genuine in the classroom. We then invite students to talk in pairs or small groups about what they have written. By utilizing these simple yet meaningful classroom practices and norms, we convey to students that they are valued members of the campus community.

Next steps toward a theory of action

The BI learning community is a unique space, and we recognize that most classrooms will have a greater diversity of student identities. In this next section, we draw on what we have learned to share recommendations for faculty and instructors to develop a ToA for their own classroom contexts. Developing a ToA begins with reflection on the knowledge, assumptions, and theory that drive practice. While the importance of race and gender in producing inequitable learning outcomes may be familiar to some, reflection specific to men of color may produce new or difficult revelations for others. The reflection questions below have been crafted not just to help faculty think more meaningfully about practice and outcomes but also to surface evidence and assumptions that can shape classroom climate and academic belonging for men of color.

Student outcomes

In developing a ToA focused on equity and learning, we encourage faculty to begin by reflecting on what they currently understand about men of color in their courses.

- What do I know about men of color as learners/participants in my classroom, discipline, and field?
- What observations inform how I understand the opportunities and challenges that men of color face in my own classroom?
- What outcomes do I want for men of color who are a part of my classroom?

Conditions for success

The academic environment includes social, emotional, and structural elements that facilitate learning. These elements form the conditions through which students engage in learning and develop a sense of belonging. Faculty can consider the questions below when designing their learning environment.

- What might my classroom feel like to students from different backgrounds? What assumptions or expectations might be present?
- What aspects of this learning environment are welcoming, and what aspects might be intimidating for men of color?

Culturally informed practice

Finally, we suggest that faculty reflect on how their current practice shapes learning conditions for men of color in the classroom. It is important to be clear about what is actually being practiced, not what faculty aspire to do, or do occasionally. While there are a variety of culturally informed approaches one may consider, the following questions focus on CECE indicators referenced in the description of the BI:

- How might the teaching strategies I use support or hinder learning for men of color?
  - How do the course assignments allow students to contextualize the course concepts through their own cultural knowledge or lived experiences?
  - To what extent do I invite culturally responsive or culturally relevant voices into my class through readings, presentations, or discussions?
  - How do I express care for my students? Does this mode of expression resonate with the students who may feel the most isolated in my class, discipline, or field?
- What evidence do I have to support teaching strategies that are best for the students I serve?
- What do I *need* to change to better support learning for men of color? What *can* I change?

After generating responses to each of the questions above, faculty can tie these considerations together simultaneously. The logic through which these responses coalesce serves as the foundation for what the Center for Educational Leadership (2014) describes as an emerging and unique theory of action story. The prompts below can be used as guides when framing this story.

- If I do: [practice]
- Then my classroom will become a space where: [conditions]
- So that students can: [student outcomes]

Note that any initial ToA will require continuous reassessment and revision as faculty gather additional evidence and observe what results materialize from the proposed actions.

Conclusion

Creating a learning environment that cultivates academic belonging for men of color, particularly in spaces where they may be one of a small few, requires critical examination, reflection, and planning. Engaging in the process of developing a ToA can uncover flaws in a pedagogical approach while also making explicit the conditions and strategies that successfully contribute to a sense of belonging. Ultimately, a well-developed ToA can serve as a roadmap for faculty as they improve their course design for multiple contexts and populations.

References

Baxter-Magolda, M. B. (2001). *Making their own way: Narratives for transforming higher education to promote self-development.* Stylus.

Bronfenbrenner, U., & Morris, P. A. (2006). The bioecological model of human development. In W. Damon & R. M. Lerner (Series Eds.) & R. M. Lerner (Vol. Ed.), *Handbook of child psychology: Vol. 1. Theoretical models of human development* (6th ed., pp. 793–828). Wiley.

Brooms, D. R. (2018). Exploring Black male initiative programs: Potential and possibilities for supporting Black male success in college. *The Journal of Negro Education,* 87(1), 59–72.

Center for Educational Leadership. (2014). *Creating a theory of action for improved teaching and learning* [Online brief]. University of Washington. https://k-12leadership.org/tools/creating-a-theory-of-action/

Cobb, P., & Jackson, K. (2011). Towards an empirically grounded theory of action for improving the quality of mathematics teaching at scale. *Mathematics Teacher Education and Development,* 13(1), 6–33.

Cole, D., Newman, C. B., & Hypolite, L. I. (2020). Sense of belonging and mattering among two cohorts of first-year students participating in a comprehensive college transition program. *American Behavioral Scientist,* 64(3), 276–297.

Davis, G. M., Hanzsek-Brill, M. B., Petzold, M. C., & Robinson, D. H. (2019). Students' sense of belonging: The development of a predictive retention model. *Journal of the Scholarship of Teaching and Learning*, 19(1), 117–127.

Freeman, T. M., Anderman, L. H., & Jensen, J. M. (2007). Sense of belonging in college freshmen at the classroom and campus levels. *The Journal of Experimental Education*, 75(3), 203–220.

Gopalan, M., & Brady, S. T. (2020). College students' sense of belonging: A national perspective. *Educational Researcher*, 49(2), 134–137.

Hausmann, L. R. M., Schofield, J. W., & Woods, R. L. (2007). Sense of belonging as a predictor of intentions to persist among African American and White first-year college students. *Research in Higher Education*, 48(7), 803–839.

Huerta, A. H., Romero-Morales, M., Dizon, J. P., Salazar, M. E., & Nguyen, J. V. (2021). *Empowering men of color in higher education: A focus on psychological, social, and cultural factors*. Pullias Center for Higher Education.

Hurtado, S., & Carter, D. F. (1997). Effects of college transition and perceptions of the campus racial climate on Latino college students' sense of belonging. *Sociology of Education*, 70(4), 324–345.

Johnson, D. R., Soldner, M., Leonard, J. B., Alvarez, P., Inkelas, K. K., Rowan-Kenyon, H. T., & Longerbeam, S. D. (2007). Examining sense of belonging among first-year undergraduates from different racial/ethnic groups. *Journal of College Student Development*, 48(5), 525–542.

Lee, J. M., Jr., & Ransom, T. (2011). *The educational experience of young men of color: A review of research, pathways and progress*. College Board Advocacy & Policy Center.

Lewis, K. L., Stout, J. G., Pollock, S. J., Finkelstein, N. D., & Ito, T. A. (2016). Fitting in or opting out: A review of key social–psychological factors influencing a sense of belonging for women in physics. *Physical Review Physics Education Research*, 12, 020110.

Lott, J. L., Bauman, K., & Yeh, T. L. (2021, October). *Introduction to BI theory of action* (BI Theory of Action Series: Brief No. 1). The Brotherhood Initiative, University of Washington.

Mata, E., & Bobb, A. (2016). Retaining and graduating empowered men of color. In V. Pendakur (Ed.), *Closing the opportunity gap: Identity-conscious strategies for retention and student success* (pp. 25–41). Stylus.

Murphy, M. C., Gopalan, M., Carter, E. R., Emerson, K. T., Bottoms, B. L., & Walton, G. M. (2020). A customized belonging intervention improves retention of socially disadvantaged students at a broad-access university. *Science Advances*, 6(29), eaba4677.

Museus, S. D., & Chang, T. H. (2021). The impact of campus environments on sense of belonging for first-generation college students. *Journal of College Student Development*, 62(3), 367–372.

Museus, S. D., Yi, V., & Saelua, N. (2017). The impact of culturally engaging campus environments on sense of belonging. *The Review of Higher Education*, 40(2), 187–215.

Nuñez, A. M. (2009). A critical paradox? Predictors of Latino students' sense of belonging in college. *Journal of Diversity in Higher Education*, 2(1), 46–61.

Pacansky-Brock, M., Smedshammer, M., & Vincent-Layton, K. (2020). Humanizing online teaching to equitize higher education. *Current Issues in Education*, 21(2). https://cie.asu.edu/ojs/index.php/cieatasu/article/view/1905

Rendon, L. I. (1994). Validating culturally diverse students: Toward a new model of learning and student development. *Innovative Higher Education*, 19(1), 33–51.

Ribera, A. K., Miller, A. L., & Dumford, A. D. (2017). Sense of peer belonging and institutional acceptance in the first year: The role of high-impact practices. *Journal of College Student Development*, 58(4), 545–563.

Strayhorn, T. L. (2008). Fittin' in: Do diverse interactions with peers affect sense of belonging for Black men at predominantly White institutions? *NASPA Journal*, 45 (4), 501–527.

Strayhorn, T. L. (2019). *College students' sense of belonging: A key to educational success for all students* (2nd ed.). Routledge.

Tachine, A. R., Cabrera, N. L., & Yellow Bird, E. (2017). Home away from home: Native American students' sense of belonging during their first year in college. *The Journal of Higher Education*, 88(5), 785–807.

Turner, P., & Zepeda, E. M. (2021). Welcoming ain't belonging: A case study that explores how two-year predominantly White colleges can foster an environment of validation and mattering for men of color. *Higher Education Studies*, 11(2), 127–138.

9

FOSTERING BELONGING IN A UNIVERSITY RESEARCH COMMUNITY OF PRACTICE

Alexandria Muller, Devon M. Christman, Jasmine McBeath Nation, Jasmine Mitchell, Kelly Vu, Nathalie Paesler and Diana J. Arya

As part of the college experience, many universities encourage their undergraduate students to engage in research (Rahman et al., 2017). Participation in research experiences benefits undergraduates by increasing engagement in coursework (Kuh et al., 2011), deepening learning through practical experiences (Laursen et al., 2012), and increasing academic success and retention (Jones et al., 2010; Russell et al., 2007). Participation in undergraduate research can also provide undergraduates with access to mentorship opportunities and hands-on experiences they might not encounter in their coursework (Linn et al., 2015).

Such research experiences can be particularly impactful for students from underrepresented communities (Cole & Espinoza, 2008; Jones et al., 2010). Students gain a sense of belonging, usefulness, and appreciation when contributing to research that centers around a common goal alongside more senior researchers (Rogoff, 2014). However, historically underrepresented students have expressed difficulties, such as finding faculty role models or mentors from similar backgrounds (Towns, 2010). The percentage of faculty who identify with historically underrepresented communities is low even among universities championed for their diversity such as Georgia State University,[1] MIT,[2] and the University of California[3] system. The number of underrepresented faculty is significantly lower than the 49% of the U.S. population who identifies with underrepresented communities (U.S. Census Bureau, 2021). Accessing quality mentoring from faculty of similar backgrounds is challenging since the availability of these individuals is limited. Connecting with faculty through undergraduate research gives undergraduates access to faculty members in ways they might otherwise not be able to. Through research, students gain access to resources and networks

DOI: 10.4324/9781003443735-12

within the academic community of practice that are not accessible to students in their traditional coursework, which helps research assistants develop a stronger sense of academic belonging (Ishiyama, 2002; National Academies of Sciences, Engineering, and Medicine, 2019; Rauckhorst et al., 2001; Russell et al., 2007).

Despite the benefits of undergraduate research engagement, students are often assigned discrete, peripheral tasks (e.g., standalone transcriptions of audio footage with no contextual information) that do not connect clearly to the broader research practice (Feldman et al., 2009). Such positioning does not foster a deep sense of belonging within the research community. Greater efforts on the part of faculty and researchers are needed to provide more enriching experiences for undergraduates. Faculty mentors play an important role in fostering a sense of belonging for underrepresented minorities as they significantly impact students' decisions in pursuing future studies and careers (Harsh et al., 2012; Towns, 2010); however, this impact is underexplored in research works. For this chapter, we took a communities of practice perspective (Lave & Wenger, 1991) in a qualitative exploration of survey and interview responses from undergraduate research assistants (RAs) about their experiences within The STEMinist Project,[4] a community-based research program that introduces young girls and non-binary youth to university scientists of similar backgrounds to foster an interest in STEM. From the perspectives of participating RAs (n = 8), we aimed to explore how faculty mentors can foster a deeper sense of belonging in academia among all members of their research team, particularly those from underrepresented communities. Fostering a deeper sense of belonging among undergraduates is likely to allow them to extend their time participating in research activities, which increases the academic and professional benefits associated with their participation (Bauer & Bennett, 2003; Cooper et al., 2019).

This chapter includes the theoretical framing that guided our reflective work and our philosophy when engaging undergraduate RAs. Also included is the historical overview of how our research team developed and how members helped shape practices related to our work. Our retrospective exploration has led to five key lessons and associated actionable steps, which are summarized toward the end of this chapter. Our chapter ends with a letter of support written by our lead faculty mentor for their peers who endeavor to foster research experiences for their students. We hope other faculty mentors can benefit from our insights in efforts to foster a sense of belonging for their RAs.

Theoretical framing

Communities of practice are joint enterprises that are continuously negotiated by members who develop a shared repertoire through mutual activities that informs how they act and speak (Wenger, 1998). In academia, our community of practice is made up of people, typically professors, who engage in systematic investigations that result in publications. Academics have a set vocabulary that members of the community of practice are familiar with but may seem foreign to outsiders. In addition, there are unspoken norms about decorum, networking, and collaborating that are unique to the academic community of practice.

New members to a community of practice enter through legitimate peripheral participation (Hoadley, 2012). Developed by Lave and Wenger (1991), legitimate peripheral participation focuses on the learning that occurs when individuals interact tangentially with a community of practice. RAs, who are generally undergraduate students, are often given peripheral roles like copying and collating interview protocols, which require minimal supervision, time, and materials and have fewer chances of error (Lave & Wenger, 1991). Under the theory of legitimate peripheral participation, such engagement in peripheral tasks allows undergraduates to learn about what researchers do, hence offering ways for them to gain further entry into the community of practice. However, research advisors often do not recognize their role as a conduit for community membership and spend little effort connecting undergraduate peripheral roles to the work of the broader research practice (Feldman et al., 2009). This lack of connection to the broader community of practice hinders the learning and development needed to foster a sense of belonging in academia.

We advocate for a more holistic type of participation in the research community that incorporates nondominant members of the community, such as undergraduate RAs, particularly those from underrepresented backgrounds. One framework that highlights holistic involvement is Rogoff's (2014) "Learning by Observing and Pitching In." Compared to the frame of peripheral participation, the holistic involvement framework provides a more expansive view of RA learning when applied to higher education. Rogoff described how people of all ages learn together by participating in ongoing events centered around a common community goal. When novices contribute productively alongside experts, they receive appreciation, acceptance, or correction as types of feedback. Participation in a shared purpose alongside rather than separate from perceived experts in an activity leads individuals to feel useful, appreciated, and successful (Rogoff, 2014), which are core elements to an academic sense of belonging. While legitimate peripheral participation is important to establish a basic understanding of the community of practice, we argue that research advisors should encourage their RAs to move beyond peripheral participation and engage in these deeper learning processes alongside them. By doing so, advisors can foster a sense of belonging for their RAs. In our retrospective work for this chapter, we worked to identify which tasks RAs participated in, both peripheral and with higher involvement in the community of practice, that contributed to a greater sense of belonging.

Program context

The STEMinist Project

In fall 2015, two faculty from our university partnered with leaders from a local afterschool organization designed to support girls and non-binary youth to develop The STEMinist Project. This program fostered sustained interest in STEM-related topics and issues for youth in Grades 4 to 6. The program was designed to position the youth participants and undergraduate facilitators as co-learners who took part in interviewing scientists. Youth participants then coauthored a book based on this research for the broader community (Arya & McBeath, 2017). Undergraduate facilitators could participate in a research component of the program by attending biweekly meetings, transcribing and coding interviews, and helping write findings for conferences. We especially needed undergraduate assistance with transcription, but their involvement didn't stop there. Our respective experiences of peripheral participation during our undergraduate studies inspired efforts to reimagine the research experience for our junior colleagues as one that would position our partnering undergraduates as integral members of our educational research community.

The structure of The STEMinist Project shifted over the years to include a teen program in 2018, but all programming ended in 2020 due to the onset of the COVID-19 pandemic and subsequent lockdowns. We maintained our connections with our undergraduate facilitators by shifting all activities to research-related tasks. Our team had 4 years of archived images, interviews, and student artifacts, all of which needed to be catalogued, transcribed, and analyzed. This transition to full research engagement marked the point where our focus on fostering belonging in a research community of practice began to take off.

Research university context

Our campus is one of several affiliated R1 universities in California claiming that students will "have the opportunity to participate in cutting-edge research" during their undergraduate program (UC Santa Barbara, 2013). Undergraduates are encouraged to apply for various research positions through a formal process (via an online submission system) or reach out to faculty directly. Undergraduates who receive RA positions can be compensated with volunteer hours or course credit. RAs are often advised by professors, members of professional clubs and organizations, postdoctoral fellows, and/or graduate students. Given the variation of potential advisors, mentorship styles can also vary according to the discretion of each advisor. The search process for a research position can be more difficult than it appears and is extremely competitive. The number of interested under-graduates generally outstrips the number of available opportunities, and there is little guidance from central university leadership on norms for men-toring undergraduate students. RAs seeking to conduct independent research projects often work in a research lab for at least two quarters before asking to conduct independent research. If the professor agrees to support an independent study, undergraduates can access resources provided by the university to support their research. However, the process for gaining access to such experiences and resources is relatively hidden, requiring students to be strategic and communicatively creative in their search.

The principal resource at our institution is the Undergraduate Research and Creative Activities (URCA) Department. URCA helps connect under-graduate students to research opportunities across campus. The primary support offered is the URCA grant, a $750 grant RAs can apply for to fund their independent research projects. Along with the monetary support, the URCA grant comes with presentation and publication opportunities. URCA hosts an annual week of events for students to present their projects includ-ing a poster and digital colloquium, conference panels, and "slam" (a quick, competitive presentation of research). All undergraduates who have com-pleted research are welcome to apply to these events, but those who received an URCA grant are automatically accepted.

Study context

Positionality statement

As a research team, we are dedicated to serving our local community and fostering connections among all stakeholders. While we are especially dedicated to supporting the voices of our underrepresented communities within our research, we recognize that our leadership team does not necessarily reflect the lived experiences of our undergraduate RAs or the youth communities that we serve. As such, given the critical focus of this chapter and its reflective nature, we maintained a mindful eye on our respective positions within The STEMinist Project research team to reduce biases placed on participant voices during analysis. Dr. Arya (using pro-nouns she/they) is multilingual and bicultural (Southwest Asian and North African and White). The graduate student coordinators include a multi-lingual speaker who identifies as White (she/her), a monolingual English speaker (she/they) who identifies as bicultural (Pacific Islander and White), and a monolingual English speaker with disabilities (she/her) who identi-fies as White. The undergraduate co-authors (all identifying as she/her) consist of one bilingual speaker identifying as Asian and two monolingual English speakers, one of which identifies as White and another as bicultural

(African American and German). Acknowledging our respective positions and backgrounds, all phases of preparing this chapter were subject to peer review and pushback from all team members.

Author and study participant information

To gain a greater perspective on how our team fostered a sense of belonging among undergraduate RAs, we invited every undergraduate researcher who participated in The STEMinist project dating back to 2016 to participate in a survey and interview about their experiences ($N = 70$). Demographic characteristics of RAs who disclosed demographic data ($n = 40$) are listed in Table 9.1. Eight former RAs responded to the survey (11% response rate), and three agreed to participate in an hour-long semistructured interview with an interviewer of their choice. We allowed the interviewees to choose their interviewer so they could speak freely about their experiences and interactions with The STEMinist Project leadership team. The survey respondents are a representative sample of the RAs dating throughout the history of our research team. All RAs for The STEMinist program identify as women or non-binary.

Responses from the survey data and interviews were transcribed for analysis and open-coded for emergent themes related to what seemed to foster belonging within our research community of practice. Pseudonyms were used for the research assistant participants to uphold participant anonymity while the names of program coordinators who co-authored this piece were preserved.

Lessons learned

Through our reflective discussions, survey responses, and interviews with RAs, we identified five key lessons we learned over the last 6 years about

TABLE 9.1 Undergraduate RA demographic characteristics.

Demographic[a]	2017–2018	2018–2019	2019–2020	2020–2021
African American/Black	1	2		
American Indian/Alaskan Native		1	1	
Chicanx/Latinx	2	2	4	2
White	2	4	7	1
Asian			4	1
Multiethnic		1	3	2

Note. Demographic information for the 2016–2017 cohort was not collected.
[a]This is the demographic label used by the university.

how to best foster a sense of belonging within our research team. We present these below with actionable steps for other research advisors to apply to their own research groups; however, we also recognize that this work is not a one-size-fits-all. As such, we recommend that research advisors consider the unique needs of their research teams when considering these lessons and adapt them accordingly.

Lesson #1: Developing community inside of the research team

Across the surveys and interviews for this chapter, collaborative members observed a convergence on the importance of developing community through a shared understanding of norms. Such norms were purportedly needed to establish a sense of community among RAs, graduate students, and faculty members. In our research group, we found two key reported actions that contributed to this development of the community.

The first action was providing intellectual support within the research group. From the perspective of coordinators and lead faculty, it was important that the RAs felt comfortable asking for help. RA Karina, for example, explained that she "felt a strong sense of belonging throughout the experience, especially because [the graduate student coordinator] worked to make us feel like we were part of one team. ... There wasn't a strong sense of hierarchy." As a result of this nonhierarchical approach, Karina said "it opened doors for me to feel more comfortable in different settings on campus and helped faculty feel more approachable." By creating an environment with no strict hierarchy, we were able to encourage deeper connections and allow RAs to feel comfortable reaching out for help. Esme, for example, commented that "we always knew we could count on you guys [graduate student coordinators]. I always feel comfortable asking either of you guys for any questions or help." Being present to respond to questions or offer guidance when needed was an important aspect of belonging in a research community for undergraduates. Often, undergraduates do not feel that they can ask faculty or graduate students for help or that their questions may come across as stupid (Wirtz et al., 2018). By actively engaging in direct communication with all research team members, a greater sense of belonging can be established.

In addition, supporting RAs at academic events greatly contributes to a sense of belonging. In our research group, our RAs were encouraged to lead an independent research project if they desired and were invited to present their findings at our departmental research symposium. Esme reflected on this experience in her survey, stating,

> One time I felt a real sense of belonging to The STEMinist research team is when [the graduate student coordinators] popped in my [Z]

oom group to watch my independent research project presentation … they did not have to go out of their way to watch mine and my other peer RAs presentations, but they did, and it meant a lot. It made me feel like my work was really appreciated.

Creating a welcoming and supportive environment includes not only being open emotionally to mentoring undergraduates as they navigate the research process but also being present to support them in academic endeavors.

The second action to foster community within research was to encourage RAs to collaborate and support each other. In research groups, community norms must be established to inform how people interact with each other. One community norm we emphasized was that the RAs themselves were a great resource to rely on and receive support from. By encouraging connections between RAs, a greater sense of community was established and thus a deeper sense of belonging. Odile reflected in her survey response that

> [m]y peer RAs also helped foster my sense of belonging because there were others of similar backgrounds to my own participating in the research team alongside me. I was able to interact and work with the RAs in the various tasks The [STEMinist Project] had.

By connecting with someone who had similar experiences, Odile was able to establish a deeper sense of belonging in our research team. Creating space for RA voices to be heard and encouraging RAs to provide feedback and remarks on each other's work allowed connections to be formed between RAs. Serena remarked that these discussions were helpful in fostering a sense of belonging since "even if we're not necessarily talking about our personal lives, it just means that we start to see each other more often. And I think that alone maybe makes me feel more like part of a group."

Lesson #2: Taking a human-centered approach to the research team

In academia, we often get caught up in the "publish or perish" mentality. This is especially true for pretenured faculty members who have additional pressures to perform well to earn tenure. As a result, RAs can be treated as tools to conduct research rather than colleagues in the research experience. Moving away from a production-centered research structure and instead recentering on the humanity of research group engagement was important when fostering a sense of belonging among all members. By recognizing that RAs have a plethora of identities and responsibilities and making space for them to be present as their whole selves, we can better foster a sense of belonging.

One way to achieve this is by encouraging non-research check-ins with team members. Taking 5 to 10 minutes at the beginning of a research meeting to receive updates from everyone about their lives can contribute greatly to a sense of belonging within the team. When asked what advice she would give faculty members advising undergraduates, Florence said, "Get to know them. Get to know the people that you're working with." By getting to know the research team members, faculty can better support their students. Florence further explained that faculty should get to know "whether or not [RAs] have access to the resources needed to be able to be the best version of themselves to participate in that research." Having these small check-ins with members of the research team can help uncover the needs and stressors, both spoken and unspoken, that RAs may be experiencing and allow research advisors to respond and offer support when needed. As a first-generation student, Esme explained that faculty should "get to know their undergraduate students because I think that was the big thing coming from a first-gen student, I was always extremely intimidated by professors."

In addition to checking-in with students, research advisors should maintain high expectations while allowing flexibility for life events. RAs join research teams to gain quality research experience and, as such, the expectations they are held to should mirror the community of practice they are adjacent to during their training. However, research efforts should not overshadow the fact that undergraduates have other obligations in life that can sometimes arise unexpectedly. In our research team, RAs recognized that while we maintained high expectations for their work, they were supported to prioritize their health and well-being. Serena reflected that our team

> emphasize[d] that you were always here for us, that we didn't have to worry if maybe we're having a bad week, and we just couldn't finish that task, or something's going on in our lives. … It takes off some of the pressure to where you're still motivated to contribute to this team. But it means that if there is that one time where you maybe fall behind, you're not going to be punished for it. You're still very much part of the team.

Allowing a space for RAs to feel comfortable sharing difficulties in their lives without fear of punishment or removal from the team added to the sense of belonging our RAs felt. By recognizing and accepting that undergraduates have other college obligations such as exams or project due dates in addition to their lives outside of college such as health or family concerns, we can create a space for flexibility that prioritizes the holistic lives of our undergraduate students.

Lesson #3: Empowering students to step outside of the peripheral zone of participation

With trust built and a transparent support system in place as established through Lessons 1 and 2, we can empower students to step out of the peripheral zone of participation to actively participate in the academic community of practice. In some instances, this transition may be achieved by inviting RAs to share their ideas and observations with the team. Rosie mentioned in her survey response how, despite being shy, she felt her voice was heard and welcome. She wrote, "I can be shy sometimes, but [the coordinators] would ensure my voice was heard at the meetings by asking me questions and about my opinions. ... They always made sure we all felt heard and seen." Encouraging RAs to share their thoughts fostered a greater sense of belonging and empowered them to participate in discussions about theories and methodological approaches. Oftentimes during our meetings, leaders made the effort to acknowledge RAs by name to ask them for their thoughts, especially when leadership members knew about the RAs and their expertise on the topic at hand.

If research advisors are in a position to know when and how undergraduate students might lead their own projects, supporting their ideas and encouraging them to take the lead can be a great way to foster confidence in academia. Serena commented that "I feel like as an undergrad, you just feel really inadequate and that you don't know much. And that you just don't feel ready to do that on your own." This feeling of inadequacy can hinder undergraduate participation in research efforts. Exploring RA research interests and ideas can help foster a sense of belonging and agency in research. Recognizing that their ideas are feasible and helping shape them into full research projects that stem from their ideas can highlight how capable RAs are. Serena further explained how being in an environment where she was supported to explore her own ideas really contributed to her sense of belonging. She remarked,

> I feel like it was just a really supportive environment to where we could explore that if we wanted to. And I think that's why everyone started doing their own projects and stuff, because I think we felt really supported.

For Serena specifically, this went one step further in her efforts to publish and present findings at academic conferences. She commented,

> Something that made me feel a lot just more like a bigger sense of belonging in the world of academia is the fact that you are willing to put your name on something that I wrote that means a lot.

Not all faculty or graduate student coordinators will be able to support research efforts to this extent; however, offering to co-author conference presentations and publications with undergraduate RAs can bolster their sense of belonging within the academic community of practice. Overall, to foster a greater sense of belonging, undergraduate RAs expressed a need to be supported and given opportunities to step out of the peripheral zone of participation and "jam with the pros" to experience the community of practice (Rogoff, 2014, p. 70).

Lesson #4: Taking the time to teach directly

While our RAs overall reported a great sense of belonging, they expressed a desire for an increased presence of the faculty member overseeing the research group. When reflecting on her experiences, Esme mentioned how she "didn't really get to know [the faculty mentor] that much, she didn't really come to all the meetings, so that would be nice." This idea of undergraduate RAs forming connections with the faculty member in addition to the connections with graduate students and fellow RAs was a common theme throughout the interviews and survey responses. While faculty may not have the capacity to attend every research meeting, it is important to make the time to show up, offer support, and foster connections with undergraduate RAs.

In our research group, this evolved into a progressive methodology training led by faculty mentor Dr. Arya, as well as feedback sessions during the development of undergraduate independent research projects. When we started a project examining undergraduate facilitators' sense of belonging in higher education, none of the graduate or undergraduate students had experience with the chosen methodology – critical discourse analysis. As such, Dr. Arya planned a four-part training sequence about how to conduct a full critical discourse analysis study for every member of our research team. Later, when undergraduate students started developing their own independent research projects, Dr. Arya requested a meeting with the RAs to hear brief presentations about their projects and offer advice. Esme reflected on this meeting, remarking, "I know we got [Dr. Arya] to come, and that was really helpful when we did our independent research. When they [listened to] all of our projects and gave us tips, it was really helpful." Serena further explained how the faculty member's presence at these meetings contributed to her sense of belonging "because you don't just feel like you're a disposable part of the team, you really do feel like you're a colleague." She further explained that

> hav[ing] someone that high up still be so sweet and willing to sit in on our meetings ... to give us advice and point us on the correct path ... kind of takes away some of the intimidation factor, and so I felt like I belonged more.

While it may be difficult to carve out the time, faculty should work to connect with their undergraduate RAs personally to offer mentorship and advice to foster a greater sense of belonging.

Lesson #5: Supporting graduate students to mentor

While faculty are valuable to the undergraduate experience, our undergraduates consistently commented on the impact of graduate coordinators. In the survey responses, all respondents identified the graduate student coordinators as having an influence on the sense of belonging they felt, while only two of the eight identified the faculty member. This was, in part, primarily because the graduate student coordinators worked the closest with the undergraduate RAs, had the bandwidth to offer training and support, and regularly met with the RAs. The quality of mentorship that our graduate student coordinators offered would not have been as high without the support and guidance of the lead faculty member. Dr. Arya intentionally positioned each coordinator as a co-leader who contributed to project decision making. She demonstrated nonhierarchical mentoring relationships and encouraged each coordinator to practice this model. The trust imbued in the graduate coordinators contributed to a sense of agency and encouraged them to show up for the RAs in the same way that Dr. Arya showed up for the graduate coordinators.

In addition, Dr. Arya worked with the graduate coordinators to ensure that the entire team was guided by the same goals and motivations. We centered around a common goal to foster rich connections between all stakeholders. To prevent negative undergraduate research experiences like those experienced by authors Jasmine McBeath Nation and Alexandria Muller, another central goal was to position our undergraduate research team in a key role that gave them a voice and agency over research efforts so they felt they belonged in the team. These goals were reiterated and revised as graduate coordinators changed over the years to focus on the area of belonging that reflected the needs of the graduate coordinators and undergraduate team at the time. By supporting graduate student coordinators and providing clear goals that everyone on the leadership team supported, Dr. Arya created an encouraging space for graduate coordinators to support RAs and maintain a safe and welcoming environment despite the changing of team members.

Discussion

This chapter involved a critical reflection on how our research team fostered an academic sense of belonging for undergraduate RAs. How undergraduate researchers are mentored influences their development of self-efficacy and identity as researchers since mentors provide guidance, information, and support (Aikens et al., 2016). Providing rich support systems that encourage holistic participation in research efforts is important for students from underrepresented communities as they have more limited networks and support systems compared with their dominant community counterparts (Aikens et al., 2017; Nelson & Rogers, 2003). As such, creating welcoming environments, planning meetings, and coordinating research activities that center undergraduate research interests that are in turn fostered to fruition is vital for the success of RAs in developing an academic sense of belonging (Cooper et al., 2019; Ishiyama, 2002).

Through discussions with our leadership team, survey responses, and interviews with undergraduate RAs, we identified five key areas that contributed to an academic sense of belonging that we presented as lessons learned:

1. Fostering a sense of community inside of the research team by establishing support systems and encouraging collaboration between all levels of the team.
2. Taking a human-centered approach to the research process to allow for the flexibility life requires at times and prioritizing well-being over work output.
3. Empowering RAs to step outside of the peripheral zone of participation and engage in deeper practices of the research community.
4. Creating time to teach and mentor students directly rather than relying solely on graduate students to mentor RAs.
5. Modeling support and mentorship for graduate student mentors that they can use to inform their mentorship practices with undergraduate students.

Our purpose for this chapter was to uncover the successes and limitations of our research group in supporting undergraduates from underrepresented communities in developing a sense of belonging within research communities of practice. Undergraduate students often are offered research positions that consist of peripheral tasks that require minimal supervision, time, and materials (Feldman et al., 2009). However, to foster a deeper sense of belonging within research communities, undergraduates need to be offered opportunities to engage in more central practices within the community. By contributing to common research goals and collaborating with more experienced team members, undergraduate RAs are further motivated by feelings of usefulness, appreciation, and success (Rogoff, 2014).

Limitations of this study include the nature of our research group. As a community-driven humanities research team, we have the benefit of having a common goal of serving our community through activist research efforts within long-term university–community partnerships. This allows for an easy transition between graduate coordinators and undergraduate researchers as we are guided by a common goal that resonates well with each of our members. Other faculty who are not as embedded in their communities or who conduct more laboratory work may have a more difficult time finding a common goal around which to base a sense of community. Despite this, we fully believe that the five lessons presented in this chapter provide a foundation to consider when fostering community within a research group, especially for undergraduate students.

Overall, running a research team is not easy work, and faculty can become overburdened by other institutional expectations, leaving undergraduate RAs to become lost in peripheral participatory tasks. Research advisors need to take the time to foster a sense of belonging for undergraduate students, especially those from marginalized backgrounds. Through having meaningful connections with faculty members and developing a sense of belonging, undergraduates have greater success in college and often feel more confident in pursuing careers within research (Aikens et al., 2017; O'Meara et al., 2017). Recognizing how difficult this work can be, we leave you, reader, with a letter of encouragement from our faculty mentor as you continue on your journey to foster a sense of belonging for undergraduates in your research community of practice.

A letter of encouragement

Dear colleagues,

We find ourselves in a new kind of peril, one wrapped in anxiety and depression caused by a confluence of political turmoil, economic instability, and environmental crises, as well as the challenges and losses from the pandemic. What has been most egregious is the institutional push for business-as-usual. Many of us are questioning the purpose of it all. Many of us feel uprooted from our starting positions as budding scholars. When thinking back to my first year as a PhD student, I am struck by how much I did not know about what faculty had to do to succeed within this profession. I had no idea about the political tensions involved in the tenure and promotion processes. I was clueless about how certain kinds of research may be valued more than others. One of the worst realizations since becoming a professor at a research-driven university is how much race and gender correlate with one's workload. I naively assumed that the biggest struggle for historically underrepresented faculty happened prior to one's entry to academia, but I have since become acquainted with the silent processes that set some of us up for failure. I have seen firsthand how expectations of exceptionalism play out among faculty who contribute to the diversity we wish to see on campus and how such tokenization can mentally and emotionally deplete one's scholarly passions and creativity.

It is with this awareness of the burdens that so many of us at research institutions carry that I share what has become one of the best, most healing experiences of my career. During the latter half of 2020 and most of 2021, we were home-bound and unable to engage in most of our community-based programming with school and afterschool sites. Two of my graduate students proposed that we take advantage of this pause by engaging the undergraduates on our team in a series of research-related workshops that would serve to foster a deeper understanding of how scholars develop lines of inquiry and how one might design an empirical exploration within a particular learning context. Together, my graduate students and I created a workshop series for our undergraduates, who crafted mini grant proposals, conference papers, and manuscripts for educational journals. This first cohort of research apprentices was given the opportunity to develop interests and confidence in doing research; several have expressed their commitment to pursue graduate studies. By listening to and working with my graduate students in developing this workshop series, I have come to realize how undergraduate students are often overlooked as budding scholars.

Fostering this intergenerational research mentoring program has helped make visible to me how little we think and converse about research mentorship for undergraduates. While there is increasing interest in developing our undergraduate courses, we seem to be missing opportunities to discuss how we can also provide meaningful research opportunities that expand beyond data collection procedures and transcribing. While a few faculty have made efforts to increase the number of research opportunities for undergraduates on my campus, such efforts have been largely developed on the backs of faculty of color. I believe that we can work to change this unfortunate pattern by raising questions about the ways in which we engage undergraduates beyond required coursework within our institutions. We can also work to normalize the idea that we benefit when we allow ourselves to learn not only from senior scholars but also from our graduate and undergraduate students.

Best,

D

Notes

1 17.5% of faculty identify with underrepresented communities (Georgia State University, 2021).
2 22.5% of faculty identify with underrepresented communities (Massachusetts Institute of Technology, 2022).
3 10% of faculty identify with underrepresented communities (Academic Student Affairs Committee, 2020).
4 The STEMinist Project is a pseudonym for the program name used to protect our youth and undergraduate participant identities.

References

Academic Student Affairs Committee. (2020). *Accountability sub-report on diversity: Staff diversity outcomes.* https://regents.universityofcalifornia.edu/regmeet/july20/a2.pdf

Aikens, M. L., Robertson, M. M., Sadselia, S., Watkins, K., Evans, M., Runyon, C. R., Eby, L., & Dolan, E. L. (2017). Race and gender differences in undergraduate research mentoring structures and research outcomes. *CBE—Life Sciences Education, 16*(2), ar34.

Aikens, M. L., Sadselia, S., Watkins, K., Evans, M., Eby, L. T., & Dolan, E. L. (2016). A social capital perspective on the mentoring of undergraduate life science researchers: An empirical study of undergraduate–postgraduate–faculty triads. *CBE—Life Sciences Education, 15*(2), ar16.

Arya, D., & McBeath, J. (Eds.). (2017). *STEMinists: The lifework of 12 women scientists and engineers.* Xochitl Justice Press.

Bauer, K. W., & Bennett, J. S. (2003). Alumni perceptions used to assess undergraduate research experience. *The Journal of Higher Education, 74*(2), 210–230.

Cole, D., & Espinoza, A. (2008). Examining the academic success of Latino students in science technology engineering and mathematics (STEM) majors. *Journal of College Student Development, 49*(4), 285–300.

Cooper, K. M., Gin, L. E., Akeeh, B., Clark, C. E., Hunter, J. S., Roderick, T. B., Elliot, D. B., Gutierrez, L. A., Mello, R. M., Pfeiffer, L. D., Scott, R. A., Arellano, D., Ramirez, D., Valdez, E. M., Vargas, C., Velarde, K., Zheng, Y., & Brownell, S. E. (2019). Factors that predict life sciences student persistence in undergraduate research experiences. *PloS One, 14*(8), e0220186.

Feldman, A., Divoll, K., & Rogan-Klyve, A. (2009). Research education of new scientists: Implications for science teacher education. *Journal of Research in Science Teaching, 46*(4), 442–459.

Georgia State University. (2021). *Fact book.* https://provost.gsu.edu/document/georgia-state-university-fact-books/?ind=1626177169766&filename=GSU%20Fact%20Book%202020-21.pdf&wpdmdl=8721&refresh=636ad21ce8e431667944988

Harsh, J. A., Maltese, A. V., & Tai, R. H. (2012). A perspective of gender differences in chemistry and physics undergraduate research experiences. *Journal of Chemical Education, 89*(11), 1364–1370.

Hoadley, C. (2012). What is a community of practice and how can we support it? In S. Land & D. Jonassen (Eds.), *Theoretical foundations of learning environments* (pp. 286–299). Routledge.

Ishiyama, J. (2002). Does early participation in undergraduate research benefit social science and humanities students? *College Student Journal, 36*(3), 381–387.

Jones, M. T., Barlow, A. E., & Villarejo, M. (2010). Importance of undergraduate research for minority persistence and achievement in biology. *The Journal of Higher Education, 81*(1), 82–115.

Kuh, G. D., Kinzie, J., Schuh, J. H., & Whitt, E. J. (2011). *Student success in college: Creating conditions that matter.* John Wiley & Sons.

Laursen, S., Seymour, E., & Hunter, A. B. (2012). Learning, teaching and scholarship: Fundamental tensions of undergraduate research. *Change: The Magazine of Higher Learning, 44*(2), 30–37.

Lave, J., & Wenger, E. (1991). *Situated learning: Legitimate peripheral participation.* Cambridge University Press.

Linn, M. C., Palmer, E., Baranger, A., Gerard, E., & Stone, E. (2015). Undergraduate research experiences: Impacts and opportunities. *Science, 347*(6222), 1261757.

Massachusetts Institute of Technology. (2022). *Diversity dashboard: Campus diversity.* https://ir.mit.edu/diversity-dashboard

National Academies of Sciences, Engineering, and Medicine. (2019). *Minority serving institutions: America's underutilized resource for strengthening the STEM workforce.* National Academies Press.

Nelson, D. J., & Rogers, D. C. (2003). *A national analysis of diversity in science and engineering faculties at research universities.* National Organization for Women.

O'Meara, K., Griffin, K. A., Kuvaeva, A., Nyunt, G., & Robinson, T. N. (2017). Sense of belonging and its contributing factors in graduate education. *International Journal of Doctoral Studies, 12*, 251–279.

Rahman, F., Hu, H., Brylow, D., & Kussmaul, C. (2017, March). Bringing undergraduate research experience in non-R1 institutions. In *Proceedings of the 2017 ACM SIGCSE Technical Symposium on Computer Science Education* (pp. 671–672). Association for Computing Machinery.

Rauckhorst, W. H., Czaja, J. A., & Baxter Magolda, M. (2001). *Measuring the impact of the undergraduate research experience on student intellectual development.* Project Kaleidoscope Summer Institute.

Rogoff, B. (2014). Learning by observing and pitching in to family and community endeavors: An orientation. *Human Development, 57*(2–3), 69–81.

Russell, S. H., Hancock, M. P., & McCullough, J. (2007). Benefits of undergraduate research experiences. *Science, 316*(5824), 548–549.

Towns, M. H. (2010). Where are the women of color? Data on African American, Hispanic, and Native American faculty in STEM. *Journal of College Science Teaching, 39*(4), 8.

UC Santa Barbara. (2013). *Undergraduate research.* https://undergrad.research.ucsb.edu/

U.S. Census Bureau. (2021). *Population estimates, July 1, 2021 (V2021).* https://data.census.gov/

Wenger, E. (1998). Communities of practice: Learning as a social system. *Systems Thinker, 9*(5), 2–3.

Wirtz, E., Dunford, A., Berger, E., Briody, E., Guruprasad, G., & Senkpeil, R. (2018). Resource usage and usefulness: Academic help-seeking behaviours of undergraduate engineering students. *Australasian Journal of Engineering Education, 23*(2), 62–70.

PART IV

Campus-wide strategies to address belonging at minority-serving institutions

10

ASSET-BASED STRATEGIES FOR ENGAGEMENT AND BELONGING AMONG LATINX STUDENTS AT AN OPEN-ACCESS, RESEARCH-INTENSIVE HISPANIC-SERVING INSTITUTION

Erika Mein and Louie Rodriguez

The demographic composition of students pursuing postsecondary education in the United States is rapidly shifting. We know that 21st-century college students are more digitally adept and more socially, economically, and culturally/linguistically diverse than at any moment historically. At the same time, college students face unprecedented social isolation and threats to mental health and well-being, particularly in the prolonged aftermath of the COVID-19 pandemic (Kim et al., 2022). Many institutions are striving to innovate and adapt to this rapidly changing landscape of higher education. Among them are Hispanic-Serving Institutions (HSIs), defined as degree-granting postsecondary institutions that enroll at least 25% Hispanic/Latinx students. As of 2020–2021, two-thirds of Hispanics enrolled in higher education (66%) attended one of 559 institutions categorized as HSIs across the country (Excelencia in Education, 2022). Notably, HSIs typically serve the highest-need students, many of whom are first-generation and low-income (Núñez et al., 2015).

The focal site for this chapter is one such HSI. The University of Texas at El Paso (UTEP) is a research-intensive, 4-year university located in the southwest corner of Texas, less than one mile from the U.S.–Mexico border. For more than 30 years, the university has maintained a commitment to open access, and the university's student composition intentionally reflects that of the region that it serves: more than 80% of UTEP students are Hispanic/Latinx, with the majority identifying as bilingual; approximately 50% of students are the first in their families to attend college; and more than two-thirds of students are Pell Grant–eligible. The university is predominantly non-residential; the vast majority of students live at home with their families, and many work while attending university. Within this context, the university has

DOI: 10.4324/9781003443735-14

developed and implemented a holistic framework for student success, known as the UTEP Edge, which is based on core tenets of asset-based teaching and learning (ABTL). This chapter will outline ABTL and present details on the university's framework for asset-based student success, which has been squarely focused on fostering a sense of belonging and increasing retention among students whose backgrounds and experiences have often been marginalized or viewed from a deficit lens.

Background

Not unlike predominantly White institutions, HSIs like UTEP face the challenge of fostering academic and social integration (Tinto, 1993) among their students, with the added complexities of serving student bodies that are predominantly commuter, first-generation, and income and time deprived. Decades of research on primarily residential campuses have demonstrated the value of academic and social integration for student persistence (Braxton et al., 2000; Ishitani, 2016; Milem & Berger, 1997). More recent approaches have come to rely on multiple dimensions to assess student success, including student demographics; institutional characteristics; student interactions with faculty, staff, and peers; and student involvement in "educationally purposeful activities" (Kuh et al., 2007, p. 38). While all of these variables are salient, the latter two – interactions with faculty and staff and participation in educationally meaningful activities – represent a significant opportunity for "institutional agents" (Harper, 2016, p. xi) to implement strategically focused efforts aimed at promoting student success – particularly among underrepresented students.

Student engagement in "educationally purposeful activities" is significant not only for its positive impact on academic and institutional outcomes (Kuh, 2001; Pascarella & Terenzini, 2005; Tinto, 2000) but also for its impact on students' sense of belonging; that is, their feeling of social support, connectedness, and mattering in a campus environment (Strayhorn, 2019). One study of first- and continuing-generation college students at five residential, teaching-focused campuses found that higher levels of daily engagement, both emotional and academic, led to greater feelings of belonging, and the effect was particularly significant among first-generation college students (Gillen-O'Neel, 2021). Higher levels of sense of belonging have also been closely tied to stronger self-efficacy and stronger academic performance among students (Freeman et al, 2007; Ostrove & Long, 2007) and ultimately to postsecondary persistence (Hausmann et al., 2007, 2009) at predominantly White, residential campuses.

While engagement and belonging have been found to be important to student success at predominantly White institutions, less is known about the practices of engagement and belonging at institutions that predominantly serve historically marginalized populations. In this chapter, we address this gap by presenting the case of one equity-focused, research-based framework for student success implemented at this open-access HSI. The framework was developed by a purposefully combined team of administrators from academic and student affairs as well as students, and utilized an asset-based lens and reflective practice for teaching and student support. The framework serves as the basis for several key institutional strategies aimed at fostering greater engagement in high-impact practices (HIPs) among a predominantly nonresidential Latinx student population.

UTEP'S student success framework

In March 2016, UTEP developed its Quality Enhancement Plan, The Next Generation of Student Engagement and Professional Preparation at UTEP, now branded as the UTEP Edge. The goal of the Edge is to prepare students for long-term success through engagement in a variety of integrated and applied learning experiences also referred to as "Edge experiences" or HIPs in and outside of the classroom.

The Edge is based on three principles (Figure 10.1): talented students, enriching experiences, and lifelong success. It is grounded on the belief that students enter the university with talents and strengths. Cultivating these attributes through HIPs makes learning relevant and concrete. Students apply their talents and learnings to future workplace/graduate school aspirations.

Degree completion, meaningful employment, and enrollment in graduate school comprise the primary intended outcomes of the Edge. HIP-specific

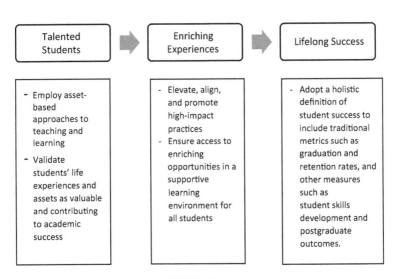

FIGURE 10.1 Core principles of the UTEP Edge.

learning outcomes and measurable learning in skill development are intended outcomes for assessing learning holistically.

The Edge is significant because it builds on student strengths, actively engages students in learning to gain a competitive advantage, and creates a shared understanding and responsibility for student success. The university community embraces its strength-based philosophy and promotes engagement in HIPs to promote student professional readiness. This approach is important to creating a sense of belonging for students who have historically been told that their assets are obstacles and whose personal experiences have been minimized.

UTEP's recently adopted 2030 Strategic Plan, America's Leading Hispanic-Serving University, incorporates the UTEP Edge under Goal 1 – Teaching, Learning, and the Student Experience: Provide students an excellent and engaged education in an inclusive university that builds on student strengths and demonstrates a culture of care. By embedding core principles of the UTEP Edge into the university's strategic plan, we ensure that the Edge is not seen as a passing fad but rather represents a culture shift in how we define a UTEP education. One example of this institutionalization of the Edge through the strategic plan is the redesign of key general education courses to provide high-impact, engaged experiences and increase student engagement from the first day of classes through graduation.

Conceptual underpinnings: Asset-based teaching and learning

Traditionally, Latinx students in the K–20 pipeline – not unlike those at UTEP – have had to contend with deficit discourses surrounding their academic performance and achievement. These discourses have placed emphasis on students' "deficiencies" – whether in terms of language, cognition, or motivation, among other factors – rather than the structural conditions, such as inequitable funding for schools, that have tended to contribute to the persistent underachievement of historically underserved groups (Valencia, 2010).

As a counter to deficit explanations of Latinx student academic underachievement, the UTEP Edge is based on an asset-based approach – ABTL – to working with students both inside and outside of the classroom. Drawing on educational research and community development literature, these asset-based pedagogical approaches emphasize students' individual and collective strengths, skills, and capacities as the starting point for learning and engagement. Such approaches do not claim to resolve the systemic conditions that contribute to persistent inequities experienced by minoritized students in the PK–20 pipeline; rather, they are focused on reconfiguring teaching and learning to promote equity and belonging at the classroom and campus level.

ABTL is defined by five distinct characteristics (Figure 10.2): inclusive, interactive, culturally responsive, linguistically responsive, and reflective. Each is described in detail in this section.

Inclusive

ABTL acknowledges that the sole reliance on more traditional forms of teaching and learning (e.g., lecture-based instruction) may not be optimal for all students all the time. ABTL recognizes that college educators need to set the conditions for optimal learning by implementing diverse teaching methods designed to reach learners representing different backgrounds, perspectives, and ways of knowing. Research tells us that when learners feel welcome, safe, and comfortable, they will learn at much higher rates than if they feel unwelcome or insecure (see Krashen, 1982/ 2009). Pedagogical methods that support inclusiveness and engagement for learners of diverse backgrounds include, but are not limited to, project-based learning, service learning, and translanguaging pedagogy. For commuter students, inclusiveness involves an awareness of the constraints related to off-campus obligations, including family and employment. On-campus activities, including coursework, can be adjusted to reflect the schedule flexibility needed by many commuter students. While inclusiveness for commuter students implies some degree of flexibility, this is also done within a backdrop of high standards and excellence expected of all students, regardless of background or commuter status.

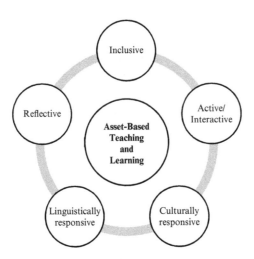

FIGURE 10.2 Characteristics of asset-based teaching and learning.

Interactive

Sociocultural theories of learning emphasize the ways in which learning is a social process, mediated and sustained through language and interaction (Vygotsky, 1978) and situated in practice (Lave & Wenger, 1991). When learners are given the opportunity to engage with content by talking and writing combined with "learning by doing," they tend to have better retention of information and higher levels of cognitive engagement. Both inside and outside the classroom, pedagogical methods that encourage active engagement run on a spectrum from individual to collective and from less to more highly structured activities. One approach to encourage active engagement with content or practice on an individual level is "writing to learn," where students engage in informal writing through "quick-writes" or exit tickets to make sense of and reflect on their learning; such writing can be a starting point for small-group dialogue and can take place in the student's preferred language. Another way to encourage active engagement at the group level is through collaboration and teamwork, which can happen in less-structured ways (e.g., small-group work related to a particular topic) or in more highly structured ways (e.g., team projects or project-based learning).

Culturally responsive

Postsecondary settings in the United States, not unlike their pre-K–12 counterparts, have typically reflected the norms and practices of middle- and upper-middle-class White populations (Conrad & Gasman, 2017). This can be seen, for example, in the emphasis on standard English in many classrooms, with little acknowledgement of students' home languages, and in the emphasis on content disconnected from students' experiences and backgrounds. In contrast, ABTL recognizes that students bring diverse backgrounds, perspectives, and practices to postsecondary settings and understands that teaching and learning should flexibly adapt to students' experiences to promote learning. Pedagogical approaches that account for culture, in all of its complexities, fall on a continuum: on one end, faculty/staff demonstrate awareness of students' backgrounds and use that knowledge as a starting point for teaching ("culturally informed"); on the other end of the continuum is "culturally sustaining pedagogy," which favors the maintenance of nondominant students' linguistic and cultural practices rather than promoting assimilation into dominant norms (Ladson-Billings, 2014; Paris, 2012; see also Chapter 4).

Linguistically responsive

At HSIs like UTEP, many students bring different levels of bilingual proficiencies (e.g., conversational and/or academic) to their studies. How we work with bilingual/multilingual students involves both stance and practice; that is, our beliefs about language(s) in the classroom and how we design our instruction with respect to language learners (de Jong, 2013; Lucas & Villegas, 2013). In many pre-K–20 classrooms in the United States, the default stance is one of monolingualism, where the assumption is that content should be taught exclusively in English without recognizing students' primary language(s) as a resource for learning (Cummins, 2005; de Jong, 2013). Alternatively, a multilingual stance recognizes the value of cross-linguistic transfer – where students can draw on what they know in one language (e.g., Spanish) and apply it in to learn content in another (e.g., English; Cummins, 2005). Instructor and institutional approaches toward language, then, usually fall on a continuum: on one end of the continuum is the monolingual stance, which emphasizes English-only instruction and neglects to see students' language backgrounds and bilingual proficiencies as a resource for learning; on the other end of the continuum is a language maintenance stance, where emphasis is placed on the development and maintenance of students' reading, writing, speaking, and listening proficiencies in two or more languages. In the middle of the continuum we find a linguistically responsive stance, where instructors leverage students' linguistic backgrounds to facilitate meaningful content learning in English. Importantly, an instructor or staff member does not need to be bilingual/multilingual to adopt a linguistically responsive stance in the classroom; rather, they need to be language-aware and to value the linguistic assets that students bring to learning.

Reflective

Despite the commonplace belief that "good teaching" is an innate talent, educational researchers have shown, repeatedly, that teaching is not, in fact, natural (Ball & Forzani, 2009); rather, teaching expertise is developed over time, through ongoing practice, feedback, and reflection. Providing opportunities for faculty and instructors to reflect on problems of practice and providing opportunities to engage in structured peer observation and feedback are two first steps to encouraging reflective practice and, in turn, the continuous improvement of teaching. In addition, another approach to help build reflective teaching at the college level includes the establishment of "communities of practice" among faculty aimed at refining their teaching. In this way, reflection becomes a collective activity, where faculty are engaged in collaborative discussion of their experiences and learn from one another.

Key institutional strategies aimed at student success

To build out this student success framework, UTEP has leveraged three key strategies. When combined, these strategies, grounded in practical application, make the conceptual concrete.

Holistic measures of student and faculty success

Traditional measures of student success often include metrics such as retention rate, 4- and 6-year graduation rates, and time to completion. While these metrics are important, they paint an incomplete picture, especially when considering the largely posttraditional student population at UTEP. Traditional student success metrics focus solely on first-time-in-college students who begin in the fall semester and are enrolled every fall and spring semester until graduation. By this measure, nearly 70% of UTEP students are excluded. The majority of UTEP students matriculate having earned some community college credits as transfer students or through the successful early college high school model that has thrived in the El Paso region. Rather than validate these students' success and commitment to their education, they are simply excluded from the traditional higher education student success story. To combat this outdated view of student success, UTEP adopts a holistic view, inclusive of but going well beyond traditional measures. UTEP values other elements of student success such as financial wellness, campus engagement, participation in HIPs, and others. When telling the story of our students, UTEP empowers faculty, staff, and students to include all of the many ways in which our students succeed, rather than be confined by a handful of traditional measures.

One specific example of how UTEP values holistic student success measures is the UTEP Edge Advantages. These skills (leadership, confidence, problem solving, global awareness, communication, teamwork, entrepreneurship, critical thinking, and social responsibility) reflect the nontechnical skills most valued by employers across industries and disciplines. Leaders of the various high-impact practices work to embed these skills into their program experiences and ask students to reflect on whether they have developed one or more of these skills and how they might apply them in other settings. A student who has successfully developed one or more of these cross-cutting skills through an internship or service-learning experience, for example, is building a more robust set of strengths and assets from which to draw throughout her academic and professional journey.

Faculty/staff partnerships

Faculty and staff partnerships are at the heart of the one-team, campus-wide approach to student success at UTEP. While the traditional silos of academia do still exist at UTEP, one institutional strategy that exemplifies our cross-campus commitment to student centeredness is the UTEP Edge Fellows. The Edge Fellows are a select group of faculty/staff committed to UTEP's model of holistic student success who collaborate toward broad implementation of the Edge through a multilevel transformational effort. This cohort of colleagues works together over a 2-year term to better understand the facets of UTEP student success and support students as they apply their unique talents and strengths to new contexts and settings. Fellows participate in professional development on topics including reflective practices, institutional data, integrative and applied learning approaches, and more. More than 60 campus departments have had at least one Edge Fellow.

Two more examples of faculty engagement in UTEP's student success work are the oversight and administration of the UTEP Edge itself and the creation of faculty Provost Fellows. Since its inception, the UTEP Edge has been co-led by a team of faculty, staff, and students, modeling cross-divisional collaboration by uniting the insight, expertise, and wisdom of both academic affairs and student affairs to better serve all students. The Office of the Provost has also created funded positions, Provost Fellows, to support student success work in a variety of ways. From direct support of the UTEP Edge to areas like inclusion, professional development, and more, Provost Fellows collaborate with diverse campus community members to advance student success.

Culturally responsive programming

Cultural responsiveness is another strategy UTEP uses to bring its student success framework to life. In serving a student population that is more than 80% Hispanic, it is the university's responsibility to provide a learning environment and experience that confronts and addresses equity gaps by recognizing the cultural knowledge of our students as an asset and then builds on that knowledge through campus engagement and classroom learning (Muñiz, 2020).

UTEP faculty and staff employ many culturally responsive strategies, including modeling high expectations for students, collaborating with families and the local community, and communicating in culturally responsive ways. One example of this is hosting sessions for parents and family, in both English and Spanish, during new student orientation. In these sessions, parents and family are introduced to or are reminded of the reality that college is very different from high school and the demands on their child's time and effort will be greater. Facilitators discuss the importance of spending time on campus outside of class, share tips on how to encourage students to seek out and participate in high-impact practices, and more. The inclusion of family-based sessions at orientation acknowledges the critically important role of *la familia* in Hispanic communities (Yosso, 2005), while the official use of Spanish in these sessions signals the importance of cultivating belonging through bilingual language practices.

Activities supporting student engagement and belonging

Finally, we present four sets of comprehensive programming that exemplify the student success framework and strategies described above. These examples could be replicated in part or whole across any campus with varying degrees of complexity and administrative restructuring.

Holistic advising model

UTEP's holistic advising model supports student success and retention through a common campus-wide undergraduate advising structure that provides equitable access to quality advising, enhances the student experience, and facilitates clear understanding of degree pathways and seamless enrollment term to term.

Three elements define this model: (a) personalized advising through a caseload model where every student is assigned their own advisor, ensuring a ratio of 350:1; (b) integrating students' academic, financial, and social realities through a framework based on students' unique assets and characteristics; and (c) engaging students immediately in developing academic and co-curricular pathways to degrees based on student aspirations and interests.

Beyond academic advising itself, a key element of the advising framework is bridging students' academic, financial, and social realities to provide meaningful holistic advising. Important student data are gathered through an entering student survey, the results of which are made available to advisors for use during advising sessions. Advisors are trained to advise students to develop academic, co-curricular, and financial aid and financial literacy plans based on the demands of their own lives.

Underpinning this advising model is a commitment to elevating the advising profession and advising community on our campus. This is accomplished through operational consistency, common evaluation metrics, and year-round training and robust professional development. To advance operational consistency, there are now common reporting structures across all academic colleges, professional staff work a 12-month contract rather than a 9-month contract, advisors have clearly defined and consistent duties and responsibilities, and there is a consistent salary and title structure. This model allows faculty who previously served in an advising capacity to focus that time and energy toward student mentoring and career preparation. The advising operation's assessment landscape includes contextual metrics, performance metrics, and accountability measures. Contextual metrics include using the holistic dimensions of the advising framework, leveraging advisor knowledge and expertise to accurately apply university and degree requirements, and establishing common processes and best practices. Performance metrics include advisor response time, student satisfaction, and timelines for outreach to key student groups to mitigate attrition. Accountability measures include retention rates, advisor accuracy and service, and time to degree. Finally, all advisors participate in a year-round, common professional development and training program focused on capacity building. This model is grounded in developing core advisor competencies but allows for deeper dives into other topics including emotional intelligence, service excellence, leadership, and more.

UTEP's approach to high-impact practices

While nearly every university offers their students access to HIPs, UTEP's student population and realities demand a different approach to HIPs. Simply making HIPs available is not enough to gain the attention and investment of students with complex and busy lives. UTEP faculty and staff work hard to connect students with the specific HIPs that best align with their goals and aspirations through personal interactions, advising, in- and out-of-class conversations, mentoring, and other avenues. It often takes careful and thoughtful exchange to help students see the value of trading off a steady part-time retail job for a short-term internship in their field of study, for example.

Getting students to participate in HIPs is only part of the work, though. HIPs must have clear value for our students to compete for their limited time and resources. A key part of demonstrating that value is to make the learning and impact of participation clear and visible. Directors of HIPs at UTEP have been provided resources and training on how to incorporate reflective practices into their programs. Ranging from simple pre- and post-participation reflective journaling to video testimonials and panel discussions, participant reflection is now a core part of participating in an HIP at UTEP. High-quality reflection allows students to make sense of their experience and cultivates an awareness of themselves as active participants in real-world experiences. The UTEP Edge aims to advance reflective practice as a campus-wide tool beyond HIPs, creating a learning culture where students are not only "consumers" of knowledge but "creators" of knowledge (Costa & Kallick, 2008).

One example of reflection being integrated into an HIP is with UTEP's undergraduate research program. All undergraduate students who participate in research must submit reflection statements throughout their experience, resulting in a draft personal statement appropriate for use in applying to graduate school. A common pair of questions students respond to includes: "What is the most important thing that you have learned this semester? Why is it important and how do you think it will be useful in your future academic/research career?" The resulting statements are often deeper and more meaningful than research-related content. So often, issues of identity, socioeconomic status, and academic belonging appear, allowing the faculty member to follow up with meaningful conversation, support, and mentoring.

Finally, given the financial realities of the demographics UTEP serves, more than 70% of students at the university report working during their time in college. Rather than be frustrated that UTEP students are pulled away to work, often to contribute to family and household expenses, the university embraces this dynamic and tries to create as many on-campus employment opportunities as possible. Departments are encouraged to budget for student employee positions beyond those funded through federal work–study, and faculty are encouraged to write student employee roles into grant proposals where feasible. Because working through college is a proud UTEP tradition, the university works to elevate the on-campus working experience so students are not only employed in a student-friendly environment but are developing professional skills and habits along the way.

At the beginning of every academic year, the university hosts "Student Worker Training," where departments can send their student employees for a full day of training and networking. Topics covered at this event have included emotional intelligence, professionalism, and communication skills. UTEP also hosts an annual training for supervisors of student employees. This event focuses on how to mentor student employees, provide helpful performance feedback, and embed professional development into the employment experience. These and other efforts help to add value to the experience of working on campus in ways that are most relevant to UTEP students.

Capacity building and faculty development

As part of its holistic student success framework, UTEP has instituted a comprehensive plan for capacity building and professional development with faculty. The plan includes touchpoints with faculty through three key mechanisms: new faculty orientation, the entry-level seminar course for students, and the university's Center for Faculty Leadership and Development. The overriding goal of these efforts is to build and enhance a "culture of care" with students, focused on their academic and professional success. Underlying the professional development is an asset-based lens for understanding UTEP students, particularly posttraditional students who juggle multiple responsibilities in addition to school, to provide a more tailored academic experience.

The first touchpoint, new faculty orientation, was revamped to include a focus on the Edge and UTEP's student success framework. Through intensive virtual and face-to-face sessions, incoming faculty engage in activities where they learn about the key pillars of the Edge. Faculty meet UTEP students who have participated in HIPs, and they are oriented to not only the outcomes of the Edge but also the ways in which their courses can be adapted to integrate HIPs. In addition, incoming faculty learn about the ABTL framework that informs the UTEP Edge and applications for their practice.

Ongoing professional development that builds on the new faculty orientation takes place through the newly formed Center for Faculty Leadership and Development. Led by a combined faculty/staff team, the Center for Faculty Leadership and Development offers credentialing and micro-credentialing programs focused on effective teaching and inclusive teaching for equitable learning.

The third mechanism for capacity building among a key subset of faculty is the entering student experience, which includes both developmental coursework for entering students as well as the first-year seminar for freshmen, known as UNIV 1301: Seminar for Critical Inquiry. The UNIV course includes structures to provide support to first-semester students, including a collaboration among instructors, peer leaders, and a dedicated librarian for each section. UNIV 1301 faculty participate in two intensive professional development sessions every year, allowing them to examine data on student performance and outcomes and to work toward greater alignment of their sections with the outcomes associated with the UTEP Edge. Faculty also participate in a Gallup StrengthsFinder training of trainers not only to reflect on their own strengths as instructors but also to integrate StrengthsFinder with their students – toward the goal of students identifying and acting on their unique strengths early in their higher education trajectory.

To strengthen the sense of both academic and social belonging among first-generation college-going students, the university offers designated sections for first-generation college students, where the instructor and support staff are all also first-generation college-going. Early impact data show that students who took UNIV 1301 in their first year were 6% more likely to be retained in their second year compared to students who did not take the course then. Furthermore, students designated to have high risk of attrition were 37% more likely to be retained in their second year if they took UNIV in their first year compared with high-risk students who did not take the course.

Building a sense of belonging

Bienvenidos campaign

Through the UTEP Edge, the university developed a campus-wide campaign called Bienvenidos to encourage students to make use of faculty office hours. The campaign was introduced to students through an engaging multiday tabling event in the center of campus with tips on how to optimize faculty interactions, what types of questions to ask during office hours, and why interacting with faculty outside the classroom is so important. To support faculty, the Edge provided materials including door hangers, posters, and window decals reading "Welcome. I'm here!" as well as topics to discuss with students during office hours beyond grades. This effort was interrupted by the pandemic but will be relaunched with new pandemic insights, including the use of virtual office hours and other ways to communicate with faculty outside of class.

Miner welcome

For the first semester back in person after the height of the pandemic, the university hosted a tabling activity during welcome week that was focused on both validating students' assets and normalizing reflective practice. In small clusters facilitated by faculty and staff, students engaged in a brief discussion about the definition and value of reflection, followed by an activity where students identified one skill they learned or enhanced during the pandemic that could help them in college. Students appreciated the chance to share the many skills they relied on, most often citing adaptability and time management as skills that would continue to serve them well during their time at UTEP. More than 1,500 students participated in the activity and shared their written reflections.

Conclusion

This chapter outlines the holistic student success framework designed and implemented by UTEP, an open-access, research-intensive HSI that serves a predominantly posttraditional student body. The majority of students at UTEP are Hispanic and nonresidential and maintain employment and additional responsibilities – including family and caregiving – outside of school. Within this context, UTEP is working to chart a new course in higher education by forging a unique approach to student success that is data informed, culturally responsive, and asset-based. The approach – implemented across student affairs and academic affairs – focuses on holistic advising, high-impact practices, ongoing capacity building and faculty development, and key activities designed to build students' sense of belonging.

As outlined in this chapter, the university has adopted holistic measures of success that go beyond traditional metrics like graduation rates. One key indicator of student success is retention, and UTEP's year-to-year retention rates are equivalent to those of peer research-intensive universities that have higher rates of selectivity. Importantly, UTEP maintains competitive retention rates without compromising its long-standing commitment to open access for students. While UTEP's approach has been successful and shown promise for even greater impact, opportunities and challenges remain. The next phase of this work will focus squarely on faculty development and curricular integration of engagement opportunities. Efforts such as redesigning the core curriculum around engaged learning and embedding transferrable skill development and assessment into courses are well underway.

While UTEP's institutional makeup differs from more traditional higher education institutions that serve a predominantly residential student body, it reflects the future of higher education, as increasing numbers of students representing diverse socioeconomic backgrounds seek postsecondary opportunities. Among institutions that serve predominantly nonresidential student bodies, the threat of attrition looms large, and the necessity for fostering belonging and engagement becomes ever more important. UTEP's focus on identifying and building on students' talents and strengths both inside and outside the classroom and on engaging students in the university experience early and often can serve as a model for other higher education institutions that serve Hispanic and posttraditional student bodies.

References

Ball, D. L., & Forzani, F. M. (2009). The work of teaching and the challenge for teacher education. *Journal of Teacher Education*, 60(5), 497–511.

Braxton, J. M., Milem, J. F., & Sullivan, A. S. (2000). The influence of active learning on the college student departure process. *Journal of Higher Education*, 71(5), 569–590.

Conrad, C., & Gasman, M. (2017). *Educating a diverse nation: Lessons from minority-serving institutions*. Harvard University Press.

Costa, A. L., & Kallick, B. (Eds.). (2008). *Learning and leading with habits of mind: 16 essential characteristics for success*. ASCD.

Cummins, J. (2005). A proposal for action: Strategies for recognizing heritage language competence as a learning resource within the mainstream classroom. *Modern Language Journal*, 89(4), 585–592.

de Jong, E. (2013). Preparing mainstream teachers for multilingual classrooms. *Association of Mexican-American Educators*, 7(2), 40–49.

Excelencia in Education. (2022). *Hispanic-serving institutions data: 2020–2021*. https://www.edexcelencia.org/research/series/hsi-2020-2021

Freeman, T. M., Anderman, L. H., & Jensen, J. M. (2007). Sense of belonging in college freshmen at the classroom and campus levels. *Journal of Experiential Education*, 75(3), 203–220.

Gillen-O'Neel, C. (2021). Sense of belonging and student engagement: A daily study of first and continuing-generation college students. *Research in Higher Education*, 62, 45–71.

Harper, S. R. (2016). Foreword. In V. Pendakur (Ed.), *Closing the opportunity gap: Identity-conscious strategies for retention and student success* (pp. ix–xii). Stylus.

Hausmann, L. R. M., Schofield, J. W., & Woods, R. L. (2007). Sense of belonging as a predictor of intentions to persist among African American and White first year college students. *Research in Higher Education*, 48(7), 803–839.

Hausmann, L. R. M., Ye, F., Schofield, J. W., & Woods, R. L. (2009). Sense of belonging in White and African American first year students. *Research in Higher Education*, 50, 649–669.

Ishitani, T. T. (2016). Time-varying effects of academic and social integration on student persistence for first and second years in college: National data approach. *Journal of College Student Retention*, 18(3), 263–286.

Kim, H., Rackoff, G. N., Fitzsimmons-Craft, E. E.Shin, K. I., Zainal, N. H., Schwob, J. T., Eisenberg, D., Wilfley, D. E., Barr Taylor, C., & Newman, M. G. (2022). College mental health before and during the COVID-19 pandemic: results from a nationwide survey. *Cognitive Therapy and Research*, 46, 1–10.

Krashen, S. D. (2009). *Principles and practice in second language acquisition*. Pergamon. (Original work published 1982). http://www.sdkrashen.com/content/books/principles_and_practice.pdf

Kuh, G. D. (2001). Assessing what really matters to student learning: Inside the National Survey of Student Engagement. *Change*, 33(3), 10–17.

Kuh, G. D., Kinzie, J., Buckley, J., Bridges, B., & Hayek, J. C. (2007). Piecing together the student success puzzle: Research, propositions, and recommendations. *ASHE Higher Education Report*, 32(5), 1–182.

Ladson-Billings, G. (2014). Culturally relevant pedagogy 2.0. *Harvard Educational Review*, 84(1), 74–84.

Lave, J., & Wenger, E. (1991). *Situated learning: Legitimate peripheral participation*. Cambridge University Press.

Lucas, T., & Villegas, A. M. (2013). Preparing linguistically responsive teachers: Laying the foundation in preservice teacher education. *Theory Into Practice*, 52, 98–109.

Milem, J. F., & Berger, J. B. (1997). A modified model of college student persistence: Exploring the relationship between Astin's theory of involvement and Tinto's theory of student departure. *Journal of College Student Development*, 11. https://scholarworks.umass.edu/cie_faculty_pubs/11

Muñiz, J. (2020). *Culturally responsive teaching: A reflection guide*. New America. https://www.newamerica.org/education-policy/policy-papers/culturally-responsive-teaching-competencies

Núñez, A. M., Hurtado, S., & Calderón Galdeano, E. (2015). Why study Hispanic-serving institutions? In A. M. Núñez, S. Hurtado, & E. Calderón Galdeano (Eds.), *Hispanic-serving institutions: Advancing research and transformative practice* (pp. 1–22). Routledge.

Ostrove, J. M., & Long, S. M. (2007). Social class and belonging: Implications for college adjustment. *Review of Higher Education*, 30(4), 363–389.

Paris, D. (2012). Culturally sustaining pedagogy: A needed change in stance, terminology, and practice. *Educational Researcher*, 41(3), 93–97.

Pascarella, E. T., & Terenzini, P. T. (2005). *How college affects students, volume 2: A third decade of research*. Jossey-Bass.

Strayhorn, T. L. (2019). *College students' sense of belonging: A key to educational success for all students* (2nd ed.). Routledge.

Tinto, V. (1993). *Leaving college: Rethinking the causes and cures of student attrition* (2nd ed.). University of Chicago Press.

Tinto, V. (2000). Taking retention seriously: Rethinking the first year of college. *NACADA Journal*, 19(2), 5–10.

The University of Texas at El Paso. (2020). *America's leading Hispanic serving institution: 2030 Strategic plan*. https://www.utep.edu/strategic-plan/

Valencia, R. R. (2010). *Dismantling contemporary deficit thinking: Educational thought and practice*. Routledge.

Vygotsky, L. (1978). *Mind and society.* Harvard University Press.

Yosso, T. J. (2005). Whose culture has capital? A critical race theory discussion of community cultural wealth. *Race Ethnicity and Education,* 8(1), 69–91.

11

CREATING HIGH-TOUCH ENVIRONMENTS FOR BELONGING IN TOUCHLESS TIMES

A Black college case study amid COVID-19

Terrell L. Strayhorn

It was Tuesday morning, 9 o'clock, and I was already on campus enjoying my first "cup of Joe" (i.e., coffee) in the privacy of my own office. According to our strategic workweek plan, it was "Leadership Tuesday," which always kicked off with executive leadership council, known elsewhere as "Cabinet." In the first half of the meeting, the vice president of enrollment management presented a snapshot of our current student profiles, offering some insights into "how the [student] market" was responding to our recent COVID-19-related decisions to dedensify campus by limiting the number of those living in residence halls, restrict campus access to full-time personnel only, and shut off universal access points, forcing everyone to enter through a centralized set of gates.

The vice president's presentation revealed that undergraduate numbers were showing some decline. However, there seemed to be rapidly rising inquiries among some student populations like off-campus residents and fully online degree seekers, to name a few. Invited into the conversation as provost and senior vice president of academic affairs, I shared plans to ensure business continuity by building eight new degree programs in high-need fields to respond to rising demands and new emerging markets, while also providing students what they need – socially and academically – despite physical displacement. Launching new, online academic programs would *not* move us away from our long-standing commitment to students' academic belonging and success. I explained how we would deepen investments in holistic support services using Title III funds and Coronavirus Aid, Relief and Economic Security (CARES) Act dollars to give students the support necessary for academic success, even in a touchless era – an unprecedented time when close proximity was classified as "high risk" by leading public

DOI: 10.4324/9781003443735-15

health experts, when direct connection could be contagious, and when personal exchange might be lethal or deadly (Strayhorn, 2020a). To be successful, we would have to heed the science about COVID-19 while ensuring that students felt connected, seen, and supported throughout their journey in ways that addressed their *academic belonging*, a combination of intellectual and social fit (Nunn, 2021).

Indeed, these were some of the difficulties presented by the COVID-19 global pandemic that delivered a serious existential threat to higher education. Consequently, the higher education enterprise has changed significantly as campuses, like the one introduced in the anecdote in the chapter opening, have been transformed from what they once were to what students always need(ed) them to be, as they chart a path forward to who they will become: truly student-centered learning spaces. No doubt, higher education learned a good deal as a system – as institutions – through the pandemic, and it is important to document the lessons learned as part of a growing playbook that can guide others in the future, challenged to lead colleges and universities through times of chaos and crisis onward to long-term planning and sustainability while, at all times, ensuring business continuity. If nothing else, we learned that higher education institutions *can* innovate, ideate, and reimagine themselves, while also doubling down on being student centered, success oriented, and laser focused on fostering conditions that offer students the gift of academic belonging. This is the subject addressed in the present chapter.

Purpose

The purpose of the current chapter is to present a case study of how a 4-year private historically Black college/university (HBCU) managed to foster and maintain students' academic belonging amid the COVID-19 pandemic, despite closures, mergers, and enrollment declines. Using sense of belonging as an industrial–organizational and social–psychological framework, the chapter demonstrates how campus leaders, faculty, and staff took intentional steps to (re)create high-touch (i.e., hi-touch) and high-tech (i.e., hi-tech) conditions for academic belonging in a touchless era when public health officials advised people to wear face coverings, quarantine, and stay at least 6 feet apart, to name a few safety measures. Strict physical distancing certainly changed how faculty and students connected during the pandemic, but the human need for connection, community, care, and belonging was no less important and will persist *well beyond* present times of crisis. Before describing the contours of the case and introducing key promising practices, the next section highlights what we know from research and scholarship about sense of belonging.

Sense of belonging

Sense of belonging is a basic human need. It is a fundamental motive that drives human behavior (Baumeister & Leary, 1995). Applied to higher education, sense of belonging reflects the availability, accessibility, quality, and usefulness of academic *and* social support that students perceive *and receive* on campus (Strayhorn, 2019). It is a feeling of connectedness, that one is important to others, that one matters, and plays an important role in relevant groups both on or off campus (Jacoby & Garland, 2004; Rosenberg & McCullough, 1981; Strayhorn 2019). Although definitions vary, scholars generally agree that *sense of belonging* is defined as "a feeling that members matter to one another and to the group and a shared faith that members' needs will be met through their commitment to be together" (McMillan & Chavis, 1986, p. 9).

Prior research on sense of belonging can be conceptualized into three major categories. First, a line of scholarship underscores the importance of sense of belonging as a critical factor in educational success (Hale et al., 2005; Hausmann et al., 2006). Sense of belonging *is* a feeling, a sensation of mattering to others such as teachers and peers, as well as identifying with a broader group, that produces an affective response in individuals (Tovar & Simon, 2010). For example, Hagerty et al. (1992) defined sense of belonging as "the experience of personal involvement in a system or environment so that persons feel themselves to be an integral part of that system or environment [i.e., academic setting]" (p. 172). Noting that belonging is something that communities provide individuals – not that individuals find themselves – Nunn (2021) described *academic belonging* as a combination of intellectual and social fit.

A second category of work aims to understand the circumstances that engender students' academic sense of belonging. For instance, some scholars uncovered the important role that peer interactions and faculty support play in facilitating college students' academic sense of belonging (Hoffman, 2002; Means & Pyne, 2017). Positive peer interactions offer opportunities to create meaningful interpersonal bonds with similarly situated peers that, in turn, can help students negotiate academic spaces and fields (Strayhorn, 2020b) through learning partnerships, study groups, and cohorts. If we know anything at all from this segment of scholarship, then we know that when students establish strong, supportive, interpersonal relationships with peers, faculty, and staff, they excel by forming friendships, attending class regularly, and engaging in campus clubs and activities. However, it's much less clear how educationally purposeful relationships were formed and sustained amid the COVID-19 pandemic when most teaching and learning took place remotely; this is an important question addressed by the study that informs the present chapter.

A third, and growing, body of scholarship focuses on sense of belonging for various student groups (Blackmon et al., 2020; Garvey et al., 2020; Strayhorn, 2021a), with a specific focus on academic life of college. For example, Garvey et al. (2020) analyzed survey data from 390 first-year, first-generation undergraduate students living in residence halls at a large public, predominantly White university in the southeastern region of the country. They found that, on average, women compared to men, high-income compared to low-income, and Christian compared to non-Christian students reported higher levels of belongingness. First-generation students who interacted frequently and positively with academic staff and peers experienced increased belonging. Academic belonging of first-generation, low-income students has also been linked to positive interactions with faculty, campus support centers, and high-impact practices (e.g., service learning) in prior research (Means & Pyne, 2017). Comparatively few studies, however, have focused on the academic belonging experiences of HBCU students, which is a gap addressed by the current chapter.

Whereas many social psychologists and educational researchers tend to focus on students' sense of belonging from a person-level or individual perspective (e.g., Anderman & Freeman, 2004; Baumeister & Leary, 1995; Fisher et al., 2015), industrial–organizational scholars call attention to the important role that sense of belonging plays at the institutional level, for instance, through studies on workplace belonging (Komisarof, 2021). Sense of belonging at the organizational or institutional level refers to alignment between an individual's personal values, commitments, and goals and those of the *employing* (or *enrolling*) institution, including one's ability to freely express important aspects of self and identity (Komisarof, 2018). Additionally, the health, safety, and security of the organization contribute to an overall sense of belonging among individuals (Komisarof, 2021). People perform optimally – whether at work or at school – when they feel physically, psychologically, emotionally, and financially secure, safe from hurt, harm, or injury. So when organizations take steps to formulate new or revise existing programs and policies to prohibit discrimination, retaliation, harassment, and/or bullying in college classrooms and departments, they create conditions that facilitate students' academic sense of belonging.

Adopting a *multilevel* perspective on sense of belonging can be helpful for examining and understanding effective ways to institutionalize strategies to foster and preserve students' academic sense of belonging in higher education, by scaling "what works" at the individual classroom, department, and program levels. A multilevel perspective on sense of belonging incorporates the seven core elements from Strayhorn's (2019) theory with seven key areas of organization-level work (e.g., policies, procedures, programs), or what is referred to as the "7 P's" (Strayhorn, in press). Figure 11.1 presents a graphical illustration of the multilevel framework.

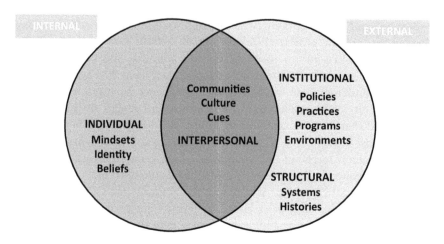

FIGURE 11.1 Strayhorn's (in press) multilevel belonging framework.

Gap identification

To recap, extant theory suggests that sense of belonging assumes heightened importance at times and circumstances when/where people are vulnerable to feeling isolated, judged, or deemed a threat to others. These are feelings that affected *some racial/ethnic minorities* long before the pandemic, according to research on stereotype threat (Steele, 1997), but were also remarkably prevalent amid COVID-19 (Strayhorn, 2021b). COVID-19, the disease caused by a betacoronavirus named SARS-CoV-2 (Sohrabi et al., 2020), posed a serious existential threat to higher education as campuses shut down, sheltered in place, restricted universal access points, and enforced strict physical distancing, mask mandates, and dedensification strategies that put many students off campus, in quarantine, out of sight (at times), and "out of touch" amid touchless times. The question arises, however, how did *some* institutions overcome the challenges posed by the COVID-19 pandemic in building and maintaining hi-touch, hi-tech environments that fostered academic belonging and kept students *connected* and *confident* academically, despite forced displacement? To be sure, a long line of research shows that students develop a sense of belonging academically "as [a] result of many and varied interactions with the college ... [which] will enhance retention" (Beal & Noel, 1980, p. 5). So, what are/were those "many and varied interactions," and how were they sustained amid the Great Pandemic? This is the core question addressed in the remainder of the chapter using a critical case study from a particular sociodemographic experience that has pedagogical influence for bigger, broader institutional contexts, in consonance with such an approach (Stake, 1998).

The case: A Black college amid COVID-19

Judging by the large volume of scholarly output, case study research design plays a central role in social sciences and education. In fact, some argue that "we are witnessing a movement away from a variable-centered approach to causality in the social sciences and towards a case-based approach" (Gerring, 2009, p. 90). Case-based approaches can be superior to others by preserving the texture and detail of individual cases; this is generally referred to as a rich, thick description (Merriam, 1998). Applied to the focus of this chapter, a *case* "connotes a spatially delimited phenomenon (a unit) observed at a single point in time or over some period of time" (Gerring, 2009, p. 94), represented by the private, 4-year, research-aspiring HBCU under study. Case study is the careful study of a single case to understand a population by answering how and why questions about the phenomenon of interest (Yin, 2002).

The critical case under study, again, is a private, 4-year, research-aspiring HBCU located in the Mid-Atlantic region of the country. Over 150 years old, part of the campus currently sits in the same physical location of a former slave jail, which has a particular paradoxical irony to it – that a site once used to imprison, shackle, and incarcerate enslaved Black people is now (and forever) a place of enlightenment, academic freedom, and intellectual liberation. The institution enrolls just under 2,000 undergraduate and graduate students, with over one-third identifying as "first-generation," and almost 80% are African American/Black. In-state tuition averages $13,530 (plus fees), and 98% of students received grant aid according to most recent data. Just over 75% of students received Pell Grants, with awards averaging $5,078. In terms of personnel, the university employs approximately 271 full-time equivalent staff according to IPEDS data. Top academic majors in terms of enrollment include psychology, criminal justice, business, and biology, to name a few. The HBCU awards several degrees including bachelor's, master's, and doctoral (i.e., doctor of ministry). Figure 11.2 presents a summary of degree production.

In keeping with the epistemological and methodological expectations of case study tradition (Yin, 2002), the balance of this chapter is based on "an in-depth, multifaceted investigation using qualitative research methods, of a single social phenomenon ... conducted in great detail and often [relying] on the use of several data sources" (Orum et al., 1991, p. 2). Specifically, three promising practices were identified that helped to foster or maintain students' academic belonging amid the Great Pandemic, by establishing new or revising existing campus services, supports, and personnel. These are discussed in the next section.

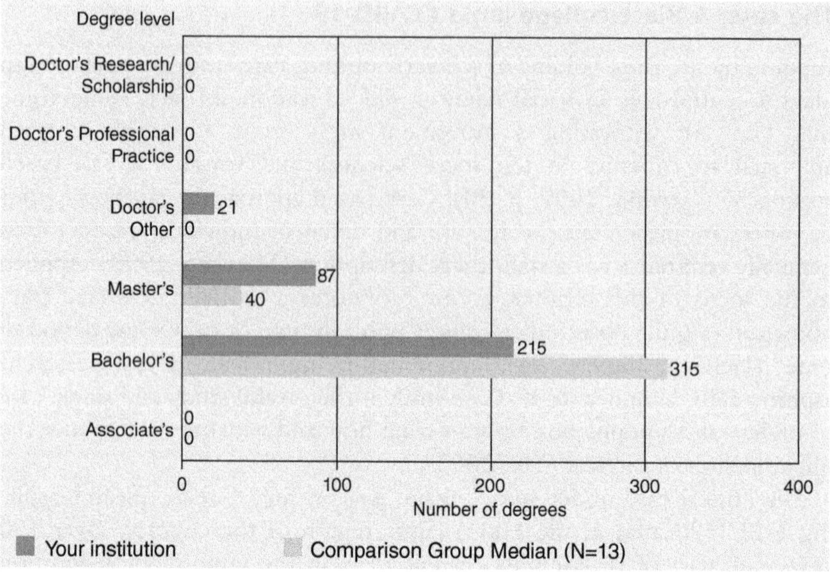

FIGURE 11.2 Number of degrees awarded, by level: 2019–2020.
Note. N is the number of institutions in the comparison group.
Source. Institute of Education Sciences, National Center for Education Statistics.
(2020).

What worked: #HBCU4Help

A major component of college students' sense of academic belonging is based on their perceptions about the accessibility, availability, quality, and utility of existing programs and support services designed to ensure academic success (Nunn, 2021). Several points deserve mention. First, as I've said elsewhere (Strayhorn, 2019), sense of belonging is *not* about the mere availability of targeted assistance or campus services. I hear time and time again from senior leaders, "Yes, we have need-based aid … we have a writing center … we have a clothing closet" and so much more. But availability does not guarantee accessibility (i.e., that students know where it is), affordability (i.e., that they can pay for it, if needed), usability, or high quality. Just as *all students* want to belong, research has consistently shown that *all students* need help at some point in their college journey; they vary, however, in the type and amount (i.e., dosage) of assistance needed (Strayhorn, 2021a). Students' need for help can be greater during moments of uncertainty, transition, and displacement, which certainly was the case for college life amid COVID-19.

To reduce feelings of academic uncertainty (Lewis & Hodges, 2015) and ease students' transition to online (remote) teaching and learning, the

HBCU under study established a #4Help campus-wide initiative, largely comprising a student volunteer–run webpage, a staff-monitored email portal, a social media campaign, and intrusive e-advising strategy.[1] For instance, we learned from analysis of "voice of customer" surveys, conducted by the institution after rolling out these new innovations, that students had a bulk of questions amid the pandemic, ranging from "How do I get my books?" and "Are academic advisors available via Zoom?" to "Can I stop by the library?" and "Where can I get tutoring?," to name a few. Each of these can have significant influence on students' academic belonging. For starters, it's hard to feel like you belong when you're filled with more questions than answers. But also, not knowing where to turn for guidance and help can undermine academic confidence and achievement.

The #4Help campus-wide initiative aimed to reduce academic doubt, uncertainty, and self-doubt at the individual level by *institutionalizing* (Kezar, 2008) fresh commitments to student success, 24/7 support, and "student-centeredness" at the organizational level. For instance, apart from working with staff in information technology to setup a "4 Help" email address that could be monitored by designated staff, the president and pro-vost helped transform the structure by communicating a clear vision, setting priorities (and goals) with solid metrics (called key performance indicators), and creating campus-wide academic support systems. Other senior leaders (e.g., deans, chairs) helped boost students' academic belonging by nudging excellent customer service among advisors, ensuring timely responses to student inquiries, and incentivizing faculty–student engagement via online service learning, research, and study away.

Ultimately, by answering their questions; providing accurate, timely academic information; and offering multiple ways for students to contact the campus remotely, the HBCU signaled to students that they matter, they're not alone, and they belong academically. One student's comment captures the heart of many others shared in online interviews:

> The pandemic made it hard for us, as students, because we were unsure about everything, all of a sudden. The #4Help campaign put a lot of those questions to rest because *finally* [emphasis added] we had some people to answer questions, email forms, reset log-ins and stuff, you know. That really helped me feel calm and better despite the world's being on fire.
>
> *(Leslie,[2] sophomore, psychology major)*

What worked: Meeting basic needs

Not only is college students' sense of belonging dependent on their ability to find answers to their questions, but it's also related to satisfying one's basic, fundamental needs. As humans, we all have basic needs – physiologically, they are as simple as air, water, food, shelter, and sleep (Strayhorn, 2019), as shown in Figure 11.3. Basic needs insecurities are a major issue facing higher education, especially among those with the fewest resources, including economically disadvantaged, Pell Grant–eligible, low-income, former foster, and/or ethnic minority students (Broton & Goldrick-Rab, 2018). When these fundamental needs are not satisfied, it's difficult, if not impossible, for such students to concentrate in class, study for tests, complete assignments, and feel like they belong academically.

Unfortunately, college students' basic needs insecurities were exacerbated by record-breaking homelessness, hunger, and (un-)/underemployment rates during the Great Pandemic. To help fight basic needs insecurities and ensure that *all students* have access to healthy food options,[3] adequate clothing, shoes, and personal hygiene products, this HBCU significantly expanded existing programs and services, namely, a campus-based pantry, through strategic partnerships with local agencies (e.g., food bank), alumni affairs, and several locally owned restaurants. Although COVID-19 protocol cut off campus access for most students and prohibited students (or staff) from entering the premises without vaccination, the dean of students was authorized to approve "temporary access" for any currently enrolled students with demonstrated need to visit the pantry located in the student union, as long as they followed all other safety procedures (e.g., face covering, temperature checks). Another component of #4Help efforts aimed to help unemployed, homeless, and/or housing-/food insecure students access and utilize Supplementary Nutrition Assistance Program (SNAP) benefits, also known as "food stamps," leveraging the expertise of social work faculty

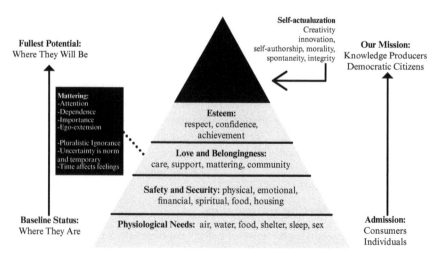

FIGURE 11.3 Strayhorn's (2019) belonging model, highlighting basic needs.

and local agencies. By ensuring that *all* students had access to food, clothing, and adequate shelter, the HBCU under study addressed students' basic needs in ways that freed up cognitive bandwidth that could be redirected or channeled toward fostering and maintaining their academic belonging.

To be sure, pantries and social safety nets are far from new or innovative. Pantries, in most cases, serve as closets or holding spaces for donated food, drinks, clothes, shoes, and supplies (Ford, 2019), provided to students free of charge (Freudenberg et al., 2019). Experts champion university-based, -funded, and -sponsored pantries (see Goldrick-Rab et al., 2021), with few exceptions. Additionally, though many more students qualify for SNAP benefits than who receive them, there are many complicated federal rules and regulations governing access to these provisions. By attending to students' basic needs and insecurities (i.e., food, housing, and otherwise) and supplying them with resources to access adequate food and clothing, this HBCU developed a multipronged strategy for giving students what they need to excel academically. The evidence is clear that satisfying students' basic needs has long-term positive associations with health and academic achievement among college students, which, in turn, facilitates academic belonging (Leung et al., 2021; Strayhorn, 2021b). The institution also exhibited the "culture of care" communicated by senior leaders, which likely signaled *institutional integrity* to students who value "keepin' it real," quoting modern vernacular. It also signaled that students are important, valued members of the institution's academic community who matter and belong, just as they are.

Data from interviews and surveys provide evidence of how students experienced these #4Help efforts. Students agreed that the #4Help online support program had a noticeable impact on their academic belonging. Students reported feeling more connected to their classmates and professors, as well as having access to helpful resources for basic needs and support from "knowledgeable [informal] mentors" through the program. Many students expressed gratitude for the emotional and academic support they received through #4Help, which enabled them to navigate the stresses of college life amid the pandemic and stay on track academically. For instance, one put it this way: "There's just no way that I could have survived the pandemic without #4Help; it was like, for the first time, I had someone on my side who was available around the clock to keep me motivated and on track, despite COVID-related setbacks."

What worked: Supplying hi-tech needs

Academic success in college requires hard work even in normal times, but the pandemic ushered in a "new normal" marked by formidable academic challenges facing faculty, staff, and students that required greater than usual hope, optimism, and resilience. For instance, it is difficult to perform well academically in most colleges without adequate technology (Kuh & Hu, 2001), but the pandemic forced teaching and learning entirely online, making stable, consistent internet connectivity (i.e., WiFi); a laptop; and, in some cases, advanced technologies that allow for video- and/or voice conferencing, high-quality audio reception (e.g., earbuds), and electronic communication absolute essentials. Technology and computer equipment are *not* free, and higher education had a "digital divide" marked by racial and socioeconomic gaps (Vinson, 2007) long before the first sign of COVID-19 appeared in spring 2020.

To help bridge the digital divide and equip students with the technology they needed to thrive during the pandemic, this HBCU established a partnership with Apple, giving all incoming, first-time, full-time freshmen a state-of-the-art iPad, wireless AirPods, and smart watch that could be used in classes. For transfer, upperclassmen, and graduate students, the institution leveraged federal CARES dollars to purchase additional iPads and expand its existing stock of loaner laptops, mobile hotspots, and learning technologies (e.g., Jenzabar modules, Canvas trainings). For instance, prior to taking these steps, over 50% of students reported difficulty accessing the learning management system (LMS), course materials, prerecorded lectures, and "live" class sessions via Microsoft (MS) Teams, Zoom, and/or Google Meet, depending on the instructor's preferred platform. The Division of Academic Affairs addressed this widespread problem by standardizing expectations for online teaching: faculty were trained, supported, and assisted in transitioning all course(s) and required materials to the university's new LMS, hosting "live" classes via MS Teams (which integrates easily into the LMS), and using lecture-capture tools like Kaltura to produce high-quality, portable videos, to name a few. Additionally, faculty were trained on holding "office hours" via videoconference and providing growth-minded feedback (Dweck, 2007) to students using "track changes" in MS Word, just as examples. All of these learning innovations were mobile device optimized, making them easy to access using students' Apple products, campus loaner laptops, or personal devices.

Benefits associated with these structural changes were many. First, analyses of data from our student information system suggested an uptick in virtual class attendance. This makes sense – by giving students the technology they need to attend class online (e.g., device, WiFi), many more were able to do so. It's not just that; data also clearly indicated that students reported feeling greater confidence in their ability to succeed in online courses as a result of these changes, which directly related to their sense of academic belonging (Means & Pyne, 2017).

Other results indicate improvements in learning engagement, as defined by (a) the number of times students log in to the LMS per week, (b) the duration of students' time in LMS per log-in, (c) percentage of students submitting assignments per class, and (d) percentage of students with complete personal profile, biography, and/or photo or avatar. All of these are important predictors of college student academic achievement, as learning engagement has been consistently correlated with grades, retention, and persistence (e.g., Cokley & Moore, 2007; Greene et al., 2008). Moreover, when students are engaged in their own learning, they are more likely to feel a sense of academic belonging (Means & Pyne, 2017; Patterson Silver Wolf et al., 2017; Strayhorn, 2019). One student said it best in a "student voice" focus group conducted by the author via Zoom:

> I would definitely say it all helped me feel like I truly belonged [academically] at [said institution] because I could stop worrying about how I would get this or get that ... or pay for this or do my homework at McDonald's so I could have good WiFi, you know. I had what I needed and could focus on class[-es] and doing good.
>
> *(Moriah, junior, criminal justice major)*

Conclusion

To wrap up, recall the purpose of the present chapter: to present a case study of how a 4-year private HBCU fostered and maintained students' sense of academic belonging, despite challenges and threats posed by the COVID-19 pandemic. Using a multilevel, multifaceted sense of belonging framework, the chapter revealed how campus leaders, faculty, and staff took intentional steps to (re)create high-touch and high-tech conditions for belonging, especially academic belonging, in a physically distanced and touchless era. Specifically, the institution took intentional steps to meet students where they were by offering 24/7 academic help (e.g., #4Help, e-advising) to satisfy their basic physiological and learning needs, while also providing the technology and support services needed to facilitate educationally purposeful faculty–student relationships, provide service-learning opportunities, and enable academic belonging in a remote learning environment.

Though hard to believe, it has been over 3 years since the first *announced* case of COVID-19 in the United States. Face masks – once worn by everyone, everywhere – are optional again. After several successful vaccination programs against Delta, Omicron, and XBB variants, the World Health Organization has declared that COVID-19 is no longer a global health emergency, shifting from pandemic to endemic status. And despite all that has changed since 2020, some lessons learned during the pandemic are not just good for crisis management; they're good for business and good educational practices. For instance, meeting students where they are, as they are, positions us to build inclusive learning spaces, formulate equitable policies, and enact supportive practices that ensure student success. Investing in faculty/staff development through technology training and upskilling in digital services is one way of showing people that you care about *them* and their long-term productivity, which is directly related to workplace belonging (Strayhorn, in press). Showing students grace in times of stress and strain, rather than merely subscribing to a purely punitive system, is educational justice at its finest. By providing help, meeting basic needs, and supplying high-tech support to students, faculty, and staff, we're nurturing strong learning partnerships, freeing up bandwidth that can be redirected to academic tasks, and accelerating the speed at which students access, assess, and acquire new information.

Lastly, evidence highlighted in this chapter demonstrates *what worked* in responding to student needs during the pandemic. That's not to say that everything worked. In fact, some things did not work or required significant (and, at times, costly) adjustments. For instance, in terms of #4Help, we learned that a single, designated point person is better than three different volunteer student workers who were likely juggling coursework, busy work schedules, and competing priorities that led to duplication of efforts, multiple responses to the same inquiry, and variable quality in terms of their responses. First-wave assessment results revealed these issues, and we course-corrected by restructuring the initiative with a single designated point person (full-time staff) who oversaw, trained, and supervised student workers paid hourly. It's also true that we saw immediate gains from the e-advising efforts, although, in some cases, we learned that the "advising trees" – a local term referring to the flow of decisions for any given program of study – were inaccurate, incomplete, or wholly incorrect, presenting students and advisors with course options that were no longer offered by the program, instructors no longer in the department, or upper-level courses without necessary prerequisites. This challenge gave us an opportunity to innovate with online advising, while simultaneously refreshing the curriculum. As an experienced chief academic officer and belonging scholar, I urge readers to remember that boosting academic belonging is a journey not a destination, full of trial and error, challenges, and successes. Using evidence-based information like that presented in this chapter and throughout the entire volume will increase the likelihood that our successes will far outweigh the former.

Notes

1 E-advising refers to a process where advisors assist, coach, or empower students with academic decisions using technology tools (e.g., text messaging, email, video conferencing), as described elsewhere (Mendez & Arguello, 2020).
2 Student names are pseudonyms, selected by either the participant or chapter author.
3 *Food insecurity* refers to "the limited or uncertain availability of nutritionally adequate and safe foods, or the ability to acquire such foods in a socially acceptable manner" (Broton & Goldrick-Rab, 2018, p. 122).

References

Anderman, L. H., & Freeman, T. M. (2004). Students' sense of belonging in school. In M. L. Maehr & P. R. Pintrich (Eds.), *Advances in motivation and achievement: Vol. 13 Motivating students, improving schools: The legacy of Carol Midgley* (pp. 27–63). Elsevier.

Baumeister, R. F., & Leary, M. R. (1995). The need to belong: Desire for interpersonal attachment as a fundamental human motivation. *Psychological Bulletin*, 117, 497–529.

Beal, P. E., & Noel, L. (1980). *What works in retention*. American College Testing Program.

Blackmon, Z. R., O'Hara, R. M., & Viars, J. W. (2020). Microaggressions, sense of belonging & sexual identity in the residential environment. *Journal of College & University Student Housing*, 46(3), 46–59.

Broton, K. M., & Goldrick-Rab, S. (2018). Going without: An exploration of food and housing insecurity among undergraduates. *Educational Researcher*, 47(2), 121–133. doi:10.3102/0013189X17741303

Cokley, K., & Moore, P. (2007). Moderating and mediating effects of gender and psychological disengagement on the academic achievement of African American college students. *Journal of Black Psychology*, 33, 169–187.

Dweck, C. (2007). *Mindset: The new psychology of success*. Ballantine.

Fisher, L. B., Overholser, J. C., Ridley, J., Braden, A., & Rosoff, C. (2015). From the outside looking in: Sense of belonging, depression, and suicide risk. *Psychiatry*, 78(1), 29–41. doi:10.1080/00332747.2015.1015867

Ford, M. (2019). Clothing closet helps students dress for success. *UWIRE Text*, 1. https://link.gale.com/apps/doc/A573871527

Freudenberg, N., Goldrick-Rab, S., & Poppendieck, J. (2019). College students and SNAP: The new face of food insecurity in the United States. *American Journal of Public Health*, 109(12), 1652–1658. https://ajph.aphapublications.org/doi/pdf/10.2105/AJPH.2019.305332?casa_token=luztZL4m-fYAAAAA:s AnbUcpTUTOInRJyn_KK9kXiO2VRky6-Ny7Rv5BJUWaYK59-d-o1m23T6kA G5JzB4n8hh0Iqw3Fm

Garvey, J. C., Arámbula Ballysingh, T., Bowley Dow, L., Howard, B. L., Ingram, A. N., & Carlson, M. (2020). Where I sleep: The relationship with residential environments and first-generation belongingness. *College Student Affairs Journal*, 38(1), 16–33.

Gerring, J. (2009). The case study: What it is and what it does. In C. Boix & S. C. Stokes (Eds.), *The Oxford handbook for comparative politics* (pp. 90–122). Oxford University Press. doi:10.1093/oxfordhb/9780199566020.003.0004

Goldrick-Rab, S., Coca, V., Kienzl, G. S., Welton, C. R., Dahl, S., & Magnelia, S. (2021). *#RealCollege during the pandemic: New evidence on basic needs insecurity and student well-being*. Hope Center, Temple University.

Greene, T. G., Marti, C. N., & McClenney, K. (2008). The effort–outcome gap: Differences for African American and Hispanic community college students in student engagement and academic achievement. *The Journal of Higher Education*, 79(5), 513–539.

Hagerty, B. M. K., Lynch-Bauer, J., Patusky, K., Bouwsema, M., & Collier, P. J. (1992). Sense of belonging: A vital mental health concept. *Archives of Psychiatric Nursing*, 6, 172–177.

Hale, C. J., Hannum, J. W., & Espelage, D. L. (2005). Social support and physical health: The importance of belonging. *Journal of American College Health*, 53, 276–284.

Hausmann, L. R. M., Schofield, J. W., & Woods, R. L. (2006, June 22–25). *Sense of belonging as a predictor of intentions to persist among African American and White first-year college students* [Paper presentation]. Biannual Meeting of the Society for the Psychological Student of Social Issues, Long Beach, CA, United States.

Hoffman, J. L. (2002). The impact of student cocurricular involvement on student success: Racial and religious differences. *Journal of College Student Development*, 43(5), 712–739.

Institute of Education Sciences, National Center for Education Statistics. (2020). *Integrated Postsecondary Education Data System (IPEDS): Fall 2020, Completions component.*

Jacoby, B., & Garland, J. (2004). Strategies for enhancing commuter student success. *Journal of College Student Retention: Research, Theory, & Practice*, 6(1), 61–79.

Kezar, A. (2008). Understanding leadership strategies for addressing the politics of diversity. *Journal of Higher Education*, 79(4), 406–441.

Komisarof, A. (2018). A new framework of workplace acculturation: The need to belong and constructing ontological interpretive spaces. *Journal of Intercultural Communication*, 21, 15–37.

Komisarof, A. (2021). A new framework of workplace belonging: Instrument validation and testing relationships to crucial acculturation outcomes. *Journal of International Intercultural Communication*, 15(3), 311–332. doi:10.1080/17513057.2021.189152

Kuh, G. D., & Hu, S. (2001). The relationships between computer and information technology use, selected learning and personal development outcomes, and other college experiences. *Journal of College Student Development*, 42(3), 217–232.

Leung, C. W., Farooqui, S., Wolfson, J. A., & Cohen, A. J. (2021). Understanding the cumulative burden of basic needs insecurities: Associations with health and academic achievement among college students. *American Journal of Health Promotion*, 35(2), 275–278. doi:10.1177/0890117120946210

Lewis, K. L., & Hodges, S. D. (2015). Expanding the concept of belonging in academic domains: Development and validation of the ability uncertainty scale. *Learning & Individual Differences*, 37, 197–202.

McMillan, D. W., & Chavis, D. M. (1986). Sense of community: A definition and theory. *Journal of Community Psychology*, 14, 6–23.

Means, D. R., & Pyne, K. B. (2017). Finding my way: Perceptions of institutional support and belonging in low-income, first-generation, first-year college students. *Journal of College Student Development*, 58(6), 907–924.

Mendez, M. G., & Arguello, G. (2020). Best practices of virtual advising: The application of an online advising portal. *FDLA Journal*, 5(6), 1–8.

Merriam, S. B. (1998). *Qualitative research and case study applications in education.* Jossey-Bass.

Nunn, L. M. (2021). *College belonging: How first-year and first-generation students navigate campus life.* Rutgers University Press.

Orum, A. M., Feagin, J. R., & Sjoberg, G. (1991). Introduction. In J. R. Feagin, A. M. Orum, & G. Sjoberg (Eds.), *A case for the case study* (pp. 1–26). University of North Carolina Press.

Patterson Silver Wolf, D. A., Perkins, J., Butler-Barnes, S. T., & Walker, T. (2017). Social belonging and college retention: Results from a quasi-experimental pilot study. *Journal of College Student Development*, 58(5), 777–782.

Rosenberg, M., & McCullough, B. C. (1981). Mattering: Inferred significance and mental health among adolescents. *Research in Community Mental Health*, 2, 163–182.

Sohrabi, C., Alsafi, Z., O'Neill, N., Khan, M., Kerwan, A., Al-Jabir, A., Iosifidis, C., & Agha, R. (2020). World Health Organization declares global emergency: A review of the 2019 novel coronavirus (COVID-19). *International Journal of Surgery*, 76, 71–76. doi:10.1016/j.ijsu.2020.02.034

Stake, R. E. (1998). Case studies. In N. Denzin & Y. Lincoln (Eds.), *Strategies of qualitative inquiry* (pp. 86–109). Sage.

Steele, C. M. (1997). A threat in the air: How stereotypes shape intellectual identity and performance. *American Psychologist*, 52(6), 613–629. doi:10.1037/0003-066X.52.6.613

Strayhorn, T. L. (2019). *College students' sense of belonging: A key to educational success for all students* (2nd ed.). Routledge.

Strayhorn, T. L. (2020a). *How we win the war against coronavirus: Staying connected while physical distancing*. Thrive Global. https://thriveglobal.com/stories/how-we-win-the-war-against-coronavirus/

Strayhorn, T. L. (2020b). Sense of belonging predicts persistence intentions among diverse dental education students: A multi-institutional investigation. *Journal of Dental Education*, 84(10), 1136–1142. doi:10.1002/jdd.12243

Strayhorn, T. L. (2021a). Analyzing the short-term impact of a brief web-based intervention on first-year students' sense of belonging at an HBCU: A quasi-experimental study. *Innovative Higher Education*, 48, 1–13. doi:10.1007/s10755-021-09559-5

Strayhorn, T. L. (2021b). Investigating the impact of COVID-19 on basic needs security among vulnerable college students: An exploratory study. *Academia Letters*, Article 1786. https://doi.org/10.20935/AL1786

Strayhorn, T. L. (in press). *Workplace belonging*. DIO Press.

Tovar, E., & Simon, M. A. (2010). Factorial structure and invariance analysis of the sense of belonging scales. *Measurement and Evaluation in Counseling and Development*, 43, 199–217.

Vinson, B. M. (2007). African American millennial college students and the impact of the digital divide. *National Association of Student Affairs Professionals Journal*, 10(1), 63–69.

Yin, R. K. (2002). *Case study research: Design and methods*. Sage.

PART V

Exploring the opportunities and limits of belonging

12

REFLECTIONS ON THE WALKING INTERVIEW APPROACH TO EXAMINING UNIVERSITY STUDENTS' SENSE OF BELONGING

Julianne K. Viola and Eliel Cohen

Contextualizing our research setting

In recent years, universities in the UK have been subject to calls to become more socially just, inclusive, and supportive institutions (Banerjee, 2018). This has coincided with, and in large part been driven by, an increasing number and range of people entering the sector, such as international students (Bolton & Lewis, 2022) and people from traditionally underrepresented groups; for example, people from low socioeconomic status backgrounds (O'Sullivan et al., 2019). Many institutions across the UK, including Imperial College London where the research in this chapter is based, are making sweeping changes across specific parts of the educational experience, partly in response to new regulatory requirements and attainment gaps across sociodemographic characteristics (Kandiko Howson & Kingsbury, 2021). Relatedly, the higher education literature has become increasingly interested in how differences in background, identity, and social capital influence students' experiences of, success in, and rewards from university (Greenbank, 2006; Harrison, 2011). There has also been a steadily increasing interest in students' sense of belonging and well-being because these factors are important to students' experience and success (Ahn & Davis, 2020; Meehan & Howells, 2019).

England's higher education regulatory body, the Office for Students, instituted Access and Participation Plans for individual universities to ensure that they improve equality of opportunity for underrepresented groups to access, succeed in, and progress from higher education (Office for Students, 2022). This chapter focuses specifically on Imperial College London, an elite, research-intensive university focused on science, technology,

DOI: 10.4324/9781003443735-17

engineering, mathematics, medicine, and business (STEMMB) subjects, where 65.8% of students come from state schools,[1] compared to 90.1% of university students across England as a whole (HESA, 2022). Imperial also has a below average percentage of undergraduate entrants from low participation neighborhoods (HESA, 2022). This is partly due to the STEMMB context of Imperial, where the courses require a higher expectation of mathematical qualification, which is difficult to attain in state secondary schools in underserved areas, which are less likely to offer higher level mathematics. Imperial is working toward making its STEMMB higher education more accessible to these groups through a variety of outreach activities, including summer schools, to help reduce these gaps (Imperial College London, 2022).

Learning and teaching strategies are common among UK universities and often provide a framework that links institutional teaching, support, and assessment practices to national-level guidelines and have benchmarks and requirements related to quality and equality. In addition to this framework, Imperial's Learning and Teaching Strategy recognized that to remain a competitive university, it required evidence-based curriculum design and pedagogy that were guided by a view of what a distinctively "Imperial Education" should look like and achieve. Imperial's Strategy was developed through extensive consultation with students and academic and non-academic staff, alongside an institution-wide review to update curricular content to foster innovation and discovery-based learning opportunities to better serve our students (Imperial College London, 2017a). Together with academic features, such as being research based, providing disciplinary depth, and increasing the use of small-group tutorials and active learning pedagogies, the Strategy committed to funding internal research to promoting an inclusive and supportive environment and enhancing belonging and well-being through, for example, teaching and assessment practices, pastoral care, and improvements in physical and social spaces (Imperial College London, 2017b).

Beyond incremental updates to curriculum, the Learning and Teaching Strategy (2017–2027) challenged the assumptions that STEMMB education utilizes specific pedagogy and that personal experiences, like identity and belonging, do not matter in an educational context. Even before the consultation phase discussed above, the Strategy demonstrated Imperial's commitment to teaching and to its students; the pedagogical research and evaluation projects that have come from the Strategy (including ours) enable a change in culture at the institution, and more widely across the sector, to recognize the importance of students' sense of belonging, well-being, and agency.

Beyond supporting research conducted by individuals within academic departments, Imperial also established the Centre of Higher Education Research and Scholarship (CHERS) to both support department-based research and conduct its own college-wide research. We, the authors, joined

CHERS at its inception. Our primary research is the ongoing "Belonging, Engagement and Community" project (hereafter the Belonging project), a mixed methods study that has captured the views and experiences of over 850 students across the university to date. In this chapter, we reflect on the methods used and key insights gained from this work and draw attention to walking interviews, which offer unique insights into student belonging.

Belonging, engagement, and community study

Since 2019, we have collaborated on the Belonging project, which is a longitudinal study conducted across all faculties and course levels at Imperial to understand how its students conceptualize belonging and the factors that influence their belonging at university. There is widespread agreement in the field that the concept of belonging is undefined (Antonsich, 2010; Healy & Richardson, 2017) and complex. At the start of our research, we conceptualized belonging as an emotional sense of connection to a community. The Belonging project found that our students experience and define belonging as shared values and interests, feeling at home, and feeling a sense of connection to others (Viola, 2021).

In their review of over 300 empirical studies within social and personality psychology, sociology, and anthropology, Baumeister and Leary (1995) concluded that belonging is a human need that can be experienced even without having things in common with the group. In the education context, we look to Goodenow's (1993) definition of belonging and apply it as:

> students' sense of being accepted, valued, included, and encouraged by others in the academic classroom setting and feeling oneself to be an important part of the life and activity of the class … it also involves support and respect for personal autonomy and for the student as an individual.
>
> *(p. 25)*

While there has been a limited focus on place and belonging at university, place is key to shaping belonging and "ways of being" at university (Habib & Ward, 2019, p. 3). Similarly, the idea of community as both interpersonal relationships (Pooley et al., 2002) and commonality (Cassidy, 2019) can also include social space, which is "created and maintained by people who have the necessity or the desire of a safe shared space" (Miño-Puigcercós et al., 2019, p. 124).

Sense of belonging is a composite construct and can be analyzed in terms of students' perceptions of what it means to belong in/to higher education, the various components of and barriers to belonging, and the various ways and places in which they do and do not feel that they belong. Accordingly, the Belonging study gave us significant opportunity to understand the multiple aspects and dimensions of students' sense of belonging. More in-depth descriptions and analyses of our research methods are available in works published previously (Cohen & Viola, 2022; Viola, 2021), but we briefly summarize them here to highlight that place is central to belonging, and the walking interview method we highlight ought to become a more broadly used method in future belonging research to capture a holistic student experience of belonging.

Overview of Belonging project methods

Since the Belonging project aims, in part, to enhance and evaluate the medium-to long-term goals of the institution-wide Learning and Teaching Strategy, we intended to be as inclusive and comprehensive as possible in recruitment. The project remains ongoing and has so far recruited over 850 students of all course levels, departments, and faculties for participation in our research across all nine Imperial campuses. We invited students to participate in either an online questionnaire, one-to-one interview, or both. The online questionnaire included a single open-ended question that asked participants to write down 10 words that came to mind when they think about belonging to Imperial (Ahn & Davis, 2020), followed by a 10-item scale drawing on preexisting validated sense of belonging scales (Gehlbach et al., 2015; Yorke, 2016). Participants chose among one of five verbally labelled response options, which allowed us to infer the extent to which students feel they belong academically and socially and to compare this with how students self-assess their overall level of belonging at Imperial (Cohen & Viola, 2022; Viola, 2021).

Interview participants were asked to choose between a standard interview or a walking interview. Both types of interviews were designed as semistructured to provide students the opportunity to discuss their experiences of belonging and not-belonging. Due to the COVID-19 pandemic, we have conducted fewer walking interviews than we would have liked (five interviews as of this publication). However, when analyzed against the backdrop of the survey and standard interview data, the walking interviews offer distinctively rich insights and a highly valuable addition to the surveys and the semistructured interviews that dominate the methods in the literature on student belonging. We discuss the method and its benefits below, along with some practical suggestions about using the method.

Walking interviews: The method

Holton and Riley (2014) used walking interviews to study students' experiences and understandings of university towns and cities. As place-based interviews embody a "sensing of place" and reveal how people and places interact (Reed, 2002, p. 129), we opted for this method to prompt participants and encourage critical thinking regarding their interpretations of the spaces they inhabit (Anderson & Jones, 2009; Porter et al., 2010).

Walking interviews normally take one of two forms: (a) following fixed routes to record a participant's first impression of a place or their response to a specific route or (b) allowing the participant to lead and move freely about the location (Jones et al., 2008). We chose the latter, asking participants to take us to parts of campus and the surrounding area that have meaning for them as part of their everyday journeys (Kusenbach, 2003) or where they go at certain times or associate with certain meaningful events, feelings, or experiences, to prompt them to describe their experience in relation to place (Holton & Riley, 2014). As we found, this can also include places that are *not* part of students' daily or regular experience but that nonetheless have important meanings for them, like symbolizing aspirations.

This approach aligns well with our project and the Learning and Teaching Strategy more broadly by positioning the student participant as co-leader of the interview, which encourages a sense of agency and an engaged reflection on their educational and broader experience at university. This generates rich qualitative data while enhancing students' sense of learner identity and development. Moreover, providing students with the opportunity to lead us to spaces that are meaningful to them, and where they experience belonging, may expand our understanding of what belonging looks like for students.

We took as neutral an approach as possible in developing and enacting the interview protocol, to best allow the participant to interpret our questions in their own way and guide us on their own path around Imperial grounds, rather than suggesting they take us to places that elicit more positive or negative emotions by being there. Our walking interview protocol is available as an appendix and includes prompts such as "Can you tell me why this place came to mind?" and "How do you think this place would make you feel if you were to revisit it years after you leave Imperial?"

Occasionally, we used additional prompts from the semistructured interview protocol to connect the discussion about the places we visited on the walking interview to the participants' experiences of belonging, such as "What does it mean for you to feel 'at home'?" and "Think about the places you call home, or 'communities' you feel a part of. Can you tell me about any involvement you have with these communities?"

Ethics and practical considerations

We obtained ethical clearance for the research from our institution's education ethics review process. We explained to participants that there may be some spaces where it might not be appropriate for researchers to enter and that if we encounter someone they know during the interview, that person would have to consent to the research before continuing to record the interview.

Should educators choose to conduct research using walking interviews, they may face an ethical barrier related to the position of power that the educators hold. As independent researchers, we did not experience this barrier, but this power dynamic is important to be mindful of, as it can lead to feelings of coercion for the student to participate, as well as potential bias in the responses. Different places also have different meanings and power relations associated with them (Elwood & Martin, 2000), prompting the researcher to take an active role in interpreting the actions of the participant and their surroundings (Anderson, 2004). These issues of power as they relate to space are important to consider (Jones et al., 2008) and can be mitigated by the method itself, which enables participants to feel more confident and comfortable in the interview through the reversal of the traditional interviewer/interviewee roles (Holton & Riley, 2014) and because they are familiar with the space (Butler & Derrett, 2014; Trell & Van Hoven, 2010).

Reflections on our walking interviews

Building rapport and student agency

We first met participants in a meeting room to review the participant information sheet and consent form. We invited participants to answer a few questions from the semistructured interview protocol before the walking interview. In some cases, this pre-walk discussion covered the standard semistructured interview protocol in such depth that we effectively conducted two interviews with the same participant, one in-office and one walking interview. In some cases, these interview encounters lasted more than 2 hours.

We found that the walking interview created a more relaxed and positive atmosphere. The conversation was more organic (Kusenbach, 2003), and because the students led the way, they had a greater amount of agency, improving our rapport with them (Holton & Riley, 2014). We believe this more relaxed, open conversation allowed the participants to engage more with the experience and may explain the higher rate of participation in follow-up interviews among walking interview participants (60% compared with an overall rate of approximately 25%).

The relaxed manner of the interview allowed students to casually take us through places important to them. Some typical examples of the organic way in which participants took control and led the walk include students gesturing to specific areas or objects and relating them to their experience as a student:

> I spend a lot of my time in the Chemistry Café. … And then come to this room, when it isn't used for tutorials, we can just go in and work. When I'm with my friends, we typically eat lunch in one of those free tutorial rooms.
>
> *(Undergraduate chemistry student)*

We noticed that over the course of the interview, we spent more time in and around the places where the student spent more of their time, which suggests a level of connection to spaces that may shape student sense of belonging. As we walked past a magazine stand in the corridor outside *The Felix*, Imperial's student newspaper, an undergraduate aeronautics student noted:

> *The Felix* is probably the best thing Imperial does. Amazing. I remember the first issue that I read was talking about all the different courses at Imperial and people were like, "Biological sciences isn't even an actual science" or something and they were ranting about how "business and biology is stupid, and maths and physics and engineering are like the future of the world." That was quite funny.

The above examples also demonstrate the importance of serendipity and the potential value of this for research findings. For example, in a standard interview in a meeting room, the meaning that the department café and the university magazine hold for students and their sense of belonging would most likely not have been revealed.

The aeronautics undergraduate student also felt comfortable sharing more about their experience of accessing mental health support, when they "struggled with the workload, drained and crying." Passing the library during the interview reminded this participant of the kindness that the library café staff shared when they noticed the student crying and offered support. Talking while walking provides many new stimulants for conversation and delays the time that the interview comes to a natural end, which allows the interviewer and participant to nurture rapport. This rapport is conducive to participants sharing about spaces and experiences that contribute to a sense of belonging in ways that may be less likely in the more formal setting of a standard meeting room interview.

Enhancing student reflexivity

Related to enhanced rapport and increased student agency, we also found that students on the walking interview became reflexive about their educational situation and experience. One undergraduate design engineering student reflected about how teaching staff's "spirit" affects students and that "the way they do things is important [for the learning experience]. Not what is taught, but the way it's done." Another participant noted that professors' focus on excitement for the subject, rather than grades, would make Imperial feel "more community-like." In our study, the notion of belonging in the academic sphere (Cohen & Viola, 2022) was clear when students discussed their interactions and relationships with teaching staff.

The value of the walking interview to understanding student academic belonging became stronger as we passed the building where chemistry labs are located, where one student described a positive relationship with her personal tutor[2] in the Chemistry Department, which began during her first week at Imperial. The tutor invited her to visit his lab, and she then applied for an Undergraduate Research Opportunities Programme (UROP)[3] in his group and was accepted into the UROP to start in the next term. The student worked in her personal tutor's lab throughout her first year and the summer holiday, which enabled her to develop a personal connection:

> I obviously chatted to him a lot about the research and science, but I also spent a lot of time just chatting about random things. ... Sometimes I'd just walk into his office and say, "Hi" and he would happily chat with me. Our relationship is even better now. I sometimes go climbing with him.

Passing the building where the student had her first interaction with her personal tutor prompted her to discuss the important connection she has with this educator, which has increased her sense of belonging within her academic discipline.

Some participants also utilized the opportunity of their participation in our study to reflect on the importance of community for their educational experience. One undergraduate medicine student was drawn to our study because "it was about communities, and I think that is possibly the most important factor in any working environment." This conversation highlighted the importance of the walking interview itself, how it enabled us to explore the places that hold meaning for students and their sense of connection to their peers, educators, and content, which is an important element of academic belonging.

Affordances of place-based interviews for understanding student agency and belonging

The decision to use this open, interpretivist research stemmed from our intrigue at its novelty and excitement about what unique findings would result from its use. One insight that we gained from using the walking interview method is that student participants tend to adopt a more critical tone when seated in the meeting room in comparison to the walk. Interestingly, three of our walking interview participants were international undergraduate engineering students, and all exhibited a pattern of spending most of the seated part of the interview criticizing their university experience as being not supportive of a sense of belonging. Then, when we moved to the walking interview, these students became balanced in discussion of their experience as the physical campus prompted their reflection on important and meaningful spaces. For example, one final-year student reflected negatively on his university experience, until we walked by the Imperial Enterprise Lab, where he said, "Ideas and people challenge the status quo." Here, he connected with new friends and collaborators with whom he worked on extracurricular projects. A second-year student first detailed her dissatisfaction with her decision to study at Imperial but while walking discussed her pride in her department's common room, how inspired she felt by certain workshops and equipment in the department, and how her relationship with library staff made her feel part of a community. A first-year student began the interview with feelings of loneliness due to lack of close relationships, and the walk prompted his reflection on common eating areas in both his university accommodation and in his department as valuable spaces for friendship and cultivating a sense of community and belonging.

Compared to traditional research methods, the walking interview provides spatial prompts to elicit participant reflections that may not otherwise come to light in a standard interview. For example, most walking interviewees mentioned the role that residence halls could play in promoting a sense of belonging, compared to only around one-third of other interviewees. One student shared how they feel part of their hall community and are "especially happy when we meet someone else from [the same hall]." Another discussed their flatmates and the time spent in their halls: "There's me and a Singaporean guy and another Chinese guy who always spend too long in the kitchen ... hours in the kitchen, just talking to each other." While other methods, like surveys, can ask students to consider spaces important to them, the walking interview enables participants to think critically about the spaces they inhabit (Porter et al., 2010). Walking interviews also allow for unique rapport building and a level of comfort in sharing these more personal spaces of living and belonging than surveys and traditional sit-down interviews may allow.

Concluding considerations for university educators who wish to use this method

When we first began the Belonging project in 2019, we interpreted our role at CHERS and Imperial's Learning and Teaching Strategy as efforts to instill a culture of ongoing educational research across the university to both improve students' educational experience and make Imperial a more inclusive and engaging environment. In this chapter, we have provided insight from our institutional context, discussed our keystone Belonging project, and detailed our experience of using walking interviews as a research method to understand student sense of belonging and simultaneously provide participants with greater opportunity to build their sense of agency in their university experience. Here, we conclude by briefly reflecting on wider work that we and others are doing across Imperial to both to contextualize and highlight the uniqueness of the insights from walking interviews.

Other work we have done to contribute to the institutional culture change includes developing an online Education Evaluation Toolkit (publicly available for internal and external use from Imperial College London, n.d.a) to encourage departments and individual academics to move beyond formal evaluation and feedback processes and to investigate other aspects of students' development and experience. We have also collaborated with educators and students in academic departments to conduct research of specific disciplinary relevance; for example, investigating how novel chemistry teaching methods can promote the self-efficacy of students with limited prior laboratory experience and promote a sense of belonging even after the sudden shift to remote teaching during the pandemic. Findings from the Belonging study have led to the development of a new module, "Learning as Belonging" on Imperial's postgraduate diploma in university learning and teaching. Ongoing research by our colleagues in CHERS works alongside the Belonging project to support the Learning and Teaching Strategy and facilitate culture change, including the Supporting the Identity Development of Underrepresented Students (SIDUS) project.

There is additional work across the university beyond our research and our Centre (CHERS), such as Imperial's recent successful application for the bronze award of the Race Equality Charter,[4] a UK sector-wide framework to promote universities' identification of and reflection on racial barriers to staff and students; educational research conducted by academics in their departments (Charalambous, 2020; Sbaiti et al., 2021); and StudentShapers,[5] which funds staff–student collaborative projects aiming to improve some aspect of the educational or broader experience of students. These opportunities are linked to institutional culture change to move the social capital of pedagogy beyond its more usual STEMMB limits.

The common thread linking this work is the genuine attempt to increase the role of students' voices and experiences in shaping the institution's understanding and improvement of students' educational, developmental, and social experience. Involving students more in conversations about and research into education is empowering and helps to develop agency, self-efficacy, and understanding of their own educational and professional goals (Neary, 2020; Oldfather, 1995). Our experience of the walking interview is that while it is too labor intensive as a single method of data collection, it is a very high "value-added" method in institutions where there already exists a motivation for research in this direction. For those who have tried understanding their students' experiences through surveys, focus groups, and interviews, we invite you consider and explore whether collecting data from walking interviews may be more illuminating than simply doing more of the same.

We encourage this kind of data collection to build understanding of students' sense of belonging at university and to contribute to building young people's self-efficacy and agency. Young people's relationships with other adults, particularly within the power structures of traditional educational settings, can influence students' self-efficacy when they view faculty and staff as having control over the institution and environment (Viola, 2020). With this in mind, we want to highlight a crucial advantage of walking interviews as a research method with university students, which is that it gives young people an opportunity to share their voice, which yields self-efficacy (Bandura, 2008). Successful experiences in sharing their voice can lead to a virtuous cycle of young people continuing to share voices and building a sense of empowerment among young people (Maddux & Gosselin, 2012; Zimmerman et al., 2019) and a sense of social support from the group they share their voice with (Guan & So, 2016). Walking interviews are therefore an important tool for understanding a broad range of student experiences and have great potential for continued investigations into student sense of belonging. Educators who are interested in doing their own research on belonging may utilize walking interviews to gain a holistic understanding of belonging and engagement among their students and advisees and to build a greater sense of community and belonging between students and educators.

Notes

1 State Schools in the UK are funded by local authorities (similar to public high schools in the United States).
2 Similar to a course advisor at an American university.
3 UROP allows undergraduate students to undertake formal research in their field to gain experience, develop/hone skills, and build their CV. More information is available from Imperial College London (n.d.c).
4 The Race Equality Charter provides a framework that encourages institutions to self-reflect on and identify institutional and cultural barriers that hinder Black, Asian, and minority ethnic staff and students. Bronze or Silver Race Equality Charter awards are given to member institutions, depending on their level of progress (Advance HE, n.d.).
5 StudentShapers was established by the Learning and Teaching Strategy and enables students to undertake projects in partnership with staff to "improve curricula, develop innovative teaching practices and make positive change to the student experience" (Imperial College London, n.d.b).

References

AdvanceHE. (n.d.). *Race Equality Charter.* https://www.advance-he.ac.uk/equality-charters/race-equality-charter

Ahn, M. Y., & Davis, H. H. (2020). Four domains of students' sense of belonging to university. *Studies in Higher Education*, 45(3), 622–634. doi:10.1080/03075079.2018.1564902

Anderson, J. (2004). Talking whilst walking: A geographical archaeology of knowledge. *Area*, 36(3), 254–261. doi:10.1111/j.0004-0894.2004.00222.x

Anderson, J., & Jones, K. (2009). The difference that place makes to methodology: Uncovering the "lived space" of young people's spatial practices. *Children's Geographies*, 7(3), 291–303. doi:10.1080/14733280903024456

Antonsich, M. (2010). Searching for belonging: An analytical framework. *Geography Compass*, 4(6), 644–659. doi:10.1111/j.1749-8198.2009.00317.x

Bandura, A. (2008). An agentic perspective on positive psychology. In S. Lopez (Ed.), *Positive psychology: Expecting the best in people* (pp. 167–196). Praeger.

Banerjee, P. A. (2018). Widening participation in higher education with a view to implementing institutional change. *Perspectives: Policy and Practice in Higher Education*, 22(3), 75–81. doi:10.1080/13603108.2018.1441198

Baumeister, R. F., & Leary, M. R. (1995). The need to belong: Desire for interpersonal attachments as a fundamental human motivation. *Psychological Bulletin*, 117, 497–529 doi:10.1037/0033-2909.117.3.497

Bolton, P., & Lewis, J. (2022). *International students in UK higher education: FAQs*. House of Commons Library.

Butler, M., & Derrett, S. (2014). The walking interview: An ethnographic approach to understanding disability. *The Internet Journal of Allied Health Sciences and Practice*, 12(3). doi:10.46743/1540-580x/2014.1491

Cassidy, K. J. (2019). Exploring the potential for community where diverse individuals belong. In S. Habib & M. R. Ward (Eds.), *Identities, youth and belonging: International perspectives* (pp. 141–157). Springer. doi:10.1007/978-3-319-96113-2_9

Charalambous, M. (2020). Variation in transition to university of life science students: Exploring the role of academic and social self-efficacy. *Journal of Further and Higher Education*, 44(10), 1419–1432. doi:10.1080/0309877X.2019.1690642

Cohen, E., & Viola, J. K. (2022). The role of pedagogy and the curriculum in university students' sense of belonging. *Journal of University Teaching & Learning Practice*, 19(4). https://ro.uow.edu.au/jutlp/vol19/iss4/06

Elwood, S. A., & Martin, D. G. (2000). "Placing" interviews: location and scales of power in qualitative research. *The Professional Geographer*, 52(4), 649–657. doi:10.1111/0033-0124.00253

Gehlbach, H., McIntyre, J., Viola, J. K., & Schueler, B. (2015). *Panorama Student Perception Survey: Psychometric properties*. Panorama Education. https://www.panoramaed.com/panorama-student-survey

Goodenow, C. (1993). Classroom belonging among early adolescent students: Relationships to motivation and achievement. *Journal of Early Adolescence*, 13(1), 21–43. doi:10.1177/0272431693013001002

Greenbank, P. (2006). Institutional widening participation policy in higher education: Dealing with the issue of social class. *Widening Participation and Lifelong Learning*, 8(1), 1–10.

Guan, M., & So, J. (2016). Influence of social identity on self-efficacy beliefs through perceived social support: A social identity theory perspective. *Communication Studies*, 67(5), 588–604. doi:10.1080/10510974.2016.1239645

Habib, S., & Ward, M. R. (2019). Youth negotiating belonging in a global world. In S. Habib & M. R. Ward (Eds.), *Identities, youth and belonging: International perspectives* (pp. 1–15). Springer. doi:10.1007/978-3-319-96113-2_1

Harrison, N. (2011). Have the changes introduced by the 2004 Higher Education Act made higher education admissions in England wider and fairer? *Journal of Education Policy*, 26(3), 449–468. doi:10.1080/02680939.2010.513742

Healy, M., & Richardson, M. (2017). Images and identity: Children constructing a sense of belonging to Europe. *European Educational Research Journal*, 16(4), 440–454. doi:10.1177/1474904116674015

HESA. (2022, February 22). *Widening participation: UK Performance Indicators 2020/21*. https://www.hesa.ac.uk/data-and-analysis/performance-indicators/widening-participation

Holton, M., & Riley, M. (2014). Talking on the move: Place-based interviewing with undergraduate students. *Area*, 46(1), 59–65. doi:10.1111/area.12070

Imperial College London. (n.d.a). *Centre for Higher Education Research and Scholarship (CHERS) Education Evaluation Toolkit*. https://www.imperial.ac.uk/education-research/evaluation/

Imperial College London. (n.d.b). *StudentShapers: Imperial's programme to support engaging with students as partners in learning and teaching*. https://www.imperial.ac.uk/students/studentshapers/

Imperial College London. (n.d.c). *Undergraduate Research Opportunities Programme (UROP)*. https://www.imperial.ac.uk/urop

Imperial College London. (2017a). *Developing our strategy*. https://www.imperial.ac.uk/learning-and-teaching-strategy/consultation/

Imperial College London. (2017b). *Learning and teaching strategy*.

Imperial College London. (2022). *Schools outreach*. https://www.imperial.ac.uk/be-inspired/schools-outreach/

Jones, P., Bunce, G., Evans, J., Gibbs, H., & Hein, J. R. (2008). Exploring space and place with walking interviews. *Journal of Research Practice*, 4(2).

Kandiko Howson, C., & Kingsbury, M. (2021). Curriculum change as transformational learning. *Teaching in Higher Education: Critical Perspectives*. doi:10.1080/13562517.2021.1940923

Kusenbach, M. (2003). Street phenomenology: The go-along as ethnographic research tool. *Ethnography*, 4(3), 455–485. doi:10.1177/146613810343007

Maddux, J. E., & Gosselin, J. T. (2012). Self-efficacy. In M. R. Leary & J. P. Tangney (Eds.), *Handbook of self and identity* (2nd ed., pp. 198–224). Guilford.

Meehan, C., & Howells, K. (2019). In search of the feeling of "belonging" in higher education: Undergraduate students transition into higher education. *Journal of Further and Higher Education*, 43(10), 1376–1390. doi:10.1080/0309877X.2018.1490702

Miño-Puigcercós, R., Rivera-Vargas, P., & Cobo Romaní, C. (2019). Virtual communities as safe spaces created by young feminists: Identity, mobility and sense of belonging. In S. Habib & M. R. Ward (Eds.), *Identities, youth and belonging: International perspectives* (pp. 123–140). Springer.

Neary, M. (2020). *Student as producer: How do revolutionary teachers teach?* John Hunt.

Office for Students. (2022). *Access and participation plans*. https://www.officeforstudents.org.uk/advice-and-guidance/promoting-equal-opportunities/access-and-participation-plans/

Oldfather, P. (1995). Songs "come back most to them": Students' experiences as researchers. *Theory Into Practice*, 34(2), 131–137. doi:10.1080/00405849509543670

O'Sullivan, K., Bird, N., Robson, J., & Winters, N. (2019). Academic identity, confidence and belonging: The role of contextualised admissions and foundation years in higher education. *British Educational Research Journal*, 45(3), 554–575. doi:10.1002/berj.3513

Pooley, J. A., Pike, L. T., Drew, N. M., & Breen, L. (2002). Inferring Australian children's sense of community: A critical exploration. *Community, Work & Family*, 5(1), 5–22. doi:10.1080/13668800020006802a

Porter, G., Hampshire, K., Abane, A., Munthali, A., Robson, E., Mashiri, M., & Maponya, G. (2010). Where dogs, ghosts and lions roam: Learning from mobile ethnographies on the journey from school. *Children's Geographies*, 8(2), 91–105. doi:10.1080/14733281003691343

Reed, A. (2002). City of details: Interpreting the personality of London. *Journal of the Royal Anthropological Institute*, 8(1), 127–141. doi:10.1111/1467-9655.00102

Sbaiti, M., Streule, M. J., Alhaffar, M., Pilkington, V., Leis, M., Budhathoki, S. S., Mkhallalati, H., Omar, M., Liu, L., Golestaneh, A. K., & Abbara, A. (2021). Whose voices should shape global health education? Curriculum codesign and codelivery by people with direct expertise and lived experience. *BMJ Global Health*, 6(9). doi:10.1136/bmjgh-2021-006262

Trell, E.-M., & Van Hoven, B. (2010). Making sense of place: Exploring creative and (inter) active research methods with young people. *Fennia-International Journal of Geography*, 188(1), 91–104.

Viola, J. K. (2020). *Young people's civic identity in the digital age*. Palgrave Macmillan.

Viola, J. K. (2021). Belonging and global citizenship in a STEM university. *Education Sciences*, 11(12), Article 803. doi:10.3390/educsci11120803

Yorke, M. (2016). The development and initial use of a survey of student "belongingness," engagement and self-confidence in UK higher education. *Assessment & Evaluation in Higher Education*, 41(1), 154–166. doi:10.1080/02602938.2014.990415

Zimmerman, L. A., Li, M., Moreau, C., Wilopo, S., & Blum, R. (2019). Measuring agency as a dimension of empowerment among young adolescents globally; findings from the Global Early Adolescent Study. *SSM Population Health*, 8. doi:10.1016/j.ssmph.2019.100454

Appendix: Belonging, engagement, and communities project walking interview protocol

Thank you for participating in this "Walking interview."

The idea is that you, the student/participant, guide me, the researcher, around parts of the campus (and perhaps the immediate surrounding area) that have been important or meaningful to your experiences as a student.

Where to go on the walk?

We ask that you lead the way! When deciding where to guide us, you might want to consider:

- places you go to (or used to go to) very often, or at regular intervals
- places that you go at particular times, such as:

a   when you meet with friends (for social or study purposes)
b   when you are, or want to be, alone
c   before, between or after your classes

- places that you have particularly memorable experiences of
- places that relate to your interests, aims, or aspirations (academic and nonacademic)

There is no need to try and cover all of these suggestions or to be restricted by them – start with somewhere that you think is most important to you and we can go from there.

Is there anywhere we can't go?

There may be some spaces on campus that it is not appropriate for me as an education researcher to enter, so in that case we may just have to approach these spaces as close as possible but remain a reasonable distance.

What happens if we see someone I know on the walk?

If we bump into people that you know and they stop to talk with you, then I will briefly explain the research to them so that they can decide whether or not to consent to me continuing the recording.

Questions/prompts to ask the participant on the walk

- Can you tell me why this place came to mind?
- How often do you come here? On what kinds of occasions do you come here?
- Do you have any particularly vivid or lasting memories of being here?
- Do you have any specific examples or memories that you can tell me about?
- How do you think this place would make you feel if you were to revisit it years after you leave Imperial?

13

REVIVING THE CONSTRUCT OF "MATTERING" IN PURSUIT OF EQUITY AND JUSTICE IN HIGHER EDUCATION

Illustrations from mentoring and partnership programs

Alison Cook-Sather, Peter Felten, Kaylyn (Kayo) Piper Stewart and Heidi Weston

The construct of *mattering* was not one we set out to research. Instead, mattering is what we heard "new majority" (Black, Indigenous, or Latinx) undergraduates who participated in student–student mentoring programs at LaGuardia Community College talk about in interviews conducted for the book *Relationship-Rich Education* (Felten & Lambert, 2020). It is also what we heard students from historically underrepresented groups (HUGs) describe in the 15 years' worth of feedback and interviews regarding their experiences in student–faculty pedagogical partnerships in the Students as Learners and Teachers (SaLT) program at Bryn Mawr and Haverford Colleges (Cook-Sather, 2020) and programs inspired by SaLT. While we concurred with aspects of "belonging" that scholars argue for in relation to student learning and experiences in higher education (Strayhorn, 2012; Thomas, 2012) and have used the construct to analyze students' experiences (Cook-Sather & Felten, 2017b; Cook-Sather & Seay, 2021; Felten & Lambert, 2020), listening carefully to what the LaGuardia, Bryn Mawr, and Haverford students were saying led us to revisit the less commonly evoked construct of mattering – which is related to but distinct from belonging.

What we heard most often from historically underrepresented students who participated in student–student mentoring and student–faculty partnerships was that their experiences, perspectives, contributions, and beings are important and significant. In one SaLT student's words: being a student partner "made me feel like who I am is more than enough – that my identity, my thoughts, my ideas are significant and valuable" (quoted in Cook-Sather, 2015). This is what scholars have defined as mattering (Flett et al., 2019; Schlossberg, 1989). The students we listened to felt that they matter

DOI: 10.4324/9781003443735-18

not because of what they have in common with others in the institution, although sometimes they do have experiences and identities in common and sometimes those shared experiences and identities promote a sense of belonging. Rather, they emphasized that what they bring to and get from the mentoring and the partnership work is affirmation of themselves as they are.

In this chapter, co-authored by two faculty members (Alison and Peter) and two students (Kayo and Heidi), we explore the overlaps and distinctions between belonging and mattering. We define mentoring and partnership as those are enacted in the programs we focus on, and we draw on the perspectives of current and former students as those are represented in data from institutional review board–approved studies and interviews with students from HUGs at several U.S. colleges and in published scholarship. For both student–student mentoring and student–faculty partnership, we provide a description of one or more college-wide programs and share outcomes of the mentoring or partnership work in relation to sense of belonging and mattering within and beyond the classroom for students from HUGs who participate in the programs. We then offer implications and recommendations for what faculty and staff can do to foster and support academic belonging and mattering for students.

Reviving mattering and reimagining belonging

The construct of *belonging* has been widely used to understand and explain college student experiences (Strayhorn, 2012; Thomas, 2012). It is typically framed as having two essential parts: fit and value. *Fit* relates to a student's sense that they share identities or other salient characteristics with others in the institution (Asher & Weeks, 2014); students sense that they fit when they feel they are similar to and connected with others at the institution. *Value* signals "students' perception of feeling valued and respected by other students" and staff at the institution (van Gijn-Grosvernor & Huisman, 2020, p. 377); students sense that they are valued when they believe that peers and others at the institution take them seriously and care about them. Belonging has been linked to a range of positive student experiences and outcomes, including transition into higher education (Meehan & Howells, 2019), academic performance (Ahn & Davis, 2020), mental health and well-being (Bye et al., 2020; Larcombe et al., 2021), and persistence and graduation rates (Gopalan & Brady, 2019; Lewis et al., 2017), including for students from historically excluded groups (Hausmann et al., 2009).

Despite its utility, the framework of belonging may contain an inherent flaw that should give higher education leaders and scholars pause. Emerging research consistently documents that students from HUGs report a lower sense of belonging (Cole et al., 2020; Eboka, 2019; Gopalan & Brady, 2019) and greater "belonging uncertainty" (Cohen & Garcia, 2008, p. 365;

Walton & Cohen, 2007) than their White counterparts. These findings are concerning because belonging is at the conceptual heart of many programs that seek to address the concerns and needs of HUGs. Can an inclusive program and institution be rooted in a construct (belonging) that often fails to account for the experiences and perspectives of students from groups that have historically been excluded from and marginalized in higher education (D. R. Johnson et al., 2007; Museus & Maramba, 2011)?

In this chapter, we invite readers to consider disentangling the two parts of belonging by separating "fit" from "value." By focusing on fit in particular, faculty and staff might misinterpret feelings of marginalization among certain groups of students and miss opportunities to understand what leads these students to learn and thrive (Cole et al., 2020). And while some students might find a social sense of connection and fit in college, that does not always translate into academic experiences. Porter and Byrd's (2021) literature review reported that Black women college students are confident they belong "within their families and friend groups" but many feel "isolated and marginal in the larger campus community" (p. 813). Former student partner Khadijah Seay concurs: "It's one thing to find your people in social spaces; it's another to feel a sense of belonging in academic spaces" (Cook-Sather & Seay, 2021, p. 742).

Additional critiques of belonging focus on the way it limits student agency, since "belonging is something that communities provide for individuals; it is not something individuals can garner for themselves" (Nunn, 2021, p. 6). Writing in the UK and Australia, Gravett and Ajjawi (2022) pointed to the necessity of "rethinking" (Thomas, 2018) belonging, particularly in "consideration of the experiences of those students who may not wish to, or who cannot, belong, as well as a questioning of the very boundaries of belonging" (p. 1386). Drawing on the experiences of students with dyslexia studying mathematics at university in Finland, Nieminen and Pesonen (2022) asked, "Might it be more desirable for disabled students *not* to belong in [certain] learning environments?" (p. 2021). Belonging can put an assimilative pressure on students to change themselves to fit the expectations and culture of the existing community.

In our research, we have observed particular struggles with both aspects of belonging as it is generally defined. The first relates to fit, especially regarding historically underrepresented college students because, by and large, these institutions were not made for them. In keeping with Gravett and Ajjawi's (2022) and Nieminen and Pesonen's (2022) points above, might encouragement to belong – for instance, for Black students at institutions built on the exploitation and destruction of Black bodies (Dancy & Edwards, 2020) – be undesirable, and indeed harmful, to those students?

The second aspect of belonging we have documented is context dependence – that one belongs in specific spaces or with certain people, as opposed to mattering in and of oneself. Even when definitions of belonging emphasize mattering – "a feeling that members matter to one another and to the group and a shared faith that members' needs will be met through their commitment to be together" (McMillan & Chavis, 1986, p. 9) – belonging relies on relationships and commitments within a given group. Context dependence is a particular limitation for belonging because if students experience belonging uncertainty in some settings (e.g., classrooms), then their sense of confidence and agency will be restricted in those settings. In contrast, if a sense of mattering can be carried across contexts (Cook-Sather, 2020; Cook-Sather & Seay, 2021; Weston et al., 2021), students will have greater confidence and agency regardless of whether they feel they fit in a specific context.

We are encouraged by Raaper's (2021) call to recognize "belonging as a dynamic, relational and nonlinear process, intersecting with pre-existing social inequalities as well as market dynamics that forcefully continue to reshape the sector and university practices" (p. 539). Complicating the focus on fit and context that many definitions of belonging reference, we re-evoke mattering as a concept related to but distinct from belonging. *Mattering* is commonly defined as "the feeling of being significant and important to other people" in a shared context (Flett et al., 2019, p. 667; see also Schlossberg, 1989), but we argue for understanding the experience of mattering not only within but also beyond any given context. In their original conception of mattering, Rosenberg and McCullough (1981) identified "three core elements: (a) the sense that other people depend on us; (b) the perception that other people regard us as important; and (c) the realization that other people are actively paying attention to us" (cited in Pychyl et al., 2022, p. 143). Feeling relied upon, important, and attended to is different from feeling one fits.

When students do not feel they matter, they may experience "a destructive state of marginalization" (Flett et al., 2019, p. 669). Yet unlike the construct of belonging, which emphasizes fit and integration as essential, mattering makes space for people to be recognized and valued as individuals with distinct identities and contributions to make to the community (Schlossberg, 1989). The inherent value and the unique set of contributions individuals bring can function as what Esteban-Guitart and Moll (2014) called "funds of identity," which they defined as "the historically accumulated, culturally developed, and socially distributed resources that are essential for a person's self-definition, self-expression, and self-understanding" (p. 31). These resources are an extension of the concept of "funds of knowledge" (González et al., 2005) – "bodies of knowledge and skills that are essential for the well-being of an entire household" – which become funds of identity "when people actively use them to define themselves" (Esteban-Guitart & Moll, 2014, p. 31). When students, particularly those from

HUGs, feel relied upon, important, and attended to for the identities and contributions they bring, not because they fit in, they feel that they matter. Mattering does not require assimilation.

Like belonging, mattering contributes to undergraduate students' psychological well-being (Flett et al., 2019), which is especially important for students from HUGs, such as Latino male undergraduates in the United States, for whom "mentoring and a sense of mattering provided opportunities … to access various forms of social and cultural capital" (Huerta & Fishman, 2014, p. 95). Based on interviews with 12 award-winning academic teachers about their views on and practices related to mattering, Pychyl and colleagues (2022) argued for "the centrality of mattering to effective teaching" (p. 154) and "that professors have a key role to play in promoting a sense of mattering in their students and that this sense of mattering is an important, if not essential, component of a safe and effective learning environment" (p. 154).

Our discussion builds on findings that positive student–student and student–faculty relationships contribute to a student's sense of belonging (Miller et al., 2019) and research that mattering influences student achievement and eagerness to excel, both in courses where they felt they mattered and in other courses (Vetro, 2021). As one student partner asserted: "Students want to feel like they matter and feeling like they matter in one class may be the catalyst to them making themselves matter in other classes" (Adams, 2023, p. 5). We focus on mentoring and partnerships as forms of what Gravett and Ajjawi (2022) called "inclusive spaces in the higher education system" (p. 1393), and we strive to attend to "the nuanced, situated and contextualised accounts of students' belonging in the learning time-spaces of the university" (p. 1393) and to the potential of mattering to relocate value within students and make it transferable.

Defining mentoring and partnership

There are many forms that mentoring and partnership can take in higher education contexts, but we offer here basic definitions of each as those inform the kinds of programs we highlight.

Mentoring

Higher education institutions often use the word *mentor* or *mentoring* to describe an array of activities, from trained students who help peers navigate their first days in college to faculty supervising a multi-semester research project (Crisp et al., 2017; W. B. Johnson, 2016). This goes far beyond the classical understanding of a long-term relationship between a mentor and a protégé. In practice, mentoring in college typically refers to a relationship that offers some combination of support and challenge to a student; mentoring might focus on academic success, social connectedness, identity development, personal well-being, or other factors – or it might integrate more than one of these into a holistic experience.

Research demonstrates that mentoring contributes to a range of positive outcomes for students and that student peer mentoring "has a double impact, helping both mentors and mentees learn new skills and develop new ... competencies" (Wu-Winiarski et al., 2020, p. 18). These gains are particularly significant for new majority students (Maramba & Fong, 2020), underscoring the significance of attention to "critical mentoring" rooted in "understanding the complexities and nuances of marginalization [experienced by students] and then explicitly moving forward to address and change them" through mentoring (Weiston-Serdan, 2017, p. 15).

Partnership

Pedagogical partnership, still relatively uncommon in higher education, refers to "a collaborative, reciprocal process through which all participants have the opportunity to contribute equally, although not necessarily in the same ways, to curricular or pedagogical conceptualization, decision making, implementation, investigation, or analysis" (Cook-Sather et al., 2014, pp. 6–7). The basic premises of partnership – respect, reciprocity, and shared responsibility (Cook-Sather et al., 2014) – require and enact the understanding that diverse individuals – "individuals from literally different places but also more metaphorically from different 'places' or positions" (Cook-Sather & Felten, 2017a, p. 182) – form relationships; negotiate across differences of power, position, and perspective; and strive *together* for deeper understanding, empathy, and informed action. Key to our understanding of partnership is that it is precisely the differences that participants bring to the partnership work – their "funds of identity" (Esteban-Guitart & Moll, 2014) – that make that work generative. Importantly, it is the affirmation of those differences – the embrace of them as resources for learning and growth – that holds such promise for realizing the potential of both belonging and mattering.

The form of student–faculty partnership we reference in this chapter unfolds outside of academic classes but informs students' experiences of those spaces. The student partners in the programs we focus on are not enrolled in the faculty partners' courses; they work in semester-long pedagogical partnerships to consider how to make the faculty partners' classrooms places of equity and inclusion (Cook-Sather, 2022). The spaces in which the faculty and student partners work are liminal or "as-if" spaces – spaces within which the typical roles and power dynamics that structure relationships and responsibilities are suspended or shifted. But they affect the academic spaces in which sense of academic belonging, as well as mattering, either gets developed or does not. Because these "as-if" spaces support students and faculty engaging with one another as partners – through affirming the value of the different positions and perspectives they bring to the partnership work – students (and faculty) can become partners beyond the liminal spaces (Cook-Sather & Felten, 2017a): they can transfer the sense of mattering through partnership work beyond any given context.

Previous research has indicated that partnership fosters a sense of belonging for faculty and students (Colón García, 2017; Cook-Sather & Felten, 2017b; Cook-Sather & Seay, 2021; Perez-Putnam, 2016). Our goal in exploring the student–faculty partnership programs we present here is to build on those findings to illustrate how partnership also fosters mattering.

Student–student mentoring

For more than 2 decades, LaGuardia Community College has centered student–student peer mentoring in its educational model and institutional priorities (Arcario et al., 2011). Located in Queens, New York, LaGuardia's students have been described by a long-time leader at the college as "first generation times two. They are not only the first in their families coming to college, they are also overwhelmingly immigrants and second language learners" (Eynon, cited in Felten & Lambert, 2020, p. 36).

To meet the distinct and varied needs of these students, LaGuardia Community College (n.d.) has developed a diverse set of peer mentoring programs that connect trained, and paid, students with others to offer support and challenge, including:

- Student success mentors, who help first-year students navigate the transition into higher education
- Peer health educators, who focus on specialized issues such sexual assault and substance abuse prevention
- *Crear Futuros* mentors, who empower fellow Latinx students to be successful academically, to build professional skills, and to establish community at the college
- Black male empowerment cooperative mentors, who engage Black men in tutoring, advising, and networking

These programs – and others like them – create an overlapping web of opportunities that enable students to have multiple chances to connect academically, personally, or professionally with peers who will contribute to their learning, persistence, identity development, well-being, and future prospects.

In our interviews with students at LaGuardia, we heard not only about the benefits and joys of individual programs but also about the importance of the college's overall commitment to peer mentoring. One student, a Black woman who had recently immigrated to the United States from a Caribbean island, explained that

> all you need sometimes, outside of math problems and psychology ter-
> minology [to study], is just to know that the college you are at cares
> about you. The community around you promotes success and wants to
> see you do great. That makes a world of difference.

Like many of her peers, she expressed the feeling that the existence of these peer programs demonstrated that she matters, even if she chooses not to join – or feel that she belongs in – any of them.

Another student, a male immigrant from South Asia, told us he never felt that he fit at LaGuardia but that the Student Success Mentors program still had been essential to him: "I told my student success mentor, 'I'm not comfortable here at LaGuardia.'" Although his student success mentor and his other experiences at the college never allowed him to overcome his belonging uncertainty, he started to feel that he mattered when that peer patiently guided him in ways that met his academic goals and personal needs, allowing him to succeed academically.

A Latino New York City native reported a similar experience. He strug-gled through high school and never felt comfortable or a sense of belonging in college classrooms. But the *Crear Futuros* Mentors program helped him feel that he mattered and that he was more capable than his teachers and classmates – or he – ever knew: "I guess in many ways, I do feel I have many talents that were unrecognized. But I think right now, after participating in *Crear Futuros*, I'm shining in ways that I never did before." The source of this student transformation is his sense of mattering, not belonging or fit. He also describes his "shining" as something that is part of him, rather than a context-dependent experience.

This is perhaps the most salient theme from our interviews with LaGuardia students; when asked what contributed to their academic and personal success in college, they almost never described the importance of feeling part of the college community – assimilation was *not* important to them. Instead, they emphasized feeling valued as students and people, which echoes the mattering component of belonging. This was illustrated by a student who moved with her family from Egypt to New York City in her teens. When she enrolled at LaGuardia, she participated in a year-long intensive English language program that included extensive peer mentoring focused on academic and personal goals. This student told her peers and faculty about her goals, and their positive reaction motivated her and helped her feel that she mattered.

I did not think that any of that was possible, especially for someone from my background and culture. But they told me that those are great ideas and we can see you achieving them. They said I'm a "shining star." When they first said that to me, I thought, "No one has ever told me that." So when they told me that, I decided, "Okay, I'm going to work for it and I'm going to work hard."

This sense of capacity and of mattering – of being "a shining star" – helped this student through her year in this program, and she carried it with her into the future: "They see that in me, and I keep that in mind whenever I'm stressed out or think that I will not make it."

Student–faculty pedagogical partnership

While the number of student–faculty pedagogical partnership programs around the world is growing rapidly, we focus here on three programs in different kinds of 4-year higher education institutions in the United States. Each took belonging as a premise of its founding; however, student comments illuminate how the construct of mattering might better describe their experiences. These programs include Students as Learners and Teachers at Bryn Mawr and Haverford Colleges, two selective, liberal arts colleges in Pennsylvania; the Student–Faculty Partnership Program at Florida Gulf Coast University, a public, state, Hispanic-serving institution in Florida; and the Student–Faculty Partnership Program at Berea College, a small, private liberal arts college in Kentucky that is one of the eight federally funded work colleges.

The SaLT program was piloted in 2007 premised on the belief that "productive reflection, dialogue, and partnership" (Cook-Sather, 2018, p. 1) between students and faculty (and between students and staff; see Lesnick & Cook-Sather, 2010) could "contribute to the creation of campuses as places of belonging" (Cook-Sather, 2018, p. 1). Developed with external grant funding as a free-standing program, SaLT supports semester-long pedagogy- or curriculum-focused partnerships between faculty members and paid student partners. One-on-one student–faculty partnerships include classroom observations, weekly meetings of student and faculty partners, and weekly meetings of student partners with Alison as the facilitator of the program. SaLT has evolved to include multiple options: new faculty orientation and pedagogy seminars (Cook-Sather, 2016; Cook-Sather et al., 2021); partnerships between individuals, pairs, and groups of student consultants and individual faculty and departments (Ameyaa et al., 2021); and pedagogy circles for diversity, equity, and inclusion (Cook-Sather et al., 2023). The explicit focus of this work is the creation of equitable and inclusive learning spaces and teaching practices. While student partners note that the partnership work "made me feel a sense of belonging," that sense is "founded in the acceptance and celebration of my identity and what it could contribute to the transformation of our classroom culture" (Colón García, 2017, p. 4).

The Student–Faculty Partnership Program at Florida Gulf Coast University (SFPP-FGCU) is "a joint faculty development and student success initiative" (Reynolds, in Gennocro & Straussberger, 2020, p. 29). It launched in the Fall-2018 semester as a collaboration between the staff and faculty of the Lucas Center for Faculty Development and the FGCU Dean of Students office. The program also receives funding from the Division of Academic Affairs. Based on the SaLT program model, the SFPP-FGCU pairs faculty members with undergraduate students, who assume the role of paid pedagogical consultant. These pairs collaborate for an entire semester to enrich teaching and learning in a particular course, and both student and faculty partners have regular meetings with the program facilitator. Faculty and student partners in the SFFP-FGCU conceptualize their work as "peer exchange" (Gennocro & Straussberger, 2020, p. 30); faculty focus as much on creating meaningful opportunities for student partners to build a sense of belonging as they do on working to make their classrooms places of belonging for enrolled students.

The Student–Faculty Partnership Program at Berea College (SFPP-BC) was launched in 2017. One of its fundamental commitments is to invite faculty members to engage in difficult conversations about identity, inclusion, educational equity, and belonging. Like SaLT and SFFP-FGCU, the SFPP-BC supports semester-long partnerships between individual faculty and student partners, but instead of earning hourly pay as in SaLT and SFFP-FGCU, student partners in the SFPP-BC enroll in a credit-bearing course. Additionally, two postbaccalaureate fellows partnered with a faculty member and teaching and learning center director to launch the SFPP-BC and to facilitate the course. In co-facilitating the course, the first postbac fellow, Khadijah Seay, drew on her commitment "to help students feel a sense of belonging on campus so they could negotiate differences of power" as they seek positive educational experiences (quoted in Ortquist-Ahrens, 2021, p. 193). The second post-bac fellow, Mia Rybeck, further enhanced the course "with an explicit emphasis on belonging through an extended unit she developed, grounded in bell hooks's 2008 book" (Ortquist-Ahrens, 2021, p. 194).

The outcomes of this student–faculty partnership work are remarkably similar across these very different institutions (and, indeed, across almost all institutions that embrace student–faculty pedagogical partnership). In relation to academic belonging in particular, student partners describe developing "the belonging of a voice" that transfers into academic contexts: "Through this partnership, I have learned how to feel a sense of belonging in my other classrooms" (Cook-Sather & Seay, 2021, p. 741). Another student said that through partnership she could "become a stakeholder in the community"; another argued: "As a Participant, I felt like I was involved as an equal member of the community, specifically when it comes to academics" (Cook-Sather & Seay, 2021, p. 742). However, another student highlighted the limits of belonging, particularly in relation to its transferability: she asserted that she "felt belonging within partnership but did not experience a 'sense of belonging on a campus-wide scale'" (Cook-Sather & Seay, 2021, p. 742).

Some student partners highlight the generative overlap between belonging and mattering, specifically in terms of confidence and agency. One student explained that partnership "helped me overcome my fear of professors therefore allowing me to be more proactive," and another wrote: "In engaging in partnership with a faculty member, I began to feel like I had more agency in my own school ... [and felt] more comfortable in navigating academic spaces as a whole" (Cook-Sather & Seay, 2021, p. 742). Yet another student partner asserted: "My partnerships gave me a seat at the table and allowed me to gain confidence, knowing my ideas and perspective held weight and had value" (Allard, 2021, p. 1).

We see in these statements evidence of mattering. These are not statements about fit and integration; rather, they are about students feeling recognized and valued as individuals with distinct identities and contributions to make to the community (Esteban-Guitart & Moll, 2014; Schlossberg, 1989). We noted in our definition of partnership that it is the differences that participants bring to the work that make it generative – differences of identity, position, and perspective – and, further, that it is the affirmation of those differences as resources for learning and growth that contribute to partnership's potential to foster belonging and mattering. When students feel that they matter, they make choices in their education that reflect a "re-prioritization of learning within education rather than a choice to continue to merely do school well" (Marcovici, 2021, p. 2). Such choices are clear illustrations that students know that they matter, not necessarily that they belong.

Implications and recommendations

In evoking the construct of mattering to analyze the experiences underrepresented students have in academic spaces, we are not suggesting that belonging in these spaces is irrelevant. Rather, we are suggesting that perhaps belonging is not the only or the most generative construct to use in analyzing students' experiences and in informing institutional practices. Mattering allows us to refocus on students' sense of capacity and agency that does not depend on – but can certainly be informed and affirmed by – fit and context. Knowing that someone at your college cares about you enough to thoughtfully guide you, to feel you can shine or, indeed, be a shining star – these are some of the ways in which peer mentoring can foster a sense of mattering without students feeling that they need or want to fit within a specific cultural or institutional context. Feeling like a stakeholder in the community, experiencing the sense of capacity transfer across academic contexts, feeling the confidence that one can contribute, and focusing on one's own learning needs and priorities – these are some of the ways in which student–faculty partnership can foster a sense of mattering without students feeling that they need or want to belong.

As an experienced student partner, Kayo notes that students who work in student–faculty partnerships feel empowered in their positions, are more likely to build connections with faculty and community members, and, if they are students from HUGs, can heal from negative social experiences in traditional gender-specific dominated departments and with non–people of color. After developing a sense that they matter through partnership, students are able to return to those situations with the language to critique pedagogical practices through a holistic and equitable lens. Kayo captures what almost all student partners express: that through partnership work, they learn how to advocate for themselves and others despite existing (and inequitable) power dynamics. Students learn through partnership how to adapt to various academic settings, to recognize when there is an issue that needs a new approach, or to find a collective solution that meets the needs and goals of all involved.

Given our findings that both build on and extend the potential of belonging in academic spaces, we recommend widening the conceptual frames used to analyze the experiences of students from HUGs to not force "fit" and to value differences that can help change the structures and practices of many higher education institutions. Student perspectives on their experiences in the peer mentoring programs developed at LaGuardia Community College and the student–faculty pedagogical partnership programs at Bryn Mawr and Haverford Colleges, Florida Gulf Coast University, and Berea College challenge us to attend to what is salient to students – to mattering. These perspectives encourage us to reconsider what we strive to support and how we conceptualize belonging. Such reconceptualization opens up possibilities because fit and context are no longer essential components of our work with students.

Conclusion

This collection includes discussions of pedagogies of belonging and promoting academic belonging in the curriculum, and it also addresses how academic belonging might be supported beyond the classroom. Mentoring and partnership programs can support these forms of attention to belonging. In our research, though, students from HUGs who participate in these programs have shown us how their experiences and feelings of mattering, rather than belonging, might be even more affirming and empowering. The "how" of supporting academic belonging, then, might include how we conceptualize what is most fundamental to student thriving. Affirming who students are – in all their diversity – and the contributions that diversity of identities constitutes, rather than striving to promote and facilitate fit in a particular context, might give individual students and the educational institutions in which they live, learn, and work greater confidence and sense of agency while they are in those institutions and after they move on from them and to develop the sense that they are worthy and that their experiences, voices, and ways of being matter consistently translates, in our research, to agency within higher education and also in the wider world beyond. We invite faculty and staff to learn from what students gain from peer mentoring and student–faculty partnership and to get involved in conversations and networks to reassert that students from HUGs matter, too, even in systems of power in higher education that can make them feel otherwise.

References

Adams, J. (2023). The F@$#-Up's guide to reclaiming and reimagining my student identity through pedagogical partnerships. *Teaching and Learning Together in Higher Education*, 38, 1–5. https://repository.brynmawr.edu/tlthe/vol1/iss38/2/

Ahn, M. Y., & Davis, H. H. (2020). Students' sense of belonging and their socio-economic status in higher education: A quantitative approach. *Teaching in Higher Education*, 28(1), 136–149. doi:10.1080/13562517.2020.1778664

Allard, S. (2021). Finding identity and agency through partnership and collaboration. *Teaching and Learning Together in Higher Education*, 34, 1–3. https://repository.brynmawr.edu/tlthe/vol1/iss34/2

Ameyaa, R. A., Cook-Sather, A., Ramo, K., & Tohfa, H. (2021). Undergraduate students partnering with faculty to develop trauma-informed, anti-racist pedagogical approaches: Intersecting experiences of three student partners. *Journal of Innovation, Partnership and Change*, 7(1). https://journals.studentengagement.org.uk/index.php/studentchangeagents/article/view/1020

Arcario, P., Eynon, B., & Lucca, L. (2011). The power of peers: New ways for students to support students. In J. Summerfield & C. C. Smith (Eds.), *Making teaching and learning matter (Explorations of educational purpose 11)* (pp. 195–215). Springer.

Asher, S. R., & Weeks, M. S. (2014). Loneliness and belongingness in the college years. In R. J. Coplan & J. C. Bowker (Eds.), *The handbook of solitude: Psychological perspectives on social isolation, social withdrawal, and being alone* (pp. 283–301). John Wiley.

Bye, L., Muller, F., & Oprescu, F. (2020). The impact of social capital on student wellbeing and university life satisfaction. *Higher Education Research & Development*, 39(5), 898–912.

Cohen, G. L., & Garcia, J. (2008). Identity, belonging, and achievement: A model, interventions, implications. *Current Directions in Psychological Science*, 17(6), 365–369.

Cole, D., Newman, C. B., & Hypolite, L. I. (2020). Sense of belonging and mattering among two cohorts of first-year students participating in a comprehensive college transition program. *American Behavioral Scientist*, 64(3), 276–297.

Colón García, A. (2017). Building a sense of belonging through pedagogical partnership. *Teaching and Learning Together in Higher Education*, 22, 1–5. http://repository.brynmawr.edu/tlthe/vol1/iss22/2

Cook-Sather, A. (2015). Dialogue across differences of position, perspective, and identity: Reflective practice in/on a student-faculty pedagogical partnership program. *Teachers College Record*, 117(2).

Cook-Sather, A. (2016). Undergraduate students as partners in new faculty orientation and academic development. *International Journal of Academic Development*, 21(2), 151–162. doi:10.1080/1360144X.2016.1156543

Cook-Sather, A. (2018). Developing "students as learners and teachers": Lessons from ten years of pedagogical partnership that strives to foster inclusive and responsive practice. *Journal of Educational Innovation, Partnership and Change*, 4(1). https://journals.studentengagement.org.uk/index.php/studentchangeagents/article/view/746/pdf

Cook-Sather, A. (2020). Respecting voices: How the co-creation of teaching and learning can support academic staff, underrepresented students, and equitable practices. *Higher Education*, 79(5), 885–901. https://rdcu.be/bQfu5

Cook-Sather, A. (2022). *Co-creating equitable teaching and learning: Structuring student voice into higher education*. Harvard Education Press.

Cook-Sather, A., Bovill, C., & Felten, P. (2014). *Engaging students as partners in learning & teaching: A guide for faculty*. Jossey-Bass.

Cook-Sather, A., & Felten, P. (2017a). Ethics of academic leadership: Guiding learning and teaching. In F. Wu & M. Wood (Eds.), *Cosmopolitan perspectives on academic leadership in higher education* (pp. 175–191). Bloomsbury Academic.

Cook-Sather, A., & Felten, P. (2017b). Where student engagement meets faculty development: How student–faculty pedagogical partnership fosters a sense of belonging. *Student Engagement in Higher Education Journal*, 1(2), 3–11. https://sehej.raise-network.com/raise/article/view/cook

Cook-Sather, A., Hong, E., Moss, T., & Williamson, A. (2021). Developing new faculty voice and agency through trustful, overlapping, faculty–faculty and student–faculty conversations. *International Journal for Academic Development*, 26(3), 347–359. doi:10.1080/1360144X.2021.1947296

Cook-Sather, A., & Seay, K. (2021). "I was involved as an equal member of the community": How pedagogical partnership can foster a sense of belonging in Black, female students. *Cambridge Journal of Education*, 51(6), 733–750. doi:10.1080/0305764X.2021.1926926

Cook-Sather, A., Stewart, K., Ameyaa, R. A., & Jones, L. A. (2023). Co-creating spaces for full selves: Student-facilitated pedagogy circles for BIPOC faculty. *Journal of Faculty Development*, 37(1), 69–71.

Crisp, G., Baker, V. L., Griffin, K. A., Lunsford, L. G., & Pifer, M. J. (2017). Mentoring undergraduate students. *ASHE Higher Education Report*, 43(1), 1–114.

Dancy, T. E., & Edwards, K. T. (2020). Labor and property: Historically White colleges, Black bodies, and constructions of (anti) humanity. In C. A. Grant, A. N. Woodson, & M. J. Dumas (Eds.), *The future is Black: Afropessism, fugitivity, and radical hope in education* (pp. 31–46). Routledge.

Eboka, T. (2019, April). Fostering student engagement with diverse cohorts: A case study of BAME undergraduate students. doi:10.2139/ssrn.3436976

Esteban-Guitart, M., & Moll, L. C. (2014). Funds of identity: A new concept based on the funds of knowledge approach. *Culture & Psychology*, 20(1), 31–48. doi:10.1177/1354067X13515934

Felten, P., & Lambert, L. M. (2020). *Relationship-rich education: How human connections drive student success*. Johns Hopkins University Press.

Flett, G., Khan, A., & Su, C. (2019). Mattering and psychological well-being in college and university students. *International Journal Mental Health Addiction*, 17, 667–680.

Gennocro, A., & Straussberger, J. (2020). Peers and colleagues: Collaborative class design through student–faculty partnerships. In A. Cook-Sather & C. Wilson (Eds.), *Building courage, confidence, and capacity in learning and teaching through student-faculty partnership: Stories from across contexts and arenas of practice* (pp. 29–37). Lexington Books.

González, N., Moll, L. C., & Amanti, C. (Eds.). (2005). *Funds of knowledge: Theorizing practices in households, communities, and classrooms*. Routledge.

Gopalan, M., & Brady, S. T. (2019). College students' sense of belonging: A national perspective. *Educational Researcher*, 49(2). doi:10.3102/0013189X19897622

Gravett, K., & Ajjawi, R. (2022). Belonging as situated practice. *Studies in Higher Education*, 47(7), 1386–1396. doi:10.1080/03075079.2021.1894118

Hausmann, L. R. M., Ye, F., Schofield, J. W., & Woods, R. L. (2009). Sense of belonging and persistence in White and African American first-year students. *Research in Higher Education*, 50, 649–669. doi:10.1007/s11162-009-9137-8

Huerta, S. M., & Fishman, S. M. (2014). Marginality and mattering: Urban Latino male undergraduates in higher education. *Journal of The First-Year Experience & Students in Transition*, 26(1), 85–100.

Johnson, D. R., Soldner, M., Leonard, J. B., Alvarez, P., Inkelas, K. K., Rowan-Kenyon, H., & Longerbeam, S. (2007). Examining sense of belonging among first-year undergraduates from different racial/ethnic groups. *Journal of College Student Development*, 48(5), 525–542. doi:10.1353/csd.2007.0054

Johnson, W. B. (2016). *On being a mentor: A guide for higher education faculty*. Routledge.

LaGuardia Community College. (n.d.). *Peer programs*. https://www.laguardia.edu/peerprograms/

Larcombe, W., Baik, C., & Finch, S. (2021). Exploring course experiences that predict psychological distress and mental wellbeing in Australian undergraduate and graduate coursework students. *Higher Education Research & Development*, 41(2), 420–435. doi:10.1080/07294360.2020.1865284

Lesnick, A., & Cook-Sather, A. (2010). Building civic capacity on campus through a radically inclusive teaching and learning initiative. *Innovative Higher Education*, 35 (1), 3–17.

Lewis, K. L., Stout, J. G., Finkelstein, N. D., Pollock, S. J., Miyake, A., Cohen, G. L., & Ito, T. A. (2017). Fitting in to move forward: Belonging, gender, and persistence in the physical sciences, technology, engineering, and mathematics (pSTEM). *Psychology of Women Quarterly*, 41(4), 420–436. doi:10.1177/0361684317720186

Maramba, D., & Fong, T. (Eds.). (2020). *Transformative practices for minority student success: Accomplishments of Asian American and Native American Pacific Islander–serving institutions*. Stylus.

Marcovici, E. (2021). Taking ownership of my learning and pushing for change. *Teaching and Learning Together in Higher Education*, 34, 1–3. https://repository.brynmawr.edu/tlthe/vol1/iss34/3/

McMillan, D. W., & Chavis, D. M. (1986). Sense of community: A definition and theory. *Journal of Community Psychology*, 14, 6–23.

Meehan, C., & Howells, K. (2019). In search of the feeling of "belonging" in higher education. *Journal of Further and Higher Education*, 43(10), 1376–1390.

Miller, A. L., Williams, L. M., & Silberstein, S. M. (2019). Found my place. *Higher Education Research & Development*, 38(3), 594–608.

Museus, S. D., & Maramba, D. C. (2011). The impact of culture on Filipino American students' sense of belonging. *Review of Higher Education*, 34(2), 231–258. doi:10.1353/rhe.2010.0022

Nieminen, J. H., & Pesonen, H. V. (2022). Politicising inclusive learning environments: How to foster belonging and challenge ableism? *Higher Education Research & Development*, 41(6), 2020–2033. https://www.tandfonline.com/doi/full/10.1080/07294360.2021.1945547

Nunn, L. M. (2021). *College belonging: How first-year and first-generation students navigate campus life*. Rutgers University Press.

Ortquist-Ahrens, L. (2021). Building partnership through partnership: Reflections on the role of post-baccalaureate fellows in program development. *International Journal for Students as Partners*, 5(2), 191–197. doi:10.15173/ijsap.v5i2.4618

Perez-Putnam, M. (2016). Belonging and brave space as hope for personal and institutional inclusion. *Teaching and Learning Together in Higher Education*, 18, 1–3. http://repository.brynmawr.edu/tlthe/vol1/iss18/2

Porter, C., &, Byrd, J. (2021). Understanding influences of development on Black women's success in U.S. colleges: A synthesis of literature. *Review of Educational Research*, 91, 803–830. doi:10.3102/00346543211027929

Pychyl, T. A., Flett, G. L., Long, M., Carreiro, E., & Azil, R. (2022). Faculty perceptions of mattering in teaching and learning: A qualitative examination of the views, values, and teaching practices of award-winning professors. *Journal of Psychoeducational Assessment*, 40(1), 142–158. doi:10.1177/07342829211057648

Raaper, R. (2021). Contemporary dynamics of student experience and belonging in higher education. *Critical Studies in Education*, 62(5), 537–542. doi:10.1080/17508487.2021.1983852

Schlossberg, N. K. (1989). Marginality and mattering. *New Directions for Student Services*, 48, 5–15.

Strayhorn, T. L. (2012). *College students' sense of belonging*. Routledge.

Thomas, L. (2012, March). *Building student engagement and belonging in higher education at a time of change*. Higher Education Academy. https://www.phf.org.uk/wp-content/uploads/2014/10/What-Works-report-final.pdf

Thomas, L. (2018). *Rethinking student belonging in higher education: From Bourdieu to borderlands*. Routledge.

van Gijn-Grosvenor, E. L., & Huisman, P. (2020). A sense of belonging among Australian university students. *Higher Education Research & Development*, 39(2), 376–389. doi:10.1080/07294360.2019.1666256

Vetro, V. (2021). College during a pandemic: A qualitative exploration of community college first-generation students' mattering and persistence experiences. *Journal of Higher Education Management*, 36, 93–103. https://issuu.com/aaual0/docs/twin_pandemics/s/11997057

Walton, G. M., & Cohen, G. L. (2007). A question of belonging: Race, social fit, and achievement. *Journal of Personality and Social Psychology*, 92(1), 82–96. doi:10.1037/0022-3514.92.1.82

Weiston-Serdan, T. (2017). *Critical mentoring: A practical guide*. Stylus.

Weston, H., Felten, P., & Cook-Sather, A. (2021, October 27). *Reviving the construct of "mattering" in pursuit of equity and justice in higher education* [Conference session]. Conference of the International Society for the Study of Teaching and Learning [virtual].

Wu-Winiarski, M. H., Geron, K., Geron, S. M., & Hoang, A. (2020). The Student Service Operation for Success Program for Asian American and American Pacific Islander students. In D. C. Maramba & T. P. Fong (Eds.), *Transformative practices for minority student success* (pp. 13–30). Stylus.

LIST OF CONTRIBUTORS

Martha Alonzo-Johnsen is a teaching faculty member in the Department of Biology at the University of St. Thomas' Dougherty Family College, USA. With an awareness of how little research is done with and for communities represented at DFC, she is passionate about showing students how and why research is conducted.

Diana J. Arya is an associate professor and founding director of Community Based Literacies (CBL) within the Gevirtz Graduate School of Education at the University of California, Santa Barbara, USA.

Kandi Bauman is a graduate research assistant for the Brotherhood Initiative at the University of Washington, USA, and teaching assistant for the Brotherhood Initiative first-year seminar. Her research interests include organizational change, public policy, and racial equity in higher education.

Dawn Berk is the founding director of the Mathematical Sciences Learning Laboratory and an associate professor in the Department of Mathematical Sciences at the University of Delaware, USA. Her research focuses on relationships between mathematics teaching, learning, and curriculum in the context of undergraduate mathematics.

Virginia L. Byrne is an assistant professor of higher education and student affairs at Morgan State University in Baltimore, USA.

DOI: 10.4324/9781003443735-19

Devon M. Christman is a PhD candidate at the University of California, Santa Barbara, USA. Her research focuses on computer science and quantum computing education in informal learning spaces and contexts.

Eliel Cohen is a research associate at The Policy Institute, King's College London, UK. He has published on higher education access, sector stratification, student experience, academic identity, and university–society relations in the knowledge economy. He currently researchers the relationship between academic governance and academic culture across different disciplinary contexts.

Alison Cook-Sather is Mary Katharine Woodworth Professor of Education at Bryn Mawr College and director of the Teaching and Learning Institute at Bryn Mawr and Haverford Colleges, USA.

Alice E. Donlan is an educational psychologist and director of research at the Teaching and Learning Transformation Center at the University of Maryland, USA.

Jessie Durk is a research associate in the Physics Education Group at Imperial College London, UK.

Peter Felten is executive director of the Center for Engaged Learning, assistant provost for Teaching and Learning, and professor of history at Elon University, USA.

Yesenia Fernández is an associate professor in the School Leadership Program in the Division of Graduate Education, California State University, Dominguez Hills, USA.

Michael F. J. Fox is a senior teaching fellow in the Department of Physics at Imperial College London, UK. He is part of the Strengthening Learning Communities project and the Physics Education Group.

Carlton E. Green operates Green Psychological Services, USA, an independent practice providing psychotherapy to diverse populations and supervision to mental health trainees.

Casey Griffin is a PhD candidate specializing in mathematics education in the School of Education at the University of Delaware, USA.

Eden Haywood-Bird is an associate professor of early childhood studies at California State Polytechnic University where she teaches math and science methods. She was a classroom teacher, serving children and families birth through age 8, for 12 years before completing a PhD in education leadership, renewal, and change at Colorado State University.

Nancy Hurlbut is an emeritus professor in early childhood studies at California State Polytechnic University, Pomona. She earned her PhD in life-span human development from the University of Wisconsin Madison. She has been a faculty member and administrator for 40 years in early childhood education in two countries and four U.S. states.

Soon Young Jang is an assistant professor in early childhood studies at California State Polytechnic University, Pomona. She obtained her PhD in language and literacies education at the University of Toronto, Canada. Her primary research interests include children's bilingualism and biliteracy, heritage language learning, translanguaging, and language policy and practice.

Camille B. Kandiko Howson is associate professor of education in the Centre for Higher Education Research and Scholarship (CHERS) at Imperial College London, UK.

Denise Kennedy is department chair and professor of early childhood studies at California State Polytechnic University, Pomona. She holds a PhD in human and community development from the University of Illinois. She completed a postdoctoral research fellowship at the University of Michigan in developmental psychology and contributed to the longitudinal Family Transitions Study.

Anna Kurhajec is the teaching professor of history at the University of St. Thomas' Dougherty Family College, USA. She has a PhD in history from the University of Illinois. Her research examines social movements and radical politics in the 20th and 21st centuries.

Joe Lott II is an associate professor in the College of Education at the University of Washington, USA, and the co-founder and faculty director of the Brotherhood Initiative.

Candice Lowe Swift is associate professor of anthropology and serves on the steering committees of Africana Studies and International Studies at Vassar College, USA.

Patricia L. Maddox is an assistant professor of sociology at the University of St. Thomas, USA. Her research interests include gender and workplace discrimination, community-engaged learning designs and first-generation college student success.

Sarah McCann is teaching faculty of theology at Dougherty Family College, University of St. Thomas, USA.

Erika Mein is associate dean of academic affairs and associate professor of literacy/biliteracy education in the College of Education at The University of Texas at El Paso, USA.

Jasmine Mitchell is an undergraduate research assistant and graduating senior from the University of California, Santa Barbara, USA, with a degree in biopsychology (BS). Her research interests include medicine, nutrition, and health and STEM education.

Amir Z. Mohamed is teaching faculty of communication studies at the University of St. Thomas' Dougherty Family College, USA. His teaching is rooted in anti-oppressive pedagogies and seeks to engender hope, solidarity, and transformation. His current research focuses on the intersection of culturally sustaining pedagogy and communication education.

Alexandria Muller is a PhD candidate at the University of California, Santa Barbara, USA. Her research focuses on creating equitable and accessible STEM education environments for all peoples, especially within informal learning contexts.

Jasmine McBeath Nation is an assistant professor in liberal studies at California Polytechnic University, San Luis Obispo, USA. Her research interests are in STEM teaching and learning, participatory design in research–practice partnerships, and equity and social justice in education.

Giselle Navarro-Cruz is an associate professor of early childhood studies at California State Polytechnic University, Pomona, where she teaches multilingualism, infant development, and early childhood education teacher practicum. Dr. Navarro-Cruz earned her PhD in education from Claremont Graduate University and her MA in child development from California State University, Los Angeles.

Nathalie Paesler is a biopsychology major and undergraduate research assistant at the University of California, Santa Barbara, USA. Her research interests include social psychology, neuroscience, and cultural psychology.

Keisha C. Paxton is professor of psychology, senior faculty strategist for the Office of Undergraduate Studies, and co-director of the Psychology MA Program at California State University, Dominguez Hills, USA.

Joanna B. Perez is an associate professor of sociology and interim associate faculty director of the Office of First and Second Year Experience at California State University, Dominguez Hills, USA.

Mark Richards is a senior teaching fellow in the Department of Physics at Imperial College London, UK.

Louie Rodriguez is vice provost for professional development, engagement, and strategic initiatives at the University of Texas at El Paso, USA.

Eréndira Rueda is associate professor of sociology and the director of the Latin American and Latinx Studies multidisciplinary program at Vassar College, USA.

Amy Smith is a PhD researcher in the Physics Education Group at Imperial College London, UK.

Kaylyn (Kayo) Piper Stewart is a member of the class of 2023 at Bryn Mawr College, USA. She completed a major in sociology and minors in education and Africana studies.

Terrell L. Strayhorn is professor of education and psychology at Virginia Union University, USA, where he also serves as director of the Center for the Study of Historically Black Colleges & Universities and principal investigator of The Belonging Lab.

Jennifer Trost is a former teaching faculty of sociology at Dougherty Family College, University of St. Thomas, USA. She currently serves as director of the Leadership Minor at the University of Minnesota–Twin Cities. Her scholarly interests include higher education transitions, first-generation college students, and culturally sustaining pedagogy and universal design.

Vijay Tymms is a principal teaching fellow in the Department of Physics at Imperial College London, UK.

Julianne K. Viola is a social scientist investigating young people's sense of belonging and political engagement at Imperial College London, UK. She is interested in youth identity development, efficacy, and community engagement and through her work aims to empower young people and inform youth-focused policy solutions to reduce inequalities.

Kelly Vu is an undergraduate research assistant and alumna from the University of California, Santa Barbara, USA. She graduated in 2021 with a degree in microbiology (BS). Her research interests are in STEM education, microbiology/genetics, and health care.

Heidi Weston is a member of the class of 2023 at Elon University, USA. She completed a major in history education and a minor in political science.

Theresa Ling Yeh is the director of research and programs for the Brotherhood Initiative at the University of Washington, USA. Her work focuses on issues of postsecondary educational access and persistence for students of color; students from low-income, first-generation backgrounds; and transfer students.

INDEX

Milton Keynes UK
Ingram Content Group UK Ltd.
UKHW020752251123
433172UK00026B/265